Crimes of
Passion

AN UNBLINKING LOOK
AT MURDEROUS LOVE

Crimes of Passion

AN UNBLINKING LOOK AT MURDEROUS LOVE

Howard Engel

Foreword by Edward L. Greenspan, Q.C.

FIREFLY BOOKS

A FIREFLY BOOK

Published by Firefly Books (U.S.) Inc. 2002

First Printing

Publisher Cataloging-in-Publication Data (U.S.)

Engel, Howard, 1931-
     Crimes of passion : an unblinking look at murderous love / Howard Engel ; foreword by Edward L. Greenspan.
240 p. :   cm.
Includes bibliographic references and index.
Summary: An exploration of crimes of passion with more than 25 classic, infamous and still unresolved cases.
ISBN 1-55297-584-3 (pbk.)
1 Crimes of passion -- Case studies. 2. Murder -- Case studies. I. Title.
364.1/ 523   21   CIP   HV6053.E54 2002

The transparencies for *Othello and Desdemona* by Eduard Buchel (p.6) and for *Paolo and Francesca* by Luigi Rubio (p. 14) are reproduced with the permission of the Bridgeman Art Library, London.

Every effort has been made to contact the copyright holders for the other photographs or transparencies in this book. Any omissions will be corrected in subsequent editions.

Published in the United States in 2002 by
Firefly Books (U.S.) Inc.
P.O. Box 1338, Ellicott Station
Buffalo, New York, USA
14205

Published in Canada in 2001 by Key Porter Books Limited

Design: Peter Maher
Electronic formatting: Heidy Lawrance Associates

Printed and bound in Canada

In loving memory of
Janet Evelyn Hamilton

With Honest Iago egging him on, whetting his jealousy, Othello murders his beloved Desdemona, as seen in this nineteenth century German engraving by Eduard Buchel.

... Then must you speak
Of one that loved not wisely but too well,
Of one not easily jealous, but, being wrought,
Perplexed in the extreme, of one whose hand,
Like the base Indian, threw a pearl away
Richer than all his tribe ...

—William Shakespeare, *Othello, V. ii.*

Contents

Acknowledgments ➤ *10*

Foreword ➤ *11*

Introduction ➤ *15*

ONE The French Have a Word for it: *Crime passionnel:*
YVONNE CHEVALLIER ➤ 27

TWO When Lovely Woman Stoops to Folly:
RUTH ELLIS; JEAN HARRIS ➤ 41

THREE Oh, beware, my lord, of jealousy.
It is the green-eyed monster...:
ALAN NORMAN; JOHN SWEENEY; O.J. SIMPSON ➤ 55

FOUR Those Old Love Letters:
EDITH THOMPSON AND FREDERICK BYWATERS ➤ 75

FIVE The Media:
THE MANNINGS; RUTH SNYDER AND JUDD GRAY ➤ 90

SIX When Newspaper Editors Were in Season:
HENRIETTE CAILLAUX ➤ 109

SEVEN Unhappy Valley and the Red Armchair: *Noblesse Oblige:*
LORD BROUGHTON; THE MARQUIS DE BERNARDY DE SIGOYER ➤ 130

EIGHT Disguises and Disappearances:
DR. HAWLEY HARVEY CRIPPEN; CYRIL BELSHAW; PETER HOGG ➤ 150

NINE The Hunger of Love and a Slice of America:
JEAN LIGER; LORENA BOBBITT ➢ 161

TEN By Love Obsessed. Hell Hath No Fury...:
PAULINE DUBUISSON; MARY ELEANOR PEARCEY ➢ 171

ELEVEN Families, I Hate You!:
ALPNA PATEL; PAULINE PARKER AND JULIET HULME (ANNE PERRY);
NATHAN LEOPOLD AND RICHARD LOEB;
LIZZIE BORDEN; SUSAN SMITH ➢ 182

TWELVE Provocation and Responsibility:
ELIZABETH MARTHA BROWN; ELIZABETH WORKMAN; VIOLET WATKINS;
RALPH KLASSEN; KENNETH PEACOCK; PATRICIA ANN HAWKINS ➢ 205

Epilogue ➢ 219

Notes ➢ 221

Bibliography ➢ 229

Index ➢ 235

Acknowledgments

I would like to thank my editor, Susan Folkins, for all her help in turning a jumbled manuscript of inchoate gibberish into a what I hope has become a readable book. I would also like to thank Gail Noble, Olga Kits and Ruth Hamlin-Douglas for their support and skills in researching much of the material herein. Thanks are due as well to Anna Porter, who put me up to this, and to Kildare Dobbs, Edward L. Greenspan, Martin Friedland, James Fontana, Arthur Ripstein and Anita Johnston who sustained me through it. I also owe a debt of thanks to Roy Krost; Noreen Taylor; Sheldon Zitner; Brian Vallée; Fred Langham; my agent, Beverley Slopen; Mary Adachi; Janet Friskney; David Mason; Mel and Lorne Tulk; and Colin and Margaret Visser. For his support and encouragement, I would like to include in this circle of thanks, Jacob Harry Hamilton Engel.

Foreword

Howard Engel, the gifted author of the famous Benny Cooperman mysteries and a recipient of the very prestigious Arthur Ellis Award for Crime Fiction, has been called by Ruth Rendell "a born writer who can bring a character to life in a few lines." His celebrated gift for narrative and his passionate curiosity produced *Lord High Executioner*, a true crime book describing executions throughout the ages, many of which were stranger than fiction.

Once again, Mr. Engel demonstrates his skills in this important, entertaining and insightful true crime book on the subject of "crimes of passion."

There is no single crime that fascinates us more than murder. The fascination that the public has with sensational murders engages public interest to a degree matched by little else. Faithfully reported, the murder trial brings us closer to life than the best literature. It is about real people. It is about life itself. The act of killing and the trial contain the essentials for great theater.

Whether it is planned and deliberate murder, whether it is murder arising out of sudden anger or uncontrollable rage, whether it is committed by a legally insane person, we have been fascinated with murder since Cain killed Abel. The fact is, murder is almost always a crime of passion and impulse where the killer seldom, if ever, weighs the consequences of his or her act at all before the killing. Crimes of passion—quarrels between husbands and wives in which wives kill husbands, husbands kill wives, where lovers kill each other—are usually the result of feelings that ultimately overflow into criminal acts and consequences do not count. And if the killer weighs the consequences at all, it is done so upon scales distorted by dark and twisted emotions. Arthur Koestler once said, "A normal person in a normal state of mind just doesn't commit murder."

As Howard Engel observes in this absorbing collection of murder trials drawn from a number of centuries and countries including the United States, Canada, England, France and New Zealand, "crimes of passion are crimes with a human perspective. We try to understand the crimes by trying to glimpse the passion that brought them about." And he does just that by bringing his own intelligent and thoroughly engaging analysis of more than twenty-five cases which will absorb any reader who has the slightest interest in what causes people to kill.

All persons are potential murderers, needing only circumstances and a sufficiently overwhelming emotion that will triumph over the restraint that education and habit have built up to control the powerful surging instincts and feelings that sometimes overwhelm men and women. Status, money, power, sex, love, jealousy—the stuff of life—are usually the stuff of murder. And that's what this book is about.

Certain killings that occur due to a sudden passion are easily understood. Rage displaces reason and judgment and all acquired restraints are submerged. Primitive and deep-seeded emotions take over. Certain killings that are provoked are more deliberate than others. Some are crimes of political passion, crimes to protect honor or, as the title of this book suggests, crimes of murderous love. Howard Engel is interested in finding patterns in these cases and he succeeds in explaining why people kill through such celebrated cases as Ruth Ellis (the last woman to hang in England), Jean Harris (the killer of Dr. Tarnower), Juliet Hulme (the writer Anne Perry), Yvonne Chevallier, Dr. Hawley Harvey Crippen, Ruth Snyder and Judd Gray, O. J. Simpson and Edith Thompson and Frederick Bywaters, to name a few. Crimes of passion give us a clear glimpse, an open window into the dark side of otherwise respectable people.

It is hard to read these accounts without feeling gripped by the sort of excitement that marks all of Howard Engel's fictional novels. The book contains many of the best murder trials in the long history of crime.

Mr. Engel shows a deep understanding of his subject. He writes with great skill about human nature and tragedy.

Enjoy!

Edward L. Greenspan, Q.C.
June 2001

The tragic love and murders of Francesca da Rimini and her Paolo is represented here in Luigi Rubio's rendition of the lovers' discovery by her irate
and vengeful husband, Giovanni Malatesta. Luckily for him, the murderer's
father was the ruling lord of Rimini and did not prosecute his son. Dante,
who knew some of the family, was only the first of many artists to bring the
story to the page or concert hall.

Introduction

In all of the annals of criminal law, there is no record more fascinating, more intriguing, than that of crimes of passion. They are interesting for a number of reasons, not the least of which is the fact that crimes of passion are offenses not normally committed by criminals, but by *ordinary people*, who are criminalized only by these acts. Both sexes and all classes and races commit these crimes. Their perpetrators are nonentities and celebrities, laborers and socialites, school-dropouts and Ph.D.'s. By *ordinary people*, I mean not some political abstraction, but rather all the rich and wide variety that people come in. The full diapason of mankind.

The study of crime offers a special tool to the social historian. Through a study of the offenses that societies, throughout history, have chosen to criminalize, prosecute and, at the end of the process, punish, we get some notion of how people behave *in extremis*. When the heat is on. Here is society caught at a disadvantage, with its hair in curlers, still in its bathrobe at eleven o'clock in the morning. The study of crime cuts a trench into the tumulus of human existence. While interesting enough in its own right, such a study allows a unique look at changing behavior. Here we can learn about the structure of the society, the classes, the power base and the mentality of not only the offenders, but also of those who judge them. Just as the archaeologist digs a trench into a mound to turn up a slice of an ancient civilization, the study of a particular crime allows the criminologist and anyone else interested in looking to see a slice of a micro-civilization that existed surrounding a peculiar group of circumstances. It's like lifting up a single rock and studying the insect life beneath it. Such an investigation interrupts a series of events and exposes a drama that would otherwise be hidden from us.

Further, such a study crosses the barriers between disciplines. Crimes of passion have inspired not only legends and literature, including the plays of great playwrights, but also novels, symphonic works, operas and the graphic arts. Think of the murder of the king that fuels the action in *Hamlet*. Think of *Carmen*. Remember Agamemnon. In fact, it is difficult to imagine art, literature or music without the violent outpouring of passion and the stories of human struggles that gave them birth. Without crimes of passion, grand opera would be impossible, and the great art galleries of the world impoverished.

Anna Freud said "a crime of passion is an action committed without the benefit of ego activity. The term means that the passion, the impulse, is of such magnitude that every other consideration apart from its fulfillment is disregarded."[1] In other words, a large part of what is regarded as normal mental functioning shuts down, becoming unavailable to the perpetrator.

The very term "crimes of passion" evokes deep-seated, atavistic responses in every reader's heart. These are the crimes that are born in the emotional core of men and women pushed to do the unthinkable. They are at the end of their tether, *au bout de souffle*. There is hardly ever any crass consideration of financial gain here, no taint of the marketplace, of reward: only release. These crimes are direct responses to unbearable betrayal, broken hearts, destroyed characters, ruined lives and injured pride. Jealousy, envy and the rest of the Seven Deadly Sins enter through this door, and, like as not, if you are looking at older records, end on the scaffold.

The passionate love of Francesca da Rimini and her tragic end have inspired artists as great as Dante, Leigh Hunt, Gabriele D'Annunzio, Ingres, George Frederick Watts, Riccardo Zandonai and Tchaikovsky to new creative heights. Shed of its thirteenth-century trapping, its aristocratic setting and well-born characters, it is story for the law courts: a murder case.

Francesca was the daughter of Guido da Polenta, lord of Ravenna, and the wife of Giovanni Malatesta, called Giovanni the Lame, an heir of

Verruchio, the lord of Rimini. An arranged marriage, it quickly went sour, for Francesca was already in love with Paolo, called Paolo the Handsome, younger brother of her husband. Giovanni trusted his wife and brother to spend time in one another's company. At last Francesca and her brother-in-law betrayed that confidence. When Giovanni discovered the young couple in *flagrante delicto*, he killed both of them on the spot. Dante, who knew some of the people in this tale, wove the tragic story into his *Inferno*. The shades of the lovers whisper to the poet as he wanders down and around the circles of Hell with his guide, the Roman poet Virgil. After a fashion, Paolo and Francesca bless Dante because he pities their perversity. He pities their present suffering, their eternal torment:

> ... if you have such a desire to know
> The first root of our love, then I will tell you ...
>
> One day, when we were reading, for distraction,
> How Lancelot was overcome by love—
> We were alone, without any suspicion;
>
> Several times, what we were reading forced
> Our eyes to meet ...
>
> That day we got no further with our reading ...[2]

The story might be taken as a paradigm of all crimes-of-passion cases. The love that they had fallen into was, in the cant phrase, "bigger than both of them." It undermined their sense of duty, loyalty and propriety. Passion undid their marriage vows and they threw caution to the winds. Dante sees their tragedy partly as the crime of allowing passion to override the dictates of reason. In the story of the opera *Carmen*, the gypsy girl goes to her doom relentlessly as she continues to spurn the love of the man she has ruined. Again, reason is the enemy. It is passion that fires and determines her short, violent life. A little more rational thought would have saved Carmen, but destroyed the story. It was passion in the loins of Paris for Helen, the wife of Menelaus, that fed the flames of the

Trojan War. And while he and his brother Agamemnon were away on the battlefields of windy Troy, Agamemnon's wife succumbed to the blandishments of Aegisthus. When the warrior returned, victorious, to Argos, Aegisthus and Clytemnestra murdered him in order to continue their torrid affair.

> A shudder in the loins engenders there
> The broken wall, the burning roof and tower
> And Agamemnon dead.[3]

Clytemnestra should have been wary of taking up with the murderer of Atreus, her father-in-law. And he, Aegisthus, should have thought twice about bedding anyone whose father was a bird.

We are all of us to a greater or lesser degree fascinated by crimes of passion. Our interest feeds the media, which produce prodigious amounts of material to satisfy our insatiable need to know more and more. The case of O. J. Simpson is still fresh in our minds. This was a sensational glimpse of the lives of the rich and famous. Millions of people sat glued to their television sets watching a slow-speed chase: a white Bronco moving sedately down the freeway as though it were the Grand Prix. Such an ecstasy of power, abuse and control is rarely seen. But sensationalism was not invented with television and the Internet: in 1849, on a cold November morning, a crowd of over thirty thousand people stayed up all night as the gallows was built on the roof of the jail, waiting to see Marie and Frederick Manning hanged at Horse-mongers' Lane Gaol for the murder of Marie's lover. The hanging of a husband and wife was a novelty not to be missed, especially when it was the ending to a sensational crime of passion that had been widely covered in the newspapers. During the 1920s, hundreds of thousands of words were written about the Ruth Snyder–Judd Gray case in which a pair of lovers murdered the spouse of one of them. Crimes of passion gave birth to and fed the tabloid newspapers that arose in the 1800s, just as more recent crimes nourish the evening news on television. Crimes of passion now have a great following on the Internet.

Everybody knows what a "crime of passion" is, but when it comes to defining exactly why one crime *is* and another *isn't* a crime of passion, the vision becomes blurred, the whole field gets murky. From a distance, nothing could be clearer, but up close the borders begin to overlap and distinctions become obscured. For instance, when two lovers quarrel and one ends the discussion, and the life of the other, with a letter-opener thrust into the heart, we can readily see both the passion and the crime it led to, but when two lovers plot to kill the spouse of one of the partners, as Ruth Snyder and Judd Gray did, a degree of premeditation is introduced as the couple plan, prepare and spring a trap to eliminate the unwanted third person. The passion that led to the murder was real enough, but it didn't blind Gray and Snyder to the need to establish alibis.

Evidently, heightened passions can lead to a well-plotted crime just as inexorably as a shouting match over a trifle in a bar or at a football game can lead to a sudden, unpremeditated one. The Mannings, mentioned above, sent several dinner invitations around to their intended victim and when he finally appeared, murdered him, a sequence of events that shouts "premeditation" in a loud voice. But must the violence always flare up immediately after the incident that provoked it? Can there be a crime of passion that contains elements of entrapment or premeditation? Could a case be made for cold-blooded passion? The Italians have a proverb that says "revenge is a dish that the man of taste prefers to enjoy cold." Is revenge a legitimate partner of passion? Might the "man of taste" also be female? The research suggests that revenge murders are a different category, related to *crime passionnel* in many ways, but not very helpful in exploring its passionate side. Significantly, the time between the provoking act and the commission of the crime is an important factor. The murderer who hears of his spouse's infidelity and catches the next available flight back home is treated differently from the murderer who books on a freighter and then takes a train from Halifax to Vancouver.

While the typical *criminelle passionnelle* is not a long-suffering wife or mistress who has finally had a bellyful and wins her release by an act of violence, this is a related category, which will be considered in the chapters ahead. Closer to the center of this category of crime is the young woman who, having been wooed and seduced by her lover, is subsequently abandoned by him, either because of family pressure or through his own irresponsibility, until the poor creature, usually with a child or at least pregnant at this stage, sees herself as a doomed heroine in a tragedy which can only be concluded with a gunshot under a street lamp, a stabbing in front of his front door, or at the very least, a flask of vitriol flung in the offender's faithless, uncaring face. I would like to test the evidence of some of these cases against the issue of provocation.

The concept of the *crime passionnel* is a romantic one. Precursors to the genre may be found in the Bible, in the plays of the Greek and Roman dramatists and poets. Hamlet says:

> Give me that man
> That is not passion's slave, and I will wear him
> In my heart's core, aye, in my heart of heart ...[4]

Yet in the battle between blood and judgment, reason and passion, passion wins: Hamlet himself is passion's slave. In modern times the crime of passion is rarely heard of before Byron and Scott. *Giaour* is a Turkish tale of love, adultery and revenge, published in 1813, six years before Scott's *The Bride of Lammermoor*, where Lucy Ashton stabs her new husband on the return of her betrothed. The romantics unbuttoned the collars and untied the tight waists of the enlightenment. Passion overruled reason. Operatic plots were played out in real life. Perhaps this came with the growing importance of the individual in society, as the calming effect of a close-knit collective society receded into history. It is a "me, me, ME!" thing. Shakespeare's Othello and a few other isolated cases in literature and in the courtrooms of Europe pioneered it, but it settled down to be a nineteenth- and twentieth-century phenomenon (so far).

There are those who believe that crimes of passion have to do with nationality. For instance, there is a traditional notion that the French, with a kind of Gallic sophistication that extends to the law courts, understand such things, while the English, whose system of laws developed in a cold, unforgiving climate, do not. But these rigid stereotypes are easily broken down by examining enough cases. Still, *le crime passionnel* does have a special place in many legal codes. Someone who has suddenly or unexpectedly been betrayed by a loved and trusted partner, even in an illicit relationship, is rarely treated as a common murderer. Why the special interest? I said above that the *criminelle passionnelle* sees herself as the heroine of a dramatic tragedy; so do many of the onlookers at her trial. Without a doubt, there is more than an element of the theatrical about these cases.

In France, the only legal justification for a "crime of passion defense" is Article 324, line 2, of the penal code, which states that a husband who murders his wife or her lover when he discovers them *in flagrante delicto* has committed excusable murder. However, the law does not show any such leniency toward a wife who discovers her husband and his lover in a similar situation; if she kills one or both of them she has committed plain, unvarnished murder. She does not share in the entitlement awarded by French law to the male. In the pages that follow, I hope to explore not only the crime that the perpetrator was provoked to commit, but also the legal ramifications of the crime of passion defense, and the characteristic emotional tangle and deadlock of the relationship of perpetrator and victim.

Perpetrators of crimes of passion are not criminals in the ordinary sense, and a previous life of crime is not usually a factor. Their violent actions originate in unique circumstances. They are like gigantic waves, the result of winds whipping up seas to great heights, and they cause huge shipwrecks. The tales of chance survivors become legendary. Nor are such offenses ever likely to be repeated. The conditions that brought them about are not the sort that come again to the same individuals.

Just as the plot of Ford Madox Ford's *The Good Soldier* would need few alterations to make it into a classic mystery novel, the plot of Verdi's *La Traviata* would need very little alteration to create a credible crime of passion: the father of the young man "of good family" convinces his son's mistress that she must do what is best for the young man's future: break off the relationship. This is only a variation on the often-used story of a father using every means, usually beginning with his pocketbook, to break up an unsuitable alliance that brings dishonor to the family. French fiction in particular is full of stories about such young men, who are sent off to the great wicked city with more money than experience, as though to be wet-nursed all over again, but this time in the demi-monde of the French capital. This is the steep, narrow back-stairs of an *éducation sentimentale*. Echoes of this will be heard in some of the following pages. In the same way, Tennessee Williams' *A Streetcar Named Desire* only needs the corpse of Stanley Kowalski to make it too a crime of passion. Stanley says to Blanche, just as he is about to rape her: "We had this date from the beginning." Elsewhere, she says, "The first time I laid eyes on him I thought to myself, that man is my executioner! That man will destroy me …"[5] I mention these cases to illustrate how closely crimes of passion resemble popular literature. Fiction takes its themes of passion from life; truth and invention are woven together.

In this book, I am more interested in crimes of love, sometimes familial love, where passion drives one or more of the people involved first to a deadlock and then to a deadly conclusion. Of necessity, the cases (with one exception) deal with homicide: murder, or at the very least manslaughter. My research has tried to seek out the Othellos and Desdemonas of the criminal courts, those who "loved not wisely but too well." I am interested in finding patterns in such cases. Is the eternal triangle always the same shape? Mathematically, since each point of the triangle may be occupied by a heterosexual or gay man or a straight or lesbian woman, there are sixty-four possibilities in the eternal triangle. When passion holds in thrall a married couple and the lover of one of them, how often is it the lover who comes to grief? And how often one or both of the two spouses?

In their 1975 book *Crime of Passion: Murder and Murderer*, the authors David and Gene Lester, both psychologists, come to the conclusion that *most* murderers, not simply those that are involved in a crime of passion, "are not ... motivated by any long-range plans or conscious desires. Most commonly, they kill during some trivial quarrel, or their acts are triggered by some apparently unimportant incident, while deep and unconscious emotional needs are their basic motivation. Most murders occur on sudden impulse and in the heat of passion, in situations where the killer's emotions overcome his ability to reason." Obviously, these killers have not been reading their Agatha Christie, Ruth Rendell or P. D. James. This is where crime fiction and true crime diverge.

While, as W. S. Gilbert observed in *Iolanthe*, "the law is the true embodiment of everything that is excellent," it is a growing and changing moral yardstick. Not even the greatest supporters of our legal system would claim that "It has no kind of fault or flaw." Our laws have always reflected the texture of the times. Rough justice suited rough, unruly times. More settled times brought in reforms and subtleties of interpretation that would only have inflamed the prejudices of an older generation. In the past, women and men who committed the same crimes have been treated very differently, the women hanged and the men receiving light sentences only, without special comment by their contemporaries. The whole evolution of the theory of sentencing for crimes also comes into play here. Do you hang A for killing B because A killed B, or so that C will not kill D, there being otherwise no horrible example to stay C's hand?

Further, the defenses offered in cases where a woman is the accused are often demeaning to women as a whole. This fact is generally ignored because such defenses are often the most successful. In French courtrooms, the concept of women as emotional creatures, given to hysteria when under stress, has won the hearts of hundreds of jurors over the years, and has not been criticized loudly or publicly very often because it is such a *useful* legal position. Should women chalk up a victory for feminism when, along with their brothers, they are treated to harsh sentences?

One commentator, Camille Granier in *La Femme criminelle* argues that French women perpetrators of crimes of passion show less imagination, less inventive subterfuge, in their crimes than their male counterparts. Women tend to murder their victims in public places and then make no attempt either to escape or to defend themselves from being taken into custody. The woman seems willing to sacrifice herself on the altar of her wrongs and at the feet of the slain author of her misfortunes. A more cynical interpretation is that she is more confident of getting acquitted in a French court of law than a man would be. Consider this after reading the strange cases of Yvonne Chevallier and Henriette Caillaux.

It is sometimes said that crimes of passion are essentially female crimes. Certainly there are plenty of examples of women who have committed what the press at least termed crimes of passion. But since only fifteen percent of all crimes are perpetrated by women, it stands to reason that most of the perpetrators of crimes of passion are men. Perhaps, within the category, the percentage of women involved in a criminal way is proportionately larger; in absolute numbers, the representation of women is low. One modern commentator observed recently that, in human society, the strong prey on those weaker than themselves: men prey on women, while women take it out on the kids.

Although both men and women have been the authors of crimes of passion, and men have statistically outnumbered women in successfully claiming this defense, it is women who have received most of the special attention given by the media to this curious branch of crime. I think the reason for this runs deeper than the peculiar, but very human, impulse that makes us unable to look away from the human fly climbing the outside of a skyscraper or the acrobat on his flying trapeze. A woman in trouble, in deep trouble, has fascinated both sexes for centuries, and of this fascination may come either a highly sensational account of a trial or, more rarely, great art. Vulnerability is the key. Women are expected by society to be meek and mild: non-physical, non-sexual, non-violent. Also kind and loving: protectors, not killers. Women commit far fewer crimes than men, and so when they do commit them the public's interest is a reaction to the rareness of the event as well as to the details of a particular crime. Kept without education and at home through the centuries, women throughout history learned little of the world beyond the management of a house. Hence their crimes tended to be domestic, involving spouses, rivals, lovers, close friends or interlopers into the family circle. Malice *domestica*.

In the thirty years from 1880 to 1910, the number of crimes of passion rose steadily in France. But so too did the total number of murders. In 1880, for instance, there were six crimes of passion committed by men, out of a total of thirty. By 1905 this total had grown to thirty-four out of ninety-six. By 1910, the figures were thirty-five out of one hundred. While *crime passionnel* never rose above a third of all murders committed by men, it was the dominant form for women: five out of six female murders in 1881, five of eight in 1895, nine of eleven in 1905; and all fourteen murders by women in 1910 were crimes of passion.

> The acquittal for women was almost customary. Of the five in 1895, three women were acquitted, one received a year in gaol, while the fate of the third is unknown. In 1905 there were seven acquittals, one unknown, and one penalty of three years. In 1910 sentences were harsher, with one life sentence and three gaol sentences of six, two, and three years; none the less in that year there were still nine acquittals and one unknown …

I owe these French statistics to Ruth Harris, whose book *Murders and Madness*,[6] has proven to be a goldmine of information. Meticulous readers might find the record-keeping at the Archives de la Seine a bit shoddy, but that hardly blurs the image implicit in the statistics. Women who killed a spouse, rival or lover in a crime of passion outside France, though, very often had a stickier time of it. Their punishments were usually much more severe than those meted out to men found guilty of similar crimes. As Jay Robert Nash has noted about a London murder in 1726:

Husband-killer Catherine Hayes, for instance, instead of merely being hanged, was strangled and burned to death before a great throng as a public warning, a governmental caution to any woman who might momentarily run a finger down the sharp edge of a kitchen knife while eyeing the throat of an oppressive spouse. ...[7]

When a usually sane and normal person is driven by panic, love or jealousy of an exaggerated or obsessive sort to kill a spouse, a rival or a lover, it is commonly called a crime of passion. It isn't exactly murder; but it isn't manslaughter either. Many believe that the law recognizes crimes of passion as a sub-category of murder, or at the very least an act whose motive deserves to be looked at more closely. But such a motive is a legal consideration only in France. In the British tradition there is no such thing as "the unwritten law" that allows a wronged spouse to take revenge; no slap on the wrist for the discarded lover who murders the abusive or neglectful former partner. The Canadian tradition, like those of other former British colonies, tends to favor gender-blind justice. In the United States, where each state has its own criminal law, traditions and practices vary. In Texas, as in some other southern states, the law has often shielded husbands who have murdered their unfaithful wives, just as it has favored a degree of vigilantism in its citizenry.

So, there it is. As you read on you will encounter, if not all aspects of passion or crimes of passion, at least a generous sample. The material collected in this book is eclectic, not systematic. It is a sampler, a pot-pourri, a medley, a *tsimes* of the many legends and legal cases of crimes of passion. In these stories, culled from a variety of sources (there are notes and a bibliography at the end of the book to guide readers who would like to know more), many aspects of the human soul in the grip of uncontrollable passion are to be seen. Read on.

ONE

The French Have a Word for It: Crime Passionnel

Yvonne Chevallier

F rance is the only country that effectively recognizes *crime passionnel*. Yvonne Chevallier's[8] murder of her war-hero husband is a classic example. It happened in the great city of Orléans on the Loire River, the city that still celebrates its delivery from an English siege by St. Joan in 1429, holding an annual "Fête Nationale de la Pucelle d'Orléans." In this story public and private lives become confused. Here public officials and private ambitions are entangled, and the use married people make of one another is mixed with an ample portion of melodrama, politics and a fair measure of irony. It is also a useful example of *timing* in a murder story: if things had not happened exactly when they did, they might not have happened at all.

Dr. Pierre Chevallier was a French war hero. He earned his reputation not at the front, but in the underground Resistance or "maquis," during the German occupation. His exploits were the stuff of the sort of movies that came out during and just after the war: *L'Arc de Triomphe, Joan of Lorraine, Casablanca, Odette, Paris Underground*. When the forces of General Jacques Leclerc's Second Armored Division and the U.S. Fourth Infantry Division broke into Paris, they found that the City of Light was largely in the hands of the Resistance. It was a similar story in cities like Orléans, seventy miles to the south. It was heroes of the Resistance who supplied the politicians for the reborn republic: men like Pierre Mendès-France and Dr. Pierre Chevallier. The doctor was awarded the Croix de Guerre and, in 1945, elected mayor of Orléans on a wave of euphoria. He proved to be a born politician, as he shouldered the huge job of rebuilding his war-ravaged city. So able was Chevallier that he was elected to the National Assembly the following year and re-elected mayor the year after that, to continue his restoration of Orléans to a peacetime economy. His local popularity recommended him in higher places. When in August 1951 France's fourteenth government since the war was being formed by the former minister of defense, who was a friend and colleague of Chevallier's, the doctor was able to help select members of the fledgling cabinet. He even was given a junior portfolio himself. At forty-two, in a country usually governed by much older men, he was young for such responsibility; Pierre Chevallier's future was assured. He was bound to succeed in politics; he seemed to have both the talent and the energy to make himself noticed.

Back in 1935, when he was a twenty-six-year-old medical student, Pierre had fallen in love with, and lived with, a young midwife, Yvonne Rousseau, the daughter of a well-to-do farmer. She was shy, stolid and, except for attractive green eyes, rather homely. Her young man, on the other hand, was attractive and outgoing enough for both of them, and in addition, he came from an old and socially prominent family in Orléans. Living together without benefit of clergy was rarer in provincial France then than it is now, but, after a rather bohemian beginning, Pierre made an honest woman of Yvonne. In the early days of their marriage, society and the greater world beyond Orléans seemed unimportant. Pierre worked hard at the hospital, completing his internship; Yvonne made him a happy home, which in due time included a bright, bustling nursery.

Then came the war and the Occupation, during which Pierre's unforeseen avocation came to the fore: he found that he had a talent for espionage and organizing guerrilla warfare. This was the beginning of Pierre's hegira from the routine career of a provincial doctor. Yvonne remained the homemaker and mother; she was happy to see Pierre's horizons widening, but when he entered politics after the war, she was left behind. She didn't think she belonged in this world. She knew little of fashion, possessed a practical but not wide education and was largely uncultured. She was, frankly, gauche and uncultivated. She retained her initial shyness, feeling uncomfortable, embarrassed and unwanted in the bigger world Pierre was discovering. As Pierre spent more and more time away from the family home—weeks at a time, when he was helping to build René Pleven's government—Yvonne became more and more despondent. She received anonymous poison pen letters saying that Pierre was not *totally* immersed in political activities, he had other interests and someone to share them with. One day, Pierre's office contacted her, telling her to get dressed for a major diplomatic evening party. She did as she was told and waited. Pierre forgot to fetch her. Then, a month before the fatal event, Yvonne discovered a crumpled letter in a pocket of one of her husband's suits. Like the wife in Truffaut's film *La Peau Douce*, she found what she'd feared she'd find. "Without you, life would have no beauty or meaning for me," it read in part. The letter began "Dear Pierre," and concluded, "Jeannette." She suspected that she knew who Jeannette might be: not a Parisian coquette or typist at the ministry, but Jeanne Perreau, the wife of an Orléans department store owner, who was several years younger than Mme Chevallier.

One can imagine Yvonne Chevallier's state of mind at this point. Like the backstage wife of a matinée idol, Yvonne found her self-worth sorely challenged. Her telephone calls to the National Assembly went unreturned. A secretary treated her calls with indifference bordering on hostility. Or so it seemed to her. She took the train northeast to Paris, but even there she could not get word through to her husband in his endless meetings that seemingly dragged on through the night, nor could she find him at the Assembly. Yvonne waited for him all night at their Paris apartment but Pierre did not come back. She returned home unsatisfied, feeling desperate. She reported to one of her maids that she had suspected that her husband was with another woman, but "I know it now," she said.

It was shortly after this incident that Yvonne applied for and got a gun permit. She explained since her husband's political success she had felt unsafe; there had been some disturbing threats both in the mail and over the telephone. She felt that their lives were at risk. Taking the permit with her to a sporting goods store, she looked at several handguns, asking which was the most dangerous, "the one which kills without any doubt." M. Meunier, the proprietor, picked out a 7.65 mm Mab automatic, a gun with a lot of stopping power. Mme Chevallier left the store undecided. The following morning, she returned to the shop and bought the "most dangerous" handgun in the store, explaining, "I'm very frightened. Who knows what may happen now that my husband is an important political figure."

Less than twenty-four hours after being given his cabinet post, on the morning of 12 August 1951, Dr. Chevallier was driven to an agricultural fair at Châtillon-sur-Loire. He stopped en route at Orléans, meaning only to change his clothes upstairs and continue on immediately. But his wife was waiting for him in the bedroom. She lit into him with a catalogue of his recent bad treatment of her and the children. She upbraided him for his neglect, his discourtesy and worst of all, his unfaithfulness. She told him that she had gone to the Chamber of Deputies and had been turned away by an *usher*. He continued to change his clothes, getting angrier and angrier as he went on unbuttoning. "You are always busy," Yvonne said. "You seem to have forgotten that I'm your *wife*."

Anger gripped both of them, mounting higher and higher. Sensing that the moment had arrived, Pierre looked at the plain forty-year-old woman; she was standing in his way, heavy in gesture and speech, an anchor dragging him down. He announced that he was going to sue for divorce. She said that she was going to shoot herself, and showed him the gun. "Good!" he said, or words to that effect. "I dare you! But wait until I get out of here." It was shortly after that that young Mathieu, their four-year-old son, and others downstairs heard four loud shots. Mathieu ran into the bedroom, where his mother stood holding a smoking gun. His father had slumped to the floor.

"Papa! Papa!" he cried, "what's the matter with your chest?" Chevallier was unable to answer. Yvonne took her son's hand and took him downstairs to a servant.

"Look after Mathieu," she said. "Let him play with your child."

"What's happening?" asked the servant.

"Nothing at all," Mme Chevallier replied calmly. She climbed the stairs again. After an interval, a fifth shot rang out. Mme Chevallier had killed her husband "without any doubt," shooting him twice in the head and three times in the body.

When she was sure that he was dead, she called a family friend in the Orléans police station. She told Commissaire Gazano to please come at once. "My husband needs you urgently." Within two hours of the shooting Mme Chevallier, wearing a black dress, was sitting in a jail cell.

When news of the death of the popular hero, mayor and deputy was published, the city of Orléans went wild with revulsion and anger. The papers of the day before were full of the triumph of Dr. Pierre Chevallier. The city had lost its favorite son. The papers called Yvonne *murderess*, without any mitigation or hedging of language. (French libel laws are more lax than they are in Britain and North America.) Local opinion supported the view that Pierre's political enemies had invented Chevallier's *affaire* to discredit him. They said that Yvonne had been brooding and morose *before* Pierre's elevation to government office. They said that it wasn't Pierre who failed to invite Yvonne to socially prominent functions, it was Yvonne who refused to go, in a marital push-me-pull-you that had eroded relations between them to a stand-off. They added, further, that irrational jealousy was stamped on her character. It was a class thing: you can take the peasant girl out of the barnyard, but you can't take the barnyard out of the girl. There didn't have to be grounds for her suspicions; she didn't need any; she was suspicious by nature. It came with her background. Public feeling against Yvonne ran so high in the area that it was decided to hold the trial in faraway Reims, in the champagne country to the northeast.

In the original police investigation and in the assembling of the case by the examining magistrate, there was no mention of another woman in Yvonne's statements. Mme Chevallier's desperate act was triggered, so she said, by Pierre's out-of-the-blue announcement that he wanted a divorce. But it was known that she had confronted Jeannette's husband,

Roger Perreau, with the accusation that her husband and his wife were having an affair. At that time she had said, according to M. Perreau, that she was going to kill her husband. He added that she knew that she could get away with it. She boasted about it to him in his own house. M. Perreau may have been speaking the truth, but he was the cuckold, after all, and he did have an axe to grind. Where would he find another friend in so high a place?

The Palais de Justice in Reims was as packed on the first day of the trial as though the venue had not been changed. It was impossible to get a hotel room. The murder of a national hero was a national concern. Everybody wanted to see, and the newspaper photographers popped their flashguns until the judge, Raymond Jadin, told them "Enough!"

The papers maintained their stance against Mme Chevallier at the beginning of the trial. She had murdered a national treasure, after all. His dalliance with Mme Perreau was either invented or exaggerated, they maintained. And, even if it *was* true, so what? Men will be men; you can't fight nature. They called Yvonne Chevallier "the Shrew," and "the Woman Who Felt Herself Inferior."

First, the judges tried to clear up the discrepancies in Mme Chevallier's statements to the examining magistrate. If she had told M. Perreau, at the time of her confrontation with him, that she intended to kill her husband, then the killing was simple murder, not a crime of passion. (She also claimed that "the gun went off by accident.") In a *crime passionnel* there can be no premeditation, no intent to kill before the fact.

When she entered the dock on Wednesday morning, 5 November 1952, Yvonne was wearing a simple light suit with a high-necked top. Her face was pale and haggard. "You are accused of murder," Judge Jadin told her. "If you are found guilty, you are liable to penal servitude for life." He then quizzed her on various points contained in the "act of accusation," which contained the case for the prosecution. The role of this judge, the *juge d'instruction*, might seem to North American or British viewers to be surprisingly prosecutorial, but this stage in the proceedings is not the trial proper, but a sort of pre-trial. This peculiarity of French procedure has led to the mistaken view that in France the prisoner is presumed guilty until he is proven innocent. However, this is no truer in France that the opposite is true in other countries, and since 1952, changes have been made to correct this impression of partiality on the part of the judge. In the case before Judge Raymond Jadin on 5 November 1952, he stated that the accused had "an animal passion" for her husband. "This passion overwhelmed your whole way of life—without your attempting to control it. I understand your Calvary, but I don't condone it."

According to David Rowan's account of the trial in his book *Famous European Crimes* (which I have relied on for much of my information about this case), early in the trial two things became clear: "Firstly, the public had so far heard only half the story, and secondly, the press had failed to realize the extent of popular sympathy for the accused."[9]

It was from the judge that the courtroom heard first about the "other woman." Spectators heard about the finding of the letter signed "Jeannette," and learned that Yvonne had found further proof as to the identity of Jeannette in the Paris apartment: a railway timetable with the town where Mme Perreau was staying clearly marked by Pierre Chevallier. This was sensational news for the press. What case is not improved by the discovery of "an unknown woman"? The judge continued his examination of the accused. He wanted to know about her meeting with M. Perreau, the other woman's husband.

"You told M. Perreau that you were going to kill your husband."

"No," answered the accused.

"You added that it would be a *crime passionnel* and you would be acquitted."

"*C'est faux!* That's untrue," she said vehemently.

The judge, Raymond Jadin, then led her through what she had previously said about buying the handgun. It was a heavy-caliber weapon with a clip holding five rounds. She had purchased twenty-five rounds altogether. Here is David Rowan's account of what happened next:

Then came the fatal morning of his return home. "According to your story," the judge queried, "he said that he was going to sue for divorce and marry Jeanne Perreau?" But Mme Chevallier was now in such a state of nervous tension that she could not reply, and when Judge Jadin began to read the account of the shooting, she fell in the dock, half-fainting. The court was cleared for fifteen minutes until she had recovered.

It was a trial that needed no Otto Preminger to enhance it. One piece of testimony would move spectators to favor the accused, while the next had them pitying the martyred hero of the Resistance again. In the end, the trial turned on the question of whether the fifth bullet, the one that followed a long silence, was fired by accident or to make sure of the work advanced by the first four. Mme Chevallier said that she intended the last bullet for herself, but on seeing pictures of her children, all the wrongs of her husband flooded back into her consciousness and she fired again at the body of her already dying husband.

An element of farce was contributed by M. Roger Perreau, the unfortunate husband of Jeannette. To the French a cuckold is always ridiculous, and they showed no pity. Even in the courtroom, smirks and laughter could be heard as he took the stand, and hand gestures signaling "horns" appeared throughout the Palais de Justice. The mention of the word *cocu* in public in France achieves an effect comparable to the sensation created by the speaking of the word *shift* on the stage of the Abbey Theatre in Dublin, in 1907. On the opening night of Synge's *Playboy of the Western World* so great a disturbance arose that the performance came to an abrupt end. We do carry about with us shreds of an earlier tribalism that no amount of sophistication can quite bury. If there is a stereotypical cuckold, Roger Perreau fitted the part to perfection—to the delight of the men and women in the court-room. He told the court that Mme Perreau had told him of Dr. Chevallier's association with her. He had decided not to make any violent objection (some observers even thought that, considering Chevallier's meteoric leap in their world, Perreau was rather pleased with his wife's affair), but for the sake of his business he had hoped that the liaison would be kept discreetly shrouded in silence.

Chevallier, he admitted, was not the first of Mme Perreau's admirers. Chevallier's predecessor had been "chased away" by the ever-vigilant husband. The first had been a cad, a bounder. "He disgusted me. But Chevallier was different."

"Why?" the judge wanted to know. "Was it M. Chevallier's higher social position?"

Perreau replied, "No ... it may seem strange, but I found him more likeable. I got on with him very well."

Laughter in the courtroom ignored the pounding of the gavel until the laughter turned to hisses as the departing witness's attractive wife took her husband's place on the stand. Jeannette was a beauty, the "other woman" of a film director's dreams. David Rowan describes her as having "long red hair under a jaunty beret, wide-set eyes and sensuous lips, her face was inscrutable as she took the oath." Boos and hisses delayed the beginning of her testimony. When asked what she did for a living, the thirty-four-year-old Mme Perreau replied that she had "no profession." She admitted that she had become Dr. Chevallier's mistress in May 1950, and that they had seen one another in Paris two or three times a week. When the defense counsel asked her scornfully whether, as a married woman and the mother of three children, she had not felt any shame in this unsanctified relationship, she whispered, "No." Maître Acquaviva was playing to the gallery, with great effect. He asked about the time Mme Chevallier had called to confront her with the affair. Mme Perreau stated, rather flat-footedly, that although Yvonne Chevallier inspired her with pity, she did not wish to end the affair with Chevallier. Once again the defense counsel rose to his feet, his righteous indignation rampant, like an American spread-eagle district attorney in an election year, thundering, "You will be responsible for your words and acts up above. Your place is there in the dock!" The applause of spectators drowned any reply coming from the witness. Once again, the judge threatened to have the courtroom cleared.

By now, only one day into the trial, it was apparent that the move from Orléans to Reims had achieved nothing. The press had managed to make the whole population aware of the details of the case. No corner of France was too remote to have formed an opinion. It was also becoming clear that, with the revelation of Chevallier's double life and the sight of his unrepentant mistress on the witness stand, the tide of opinion had shifted from the victim to the accused. The seven men on the jury were theoretically isolated from knowledge of this shift in public opinion, but in reality they could hardly be unaware of an opinion that was being so noisily expressed in the courtroom. Had their sympathies been swayed?

On the second day of the trial, Maître Mirat, counsel representing the interests of Dr. Chevallier's parents, began to question the saintly character of the accused as a good wife and homemaker. The parents were not out for vengeance, he declared; there was no vindictiveness intended in his presentation. The court had heard that Yvonne had been a good and faithful wife and mother, but had she been the appropriate wife for Pierre Chevallier? Did she make him happy? He read statements from the family caretaker, who admitted that Madame was not sociable. Friends of the couple remembered her as cold, suspicious and standoffish. They said that she "wanted to create a vacuum around her husband."

Maître Mirat went on to say that the accused had given several versions of what happened in the bedroom at the time of the shooting, no two versions the same. "She never gave the same truth." Counsel had achieved his objective. Once more public sympathy moved away from Yvonne Chevallier. This shift was further aggravated when the secretary-general of Orléans Town Hall told the court that the accused seemed neither upset nor moved by the shooting. Affect, appropriate emotion, is very often totally absent in cases like this, as we shall see in other cases discussed in this book. Anna Freud has said that the ego, the self, is absent, entirely missing, as an element in a crime of passion. Emotion obliterates conscious choice; it is as though the perpetrator does not exist. The assassin "becomes" the gun or the knife, which then kills apparently of its own volition.

But the courtroom did not hear evidence from psychiatric professionals. The only medical evidence heard, apart from a description of the fatal bullet wounds, came from a doctor who stated that Yvonne had "retained the mentality of a teenager in love with a student." He stressed her feelings of social, physical and intellectual inferiority and concluded that at the time of the shooting she was suffering from "physical depreciation [*dépréciation*: a sense of diminished worth] because her husband refused to make love to her. She despaired of ever being the equal of the man whom she had never stopped loving."

A neighbor of the Chevalliers, a Mme Allemand, may have remedied the impact of Yvonne's differing accounts of the tragedy when she testified that Yvonne had told her that she wanted to commit suicide. "She told me," she continued, "'Mme Perreau is better dressed than me. She has money to burn. She introduces my husband into literary circles, and he likes that.'" This helped correct the balance of opinion, which was altered further when the defense counsel asked the witness:

"Did she not add that her husband told her, 'You disgust me?'"

"That is correct," Mme Allemand answered.

Sensing that his case had been weakened by revelations of personal misconduct in high places and that the accused had been in many ways abused by the victim, while she continued to care for the children and maintain their home in Orléans, the prosecuting attorney introduced as much evidence as he could that tended to mitigate the guilt of the accused. At times it seemed that he was stealing the thunder of the defense counsel. M. Lindon read from a letter written by Chevallier to Jeanne Perreau: "I haven't even any feeling of pity left for my wife." These two, Pierre Chevallier and Jeanne Perreau, he said, were the true authors of this tragedy.

"Such cynicism," the state prosecutor continued, "fell on the heart of Yvonne Chevallier like drops of boiling oil on wax. Pierre Chevallier was avid for everything—for honor, glory and the embraces of his mistress. Yvonne Chevallier thought only of the home. When she tried to win back his love, he thrust her aside. Do I need to add that she must be pitied?" Then he began to make noises that sounded less unusual coming from a prosecutor. Despite her suffering, he told the court, she should not have killed her husband. She should have put Pierre's outstanding qualities of leadership above her own personal anguish. This brought a loud protest from the crowd, but M. Lindon's voice rose above the din of the unruly gallery: "Gentlemen of the jury, do not allow yourselves to be influenced by the public demonstrations in favor of Yvonne Chevallier. You must determine whether this adultery merited murder." But the outcry seems to have influenced the final part of his summation. He could have demanded the heaviest penalty of the law and thus ensured an acquittal of the accused. In fact, he took the opposite line, asking for a token verdict of guilty, with a token sentence of two years, all because of the many mitigating circumstances. He said that "justice" demanded a guilty verdict. "To ask for a conviction is not always to condemn but to seek the truth. Must one pity her? Yes. Absolve her? No." He reminded the jury that they had to decide whether the fifth bullet was an accident as claimed. And if it was not, was it intended? Did she buy the gun "to kill herself or someone else?"

This was a fine, passionate final speech, in the best traditions of French jurisprudence. But it was his friend Maître Acquaviva's speech that achieved the full diapason of dramatic effects. Here was tear-jerking oratory of a sort that cracks granite and melts steel hearts. Again and again he demanded that Mme Chevallier be returned to raise her two sons. "Gentlemen of the jury! Think of this woman who bears the heavy burden of making men of her two sons. Think of this and acquit Yvonne Chevallier." In the prisoner's dock, Mme Chevallier was completely overcome by the strain of the trial. She sobbed again and again, "I'm sorry, I'm sorry." She was asked if she wished to address the court herself before the jury retired, but, as everyone could see, she was in no state to say anything.

The jury retired. They had to answer three questions with a "Yes" or "No." (1) Did the accused intend to do bodily harm to her husband? (2) Did she premeditate the deed? (3) Did she fire with the intention of killing him? If their answer to all the questions was "Yes," then Mme Chevallier was a deliberate murderess, and in theory at least was subject to the extreme penalty of the law, which in 1952 remained the engine of public justice named after Dr. Guillotin. I say in theory, because in practice no woman had been executed in France since the fall of Pétain in 1945. (The last woman executed was a some-time abortionist who ran into judges trying to demonstrate their independence from their German or collaborationist overlords during the Occupation.) If the jury answered yes to the first and last of these questions, then the responsibility of the accused would have been reduced to the equivalent of murder in the second degree, "murder two." If the decision was yes to the first question alone, then a verdict of manslaughter (as it is known in Britain and North America) would have resulted.

Forty-five minutes after the jurors retired, they returned to the court-room to declare Yvonne Chevallier not guilty on all of the charges against her. The gallery went wild at the news. Reporters rushed out to call or wire the news to their waiting editors. The jury had voted no to all three questions put to them. Mme Chevallier was acquitted. The press widely condemned the verdict. Opinions printed in the estab-lishment papers and mostly written by men saw Mme Chevallier as the promoter of capital punishment for adulterers. In the left-wing papers *L'Humanité* and *Libération* women writers declared Mme Chevallier's acquittal as a great victory for the female sex. One writer in *Le Figaro*, whose identity and gender were shielded by the Proustian *nom de plume* "Guermantes" contrasted this verdict with one given two weeks previously in Lyons. In that case a girl had played an important role in a murder for motives of theft. In her first trial, which was declared null and void on a technicality, she was given a life sentence. In her second trial, she was given twenty years at hard labor, a far heavier penalty. On this occasion the judge had said, "I am not here to favor pity. I am here to defend property and persons."

"Guermantes" said of this, "Between the severity of the tribunal of Lyons and the indulgence of that at Reims, the space is so vast that both reason and feeling are put out of countenance." For a few weeks after the verdict, barmen, innkeepers and proprietors of cafés all over France noted that business was off. Husbands were hurrying home to their wives for a hot dinner, not leaning against the bar in some estaminet or boîte, hoping to get lucky. Of course, this was merely a ripple in the normal pattern, to which they returned in time. The lesson, such as it was, was soon lost on them once again.

But what of Yvonne Chevallier? She was reunited with her sons. She promised to take them to Chamonix for the skiing. She did that. Her friends and neighbors stood by her in the main, but in the end it wasn't enough. Even after the Church exonerated her of the crime for which she had been tried, she was shadowed by guilt, not an unusual concomitant in a crime of passion. There had always been an element of self-destruction about the case. However, Yvonne Chevallier surprised many avid *amateurs* of the proceedings when she flew to the penal colony in New Guinea to work out her penitence among the convicts. This was a sentence she imposed on herself after the established institutions had cleared her. Could she have been carrying a guilty secret about with her? Was M. Perreau, Jeannette's husband, simply stating a fact when he told the police that she had boasted to him that she knew that she would get away with it?

TWO

When Lovely Woman
Stoops to Folly

Ruth Ellis

Ruth Ellis, a London nightclub manager, shot her lover dead outside a Hampstead pub called the Magdala in 1955.[10] Ellis holds the dubious distinction of being the last woman hanged in England. A reading of her trial transcript, from the limp defense to her lawyers' failure to appeal the guilty verdict, suggests that she may have used the state as a means of committing suicide. Not only did she reject the idea of an appeal against the death sentence, she even refused to associate herself with any of the efforts that were made to obtain a reprieve. As she said herself in one of her last letters, "I did not defend myself. I say a life for a life. I am quite well and not worrying about anything." When the then Home Secretary was questioned about the Ellis case, ten years after her death, he said that he had not reprieved Ruth Ellis because

> … We can't have people shooting off firearms in the street. This was a public thoroughfare where Ruth Ellis stalked and shot her quarry. And remember that she did not only kill David Blakely; she also injured a passerby. …

True. A Mrs. Gladys Yule was injured in the thumb by a stray bullet. But Lord Tenby—then only Sir Gwilym Lloyd George[11]—made no reference to Ellis's recent miscarriage or to her excited and irrational state, both of which considerations might have mitigated his zeal to uphold standards. There was to be no exercise of the royal prerogative in this case.

> … As long as I was Home Secretary I was determined to ensure that people could use the streets without fear of a bullet.

After 1922, the majority of women who murdered their infant children were sentenced to death, but always reprieved. After 1938, women who killed their babies were not even sentenced to death. Somewhere in the collective legal mind, the British bar decided that women who had recently given birth were not entirely responsible for their actions. It would take some time for this understanding to extend to those who had recently miscarried. But while a miscarriage close to the time of a homicide tended to bring a certain amount of mitigation to bear on a Home Secretary, it did not in this case. As Patrick Wilson says in his book *Murderess*:

> Reasons which might cause a French jury to acquit or find extenuating circumstances in a *crime passionnel* rarely influenced a Home Secretary. Indeed it appears that the English scorn for what is considered this peculiarly Latin manifestation of ardour provoked severity rather than leniency.

To be quite fair, it must be said that Ruth didn't try to save herself. When her attorney tried to get a verdict of manslaughter, he was frustrated by Ruth's unambiguous answers on the stand. "I had a peculiar idea that I wanted to kill him," she said.

Her responses under cross-examination made her an even worse witness in her own defense. "When you fired that revolver at close range into the body of David Blakely, what did you intend to do?'

"It's obvious," she said with cool logic. "I intended to kill him." She should have been treated as hostile by her own counsel. In a *voir dire*, a discussion before the judge without the jury hearing, the Crown maintained that it had a solid, unanswerable case and would be able to convict the defendant not of manslaughter but of murder. He felt certain that if convicted of murder, Ellis would surely be reprieved. He said:

> I accept fully that there is evidence that this woman was disgracefully treated. I accept that it would tend to lead her into an intensely emotional condition. These conditions may well apply elsewhere.

By "elsewhere" he meant in the court of appeal or in any humane review of her death sentence. The learned judge declared, as he had to prior to 1957, that there was no way he could allow a verdict of manslaughter. So murder it had to be. Neither defense counsel nor Crown made closing arguments. The jury, which found Ruth guilty, made no recommendation for mercy.

On 13 July 1955, Ruth Ellis was executed for a crime that, in France, would have earned her a short jail term at the most. But England after the war was decidedly not France, and the Ruth Ellis case played an important role in bringing Britain closer to the European standard of criminal justice. This is a classic crime-of-passion case from Britain, in spite of the severity of the sentence.

Her case is perhaps too well known because of the newspaper coverage at the time of her trial and execution, involving as it did appeals from such literary celebrities as Raymond Chandler and Victor Gollancz, and because of the film, *Dance with a Stranger*, to require a detailed description here. However, for the uninitiated, I will supply a précis of the events and people involved. Even after the passing of forty-six years, the case, apart from its sensational aspects, is an absorbing one, which brought changes to the criminal law in its wake.

Ellis, a hardworking and hard-playing party girl, with platinum hair and an attention-getting figure, had been making a career for herself in London, with nothing but her looks and her wits to support her and her young son (born in 1945 and fathered by a Canadian soldier who had a wife and two children back in Canada). After working as a photographer's assistant around the clubs and doing a little modeling, Ruth met Morris Conley, a property developer, clubowner and pimp; a man the press liked to describe as "Britain's biggest vice boss." He put her to work in one of his West End clubs, and soon, as a birthday present to her, he made her the manager of one of them, the Little Club in Knightsbridge. Soon she was making more than ten times the national average income every week, and all she had to do was to flirt with the members and encourage them to buy the overpriced champagne. It was here, in this sordid side of clubland, that she met an alcoholic dentist named George Ellis, who gave her his name, a daughter named Georgina, and little else. Ruth had hoped that marrying a professional man would give her the middle-class life she longed for. But, George was set in his ways as a drinker, and after a token gesture in the direction of reform, gave it up as a bad job. They separated in 1951, Ruth taking her infant daughter with her. Shortly after their divorce became final in February of 1955, George killed himself in a Jersey hotel room.

Meanwhile, Ruth was not staying at home watching the baby. In fact, the baby was put up for adoption, while Andria, her son, was looked after by an assortment of friends. At the club, Ruth met twenty-five-year-old David Moffat Drummond Blakely, a wealthy, handsome, spoiled racing-car driver, who parked his fiancée while making time with Ruth. That was in 1953. He was the chief, but not the exclusive, romantic interest in Ruth's life after George Ellis's departure. For a time they lived together in an apartment in Egerton Gardens, Kensington. Their roller-coaster affair had no middle ground of calm; they were either in one another's arms or punching and pounding one another. Blakely sponged off Ruth shamelessly and beat her up when he was drunk and angry. The third figure in this ill-fated relationship was Desmond Cussen, a company director smitten by Ruth's good looks and her flattery at the Little Club, who usually took in Ruth and Andria after she had had a spat with Blakely. Blakely and Ellis's overheated love-hate relationship went on many months, during which time the loutish Blakely exploited Ellis's trust and friendship. He made her pregnant, then beat her so badly that she suffered a miscarriage just before Easter, 1955. To follow the twists and turns in their relationship is to write a gloss to the heady, gin-soaked post-war years in London when the city tried, after six years of war, to remember how to enjoy itself. Drink, once more freely available, although ration books were still required for many food items, helped this stormy romance to degenerate into arguments, brutal beatings and untethered jealousy. Neither victim nor murderer can escape criticism here, although Ruth, with a child dependent on her, was usually in the more vulnerable position.

Their turbulent affair came to an abrupt end on the Easter weekend, 1955. Still not completely recovered from the miscarriage, Ruth had agreed to meet David Blakely on Good Friday. For the moment at least, Blakely had decided to make a complete break from Ruth, and had found temporary shelter with racing-car enthusiasts Anthony ("Ant") and Carole Findlater, who lived in Tanza Road not far from the Magdala pub on the edge of Hampstead Heath. Intoxicated by alcohol and, one might add, with frustration and jealousy, Ruth pursued him to the Findlaters' house where, hearing sounds of a party upstairs, she banged on the door and finally smashed the window of Blakely's car parked outside. She caught sight of Blakely and others in a party mood. Perhaps she mistook the Findlaters' *au pair* for Blakely's newest conquest. Twice the Findlaters called the police to remove Ruth from their doorstep. On the evening of Easter Sunday, Ruth was again on David's trail. This time she brought a gun with her. She followed Blakely and a friend from Tanza Road to the Magdala, a Charrington's public house at the bottom of South Hill Park, in North London. Alan Thompson, an off-duty policeman, was inside enjoying his pint when he saw a woman who might have been Ruth Ellis staring at Blakely through the pub's window, as Blakely was buying a few bottles at the off-license counter. Shortly afterwards, Thompson heard shots, and running outside to investigate, found Ruth standing over the prostrate body of her lover with a smoking gun still clutched in her hand. She had emptied the gun at Blakely, calmly telling his friend to stand clear. In the fusillade, a bystander, a Mrs. Gladys Kensington Yule, was hit in the thumb by one of the six bullets fired. At least one observer saw Ruth put the .38 Smith and Wesson to her head and pull the trigger.

When Ruth handed PC Thompson her empty gun and asked him to call the police, he identified himself as a constable and took her into custody. As is typical of many people who kill while in the grip of heightened emotions, she made no attempt to escape. Indeed, she seemed to welcome the opportunity to pay for her deed and expiate her sin; she even thanked the judge who sentenced her to death. (The trial was a perfunctory one, in which only a modest defense was offered, concentrating on the events of that Easter weekend and not going into the background of abuse and alcoholism. The jury took twenty-three minutes to find her guilty.) Ellis would not allow her lawyers to appeal her case. Nor would she have anything to do with the many petitions that circulated after her trial asking for clemency. Her letters from Holloway indicated that she wanted to pay for her crime.

Meanwhile, all around her, efforts to save her life continued, among them those of the mystery writer, Raymond Chandler. In his biography of Chandler, Frank MacShane writes:

> During the summer of 1955 Chandler also became involved in a heated public controversy. He wrote a letter to the *Evening Standard*, protesting the imminent hanging of Ruth Ellis, a condemned murderess. There was no doubt she was guilty, but Chandler's Galahad instincts were offended by "the idea that a highly civilized people should put a rope around the neck of Ruth Ellis and drop her through a trap and break her neck." He did not quarrel with the official court judgement, but the "medieval savagery of the law" struck him as being obscene. The letter was published at a time of considerable public outcry over capital punishment, and many other prominent persons, including Members of Parliament, wrote in support of Chandler's position.[12]

But it was all to no avail. On the appointed day, 13 July 1955, Ruth Ellis was hanged by the neck until dead according to the letter of the law, under the supervision of the unfortunately named Dr. Charity

Taylor, governor of Holloway Prison. Since that date, the case has been tried and retried in many different forums. New evidence has come to light, and the majestic figure of impartial "Justice," with her blindfold and her balances, has been besmirched by complicity in this sorry tale of a near call-girl murderess who tricked the justice system into completing her attempted suicide.

Shortly before the execution an attempt was launched by Granville, Ruth's brother, to trace the gun that Ellis had used. Her story of how she had acquired the weapon was never satisfactory or fully believed. Now we hear about a mysterious stranger—perhaps Desmond Cussen—who put the loaded gun into her hand, took her to a quiet woodland where she fired a few rounds, and then drove her with the reloaded gun to Tanza Road on that fatal Easter Sunday, where the deadly drama began to unfold. Without naming the guilty man, who must have hated Blakely as much as she did, Ellis gave a version of this explanation of where the Smith and Wesson had come from in her statement to her counsel. Unable to locate anyone who might confirm the story, her attorney could not use it to influence the Home Secretary in the time available.

Frank Owen, a former Liberal MP and later a respected journalist, urged the Home Secretary to consider the interval between Ruth's miscarriage and the murder. He pointed out that had she killed her own newborn child, the crime would not have been murder under British law. The Infanticide Act understood the concept of diminished responsibility in the case of a recent mother killing a newborn child. But this cut no ice with Major Gwilym Lloyd George, who was more concerned with the fact that Mrs. Yule, a bystander, had been shot in the thumb.

Patrick Wilson, the author of *Murderess*, has said of Ruth Ellis:

Ruth Ellis is assured of her small place in history, not only because she was the last woman to hang, but because her execution, considered barbarous by many, placed her in that group of murderers, together with Derek Bentley and Timothy Evans, whose executions were constantly cited by those seeking the abolition of the death penalty, in the limitation and eventual disappearance of which Ruth Ellis's death played no small part …

Part of the blame for the fatal outcome for Ruth Ellis may be placed at the door of Lord Tenby, as Gwilym Lloyd George became after he resigned as Home Secretary. Called "the unsuccessful son of a famous father," he was a dullard who was once quoted as saying that he thought it would be a good thing if the Russians and Chinese learned to play cricket. "Only Heaven help the fellow who ran his Captain out!" He retired to the House of Lords, where he told cricket stories to all who would listen to him.

Fifty thousand people signed a petition demanding that Ellis be reprieved. The execution profoundly shocked the public. As Patrick Wilson says: "… it is difficult not to conclude that the provocation she had received and the fact that she had recently miscarried should have caused her to be reprieved." The present author is not the first to say that more miscarried here than the unfortunate Ruth Ellis.

Jean Harris

Ruth Ellis was English and she was tried in an English court of law. Across the water in North America, Americans have their own traditions and legal history involving men and women at the end of their tether. One case that illustrates many of the legal implications of the *crime passionnel* is that of Jean Harris[13] and her lover, Dr. Herman Tarnower, the man behind the famous Scarsdale Medical Diet. Both were well-educated, sophisticated, privileged people, who had known success in their lives. Ruth Ellis was a badly educated woman from a working class Manchester background. Jean Harris was the headmistress of an exclusive Virginian girls' school; Tarnower a millionaire doctor, head of a successful medical clinic in Purchase, New York, and co-author of a bestselling diet book. She was a fifty-seven-year-old divorcée, he a bachelor of sixty-nine. Their affair had been going on for fourteen years.

Tarnower was a wealthy cardiologist with affluent patients when his neighbor, the head of Bantam Books, suggested to him that the two-page diet typescript that he had been giving away free to patients for the past twenty years might be expanded into a book. With the right co-author, it became an enormous success, turning a wealthy suburban doctor into a very rich celebrity. Hy Tarnower was a career bachelor, whose comfortable solitude was punctuated by many long and short involvements with younger women. He was generous and loving during the life of his affairs, but rather cowardly when they came to an end. Jean Harris had been aware for some time that Tarnower was seeing Mrs. Lynne Tryforos, a thirty-seven-year-old divorcée with two children, and had invited her, instead of Mrs. Harris, to an exclusive and prestigious dinner in his honor. At the same time, Jean Harris's hold over the teenage girls under her care at the Madeira School was becoming complicated. As her contacts with Tarnower became less frequent, she no longer had access to the tranquilizers that he had prescribed for her over the years, and she became less able to cope with her professional responsibilities. On 10 March 1980, after sending a registered letter to Tarnower, she spoke with him briefly on the telephone, wrote her will, and set out to drive northeast from McLean, Virginia, to Dr. Tarnower's house in Purchase, New York. The five-hundred-mile journey took more than five hours. With her in the car she had a pot of daisies, thirty-four rounds of ammunition and a fully-loaded .32 caliber Harrington and Richardson revolver.

Exactly what happened when she awakened him in his bedroom is only partly known, patched together from what a servant said she overheard on the telephone connected to the bedroom and a police reconstruction based on blood splattering and fingerprints. Jean Harris's own account changed somewhat as the case developed. The final version was that when she got to the house, she entered his bedroom in the usual way, taking with her the flowers, the gun and five extra bullets. She turned on the lights in the bedroom, insisted on speaking with the bewildered doctor, whose comment was, "Jesus Christ, Jean, it's the middle of the night!" Finding her rival's nightclothes and curlers in the bathroom, she pitched them through the window.

It was a furious Tarnower who confronted Jean Harris when she returned to the bedroom. He slapped her face twice. This calmed her, but only momentarily. She reached into her handbag and produced the revolver, which she held to her own head. The diet doctor tried to wrest it from her hand. They struggled. The gun went off, shattering the doctor's hand. In spite of the pain, he held on to the weapon and buzzed for a servant on the intercom at the same time. He had just picked up the telephone when Jean renewed her struggle for the gun. The servant heard screams, shots, Harris's voice and another struggle. The gun went off. Harris's finger was on the trigger. Tarnower, his blood staining both himself and his killer, dropped between the two beds in the room, where he slipped into unconsciousness and death.

The following day, Jean Harris was formally arraigned for the murder of Dr. Tarnower in the courthouse at Harrison, New York. The case quickly expanded into a media circus, which would occupy the international press and television screens for months. Why? Possibly because of the celebrity of Tarnower, the diet doctor, and the implication of sexual jealousy in a proper, well-bred, middle-aged, middle-class woman; partly, too, because of the glamor of the surroundings: Scarsdale, Purchase and the rest of Westchester County, New York, make up an enclave of the very rich (the Rockefellers lived nearby), and this was a crime that had nothing to do with mean streets and badly educated, disaffected, underprivileged or poor people. The Tarnowers and Harrises are the models of American society. And here the model had gone very wrong.

The trial lasted fourteen weeks; a week for every year Jean Harris and Hy Tarnower were lovers. It took place in White Plains, New York, and was never out of the glare of the media. A clever woman, Harris quickly learned how to manipulate the television interviewers and reporters to her advantage. She was polite and gracious to the throng of journalists. She appeared in court dressed conservatively and immaculately. She appeared calm and collected. She played the part of the wronged party: the jilted lover of a heartless beast who had cast her away after having had his way with her. She appeared to have taken the press into her confidence, talking about the case, the legal battles, the quality of the witnesses. She half convinced them that she was being abused by the criminal justice system. The impression she made on the jury was equally well contrived. Here too she was the wronged woman, the cast-off plaything of a powerful and wealthy bully.

In the United States, murder comes in two kinds: murder in the first degree ("murder one") and murder in the second degree ("murder two"). The only other charge involving the loss of life is manslaughter. Murder two, the charge under which Jean Harris was held, carries a minimum sentence of fifteen years on conviction without any chance of parole. Murder two is defined as murder without premeditation, but it does not preclude intent, which is defined as the overpowering urge to kill someone when a weapon, by chance, becomes available.

It might be interesting to compare Jean Harris and Ruth Ellis with regard to the impression each made on the jury in her case. Jean Harris appeared to be a highly intelligent, well-dressed professional matron, calm and confident in the rightness of her cause. She wept appropriately at times, but her demeanor was always dignified. She was a lady. Ruth Ellis, a quarter-century earlier, appeared to be what the Crown described her as: a rather cheap manager of drinking clubs and no better than she should be. The governor of Holloway Prison, where Ellis was confined before her trial, allowed Ellis to have her hair bleached, so that the platinum blonde who in custody had become a mousy, uncoiffured waif, was restored to her youthful, confident, rather provocative self before she first faced her jurors. In both cases these impressions went badly awry as the trials progressed. Ellis appeared hard and brassy, a tough old boot, in no need of mercy from the jury, while Harris's air of being a lady from her chignon to her insteps was contradicted by her own screeching letter to her victim. Will the *real* Jean Harris please stand up?

To defend her, Harris retained the able services of Joel Aurnou, a beefy bantam in the courtroom, and the cigar-smoking head of an impressive defense team in chambers. She was charged with second degree murder, that is, murder without planning or premeditation, illegal possession of a firearm, and possession of a firearm away from her home or business. (The gun had a Virginia registry but was used in New York.) The defense team tried to prove that Harris had made her pilgrimage to Dr. Tarnower's house in order to say goodbye to him before committing suicide. The team maintained that Tarnower's death was caused accidentally when he tried to disarm Harris. One of the arresting officers testified that Harris had told him that her wish had been for Tarnower to shoot her, since she had been discarded and could be of no further use to anyone. Harris denied saying this as stoutly as she denied having formed the intention of killing Tarnower at any time during her long drive or in the doctor's bedroom as she flicked the switch, turning the lights on the sleeping doctor. The defense also tried to show that Harris's acts before her drive were consistent with those of someone contemplating suicide. She resigned from her job, put her papers in order, and made her will. Much trial time was taken up with tracing the descending spiral of Harris's depression as her affair languished. Here we have the doctor as both lover and dispenser of the pills that made her life tolerable. The defense team was successful in conveying the impression that Dr. Tarnower had treated her abusively and without pity. Further, the defense showed that Jean Harris had devised a scenario of her own martyrdom to be enacted at the feet of her lover. The idea being promoted was that in such a climate of rejection, Jean Harris's intention to kill herself became overwhelmed by emotion. She snapped, and committed entirely unpremeditated murder instead. The jury appeared to buy it, for the moment.

George Bolen, the assistant district attorney, acting as prosecutor, asked Harris why, once Tarnower could no longer stop her, she didn't continue with her design, that is, why hadn't she killed herself? She had no pat answer to that, which weakened the suicide defense. Jean Harris's presentation of herself as a capable, sensible person was weakened by her confused testimony about what happened in the fatal bedroom. Apparently Tarnower had three wounds, not two, although the original medical evidence introduced by the state indicated that there were *four* wounds. She failed to explain the third shot. She and her defenders also failed to make significant use of the fact that Harris was suffering from painful withdrawal symptoms at the time of the shooting. Tarnower had been giving her tranquilizers and stimulants for at least ten years, and she was coming off her dependence on all of them "cold turkey." Further, the defense omitted to call into evidence a psychiatric report of Harris's mental state at the time of the shooting—she had been examined by a psychiatrist shortly after the killing—an omission that even the jury remarked on as unusual. Another prosecution ploy was to introduce evidence that the wound to Tarnower's hand was caused as he held it up defensively in front of him as the lethal shots were fired. A parade of medical expert witnesses managed to confuse everybody about whether or not flesh from Tarnower's palm had entered the chest wound. If true, it would make a mockery of Harris's story about Tarnower's attempt to wrest the gun away from her in a struggle.

The most damning piece of evidence against Jean Harris was the letter she sent by registered mail to Dr. Tarnower before she began her drive from Virginia to Purchase, New York:

> Twice have I taken money from your wallet—each time to pay for sick damage to my property by your psychotic whore. I don't have the money to afford a sick playmate—you do ...

The letter, with its paranoid obsession with money matters, its vicious insults aimed at her rival, Lynne Tryforos, its demeaning groveling and bad language, showed the jury a different Jean Harris, far different from the quiet, composed lady they could see at the defense table. It was enough to give them pause, enough to make them ask "Which is the real Jean Harris?" The letter showed the depth of rage and jealousy the woman was capable of. While the jurors were free to sympathize with the accused, they could hardly fail to notice, in all the wallowing self-pity, that here was a highly plausible motive for murder. Nor was she able to offer to the jury any explanation for the savagery of the letter, or evidence of an emotional state that might tend to mitigate its powerful effect.

The jury retired on 20 February 1981, and took eight days to return a verdict of guilty on all three charges. Exactly a month later, Judge Russell Leggett sentenced Jean Harris to the minimum sentence under the law: fifteen years. She began serving her sentence at Bedford Hills Correctional Facility, New York, immediately after the trial. In 1982, an appeal for parole was unsuccessful. Two years later, she suffered a heart attack, from which she recovered. In 1988, she became eligible to make a Christmas-time appeal to New York Governor Mario Cuomo for clemency (Christmas was the traditional time for such requests). No clemency was granted. In 1996, when she was seventy-two, she came up for parole. As a well-educated, white middle-class woman, Jean Harris used her skills and notoriety to attract attention to the many poor, badly educated black and Hispanic women incarcerated along with her. Although the facility in Bedford Hills is called a "correctional facility," few resources for rehabilitation are available to the inmates. Harnessing her literary abilities in a positive way, Harris has written two books, *Stranger in Two Worlds* and *They Always Call Us Ladies—Stories from Prison*, which dramatically convey the plight of her fellow inmates. She was partly responsible for setting up a scheme whereby prisoners could visit with their young children.

Now seventy-four and living quietly near the Connecticut River, where all she can see from her cabin is "trees and water," Jean Harris is still working for the improvement of conditions for the inmates of prisons she didn't even know existed twenty years ago.

THREE

Oh, beware, my lord, of jealousy. It is the green-eyed monster ...

Alan Norman

> There's a seaside resort-place called Blackpool,
> That's noted for fresh air and fun ...

S
o begins the old music-hall rhyme, *Albert and the Lion*, written by Marriott Edgar and immortalized by Stanley Holloway. In the early 1990s, Alan Norman operated a fish-and-chip shop in Blackpool, but he didn't see much of the fun.[14] The Pennines Fish Bar was a marginal operation, and he and his wife, Patricia, put in long hours and saw little profit. They were bewildered by the value added tax, which remains the bane of many European small business people. Patricia, for her part, had something more to put up with: her husband's insane jealousy and abuse, which had gone on throughout a marriage that lasted twenty-five years. Twice a grandmother at thirty-eight, she had to do most of the business arrangements for the chip shop, because Alan had never learned to read or write. Finally, unable to put up with the abuse and the near-slavery conditions of her life with Norman, she found the courage to leave him, escaping to a

women's shelter where she thought that she would be safe from his beatings and intense scrutiny of every aspect of her life. She had every right to believe that having made her escape, she would be free to breathe easily once again. But it was not to be.

Norman told a pathetic story to the newspapers about being abandoned by "Trish," as he called her. He told the same story on television, to the police and on the radio. He announced that should she return under his roof again, all wrongs would be made right and there would be no repercussions. According to him, Trish had run away to escape the ever-mounting debts at the chip shop. They owed their creditors £114,575.81, including £10,000 to the VAT. He still believed the shop could be a gold mine, but his illiteracy and bull-headed certainty that he had the right end of the stick in all matters and at all times led him to a ridiculous conclusion. It was time to start a new business, try something else. Alan never got it through his head that Trish had not run away from the business or from money troubles; she had run away from Alan.

But while Alan Norman would have been lost in a library, he was clever at some things: he got the phone number of the refuge from Olga, his wife's sister and his sometime mistress. (It wasn't exactly incest, and it certainly wasn't love: Norman *paid* Olga for their secret meetings.) He then appealed to a friend to find the address that matched the phone number. He told the friend that he was "sick with worry about her." This wasn't exactly true. When he had gone to the police after Trish went missing, they informed him on several occasions that his wife was safe and well. At *his wife's* request, they had refused to give Alan her present address.

Out of sympathy, the friend found a pal at British Telecom, the phone company, and got him, as a special favor, to match the phone number to an address. Later, the friend passed on to Alan not just an address but a map of how to find it. That same night, Alan arrived at the shelter, broke in and murdered his wife in front of a group of other abused and runaway wives and children, after battering down the bathroom door behind which they were cowering in fear. After the killing, Alan Norman made a pathetic attempt to cut his wrists. Like most perpetrators of crimes of passion in the classical mold, Norman made no other attempt to avoid the consequences of his act. He didn't try to escape. To him, the murder of his wife implied the sacrifice of his own life shortly afterwards. There was no plot to escape justice. His own fate was outside his vision.

According to Elliott Leyton, in his excellent book *Men of Blood: Murder in Modern England*, an average of 127 spouses and lovers are murdered every year in England. Most of these are women. Half of the women murdered in Britain are killed by their husbands or lovers. This is simply a special case of the old homicide truism that most murders are committed by people well known to their victims.

When Trish Norman entered the women's shelter, she was asked to make a list of the abuses that her spouse had heaped upon her. Believing—falsely, as it turned out—that she was at last safe from Alan's brutal blows, she wrote out a list, in her own untutored hand, in ballpoint on lined paper:

Mental cruelty
Sexual arrisment
Dident have any privacy. Couldnt take a bath without being inter-
    rupted.
Couldn't have any mony for my self.
Worked 10–12 hours a day 7 days a week.
Shown up all the time in front of his friends.
I couldent have any friends.
Wouldent let me visit my sister or mother.
Wouldent let me go out, only could go out with him (dident go out
    drinkin', just visiting his friends).
If he did go out for any reason, such as fishing haveing a hour
    with is friend when he came home he accused me of having
    men in the house and going to bed withe them.
Didn't dare bye any new underwear. If I did he would say who you
    bought them for

He checked my underwear for any stains. I had to keep checked my underwear myself for stain, If there was any I had to try and clean it with toilet paper before he seen it, dident dare change them because he checked to see what I put on in the morning.

On the afternoon before the murder, Trish Norman tried to put her feelings about her husband and his longtime abuse of her body and her identity as a separate individual in a letter addressed to Alan. I am quoting from the letter at length because it gives an uncommon glimpse of the life of the unhappy Normans. The letter reads:

> Alan
>
> I shall not be coming back. I hate you for what you have done to me, made me leave my home, my family my grankids, the village I lived in. Why did you drive me away
>
> Why did you make my life like hell
>
> Why was you so hateful to me.
>
> I did love you.
>
> Was it my fault you became like this. Tried to tell you what you was doing to me but you wouldent lisen would you always tried to make a big thing about everything, dident you. Twisted everything even twisted my mind. you even manage it for me to be taking in to hospital dident you. Couldent take any more pressure from you, oh dont worry Im out know.
>
> What joke have you telled your mates. I bett you havent telled that I had to run away from you. you will never do this to me again, for thesimple reason is that I shall not see you again. Hope you are suffering like I have. Whats it like not having knowone to moune at.
>
> Oh by the way dont think I have gone away with someone eles. anyway who would have me the state you have put me in. Why did you do it to me. Now I'm all alone dont know anyone don't know what to do. Keep haven blackouts. dont know what

I am doing you really did a good job dident you.

Why should I be crying like this Ive done nothing wronge. if I have I don't know about it. You couldent even be a husband or a father could you. over 20 years we have been together what for all them years just gone waisted.

I can remember when I really loved you. Couldent get enough of you, but now I want to forget try and make a new life for myself. When I get well enough. Woke up last night thinking you was shouting me. you see you are just playing on my mind. haved to try a forget what it is you have done to me. hope you find yourself alone. the way you are, probly you will. never had a kind word for me did you. dont know how I lasted so long these poast few years living with you, it was horrible for me, it seemed as if everything was closing in it seamed as if you were trying to get into my mind.

I just couldent escape you—I was thinking all the time what will he be mouning about next. Should I do this before he starts should I do that thinking about what you would say next. I am just like a nervous wreck. Thats it have a good laugh. You could show all your mates this letter then you can all laugh. don't try and find me. I am in no Fit State to be able to cope with you. If it wasent for the staff in this place I don't know what I would hae done. So stop looking because no one will tell you were I am I am even having my name changed. I did keep telling you that you was going to far with me dident I.

It better this way me laving. If I'd had stayed I would have proberly have killed myself. Can you remember when I got those sleeping table[ts] from the doctor I did take all the table[ts] but I dident exseed did I in dying. Think back what life did I have with you not very good was it wasn't alound a money to spend on my self. not being able to go out. well dident hae any friends to go out with did I I dident have any privacy had to work all hours accused of going to bed with everybody had to have sex everytime you felt like it. If you worked as many hours as I did you wouldent have had ther strength to do it—next thing is becoming a alcoholic all because of you ...

Within a few short hours of writing this, Trish was dead, murdered by a man who had no capacity to read, let alone understand the letter his wife had left unfinished. When she was questioned, the nineteen-year-old daughter of the couple couldn't recall any incidents of violence in her parents' happy home. "From as far back as I can remember they appeared to be happy. I cannot remember any real domestic arguments between them. ..." At the police station Alan Norman explained to her, "I only wanted her back. I loved her so much I didn't want anyone else to have her." Looking at what Trish wrote, it is easy to see that Alan's active imagination had transformed his wife into a highly desirable sex object, whose amorous activities would make the whores of Babylon look like rank amateurs. He thought that the moment his back was turned, Trish was having it off with one or another of his mates hanging around the chip shop. Like Othello, the Moor of Venice, Alan Norman—who incidentally hated blacks and foreigners—was made jealous:

> I kissed thee ere I killed thee. No way but this,
> Killing myself, to die upon a kiss.

Unlike Othello, Alan Norman had a long history of abusing his wife and being obsessed with the details of her life. Desdemona never made that charge against her soldier husband.

Norman told the police, "I only struck her once. Stabbed her with that knife. I know what I've done. I just want to die." Again he said to the investigating officers:

> Excessive force? No, I didn't want to hurt her, I laid down kissing her after I'd done it. I kissed her twice, put my arms round her and said, "I'm sorry, duck, I'm ever so sorry," and she kept

saying to me, "You don't realize I loved ya, you don't realize I loved ya, give over please" and then I ran out, ran down to the bottom of stairs and slashed me wrist … I wanted to die with my wife. I didn't want to live no more. I knew I'd done injuries to her and I thought, Well, look, do injuries, do yourself now. I didn't want 'em to save my life. [His injuries were not remotely life-threatening.] I wanted to die, I still want to die …

Unfortunately for Alan Norman, his end wasn't as tidy as Othello's.

I think there's something up, up in my head, there's something wrong. I just can't understand it, it's like you say she was happy and I couldn't stand it for her to be happy. I wanted her with me. It kept ticking over in my brain, you know. I know there's something up there, but I've tried three appointments at the doctor's, freeze every time I got there, I just said, "It's chest pains, I think I'm going to have a heart attack." They just checked me and said there was nothing wrong with me.

In the words of Professor Leyton:

The man who was raised "in care" [that is, in an orphanage], the illiterate businessman murdering his wife in the presence of screaming women and children—themselves in the care of a protective institution—made no attempt to deny his guilt in court, and was sentenced to indefinite detention under the Medical Health Act.

Like Othello, again, Alan Norman loved not wisely but too well. Both had taken to themselves the very being of their spouses. They could not conceive of their wives having any existence apart from them. Trish and Desdemona were wholly owned by their husbands. Their imagined transgressions reflected not upon themselves but upon their men. Alan Norman's twisted mind, distracted and stressed by business worries, corrupted and abused in an orphanage that failed to teach him his letters, acted as his own Iago. Iago too treated his wife, Emilia, as an appendage to himself. He says, early in the play, that Cassio is "A fellow almost damned in a good wife." From the beginning Iago seems obsessed with the condition of marriage. Marriage is man's undoing. He proves it on Othello. As Emilia says to the betrayed Moor moments before Iago, her husband, stabs her:

> O murderous coxcomb, what should such a fool
> Do with so good a wife?

Because Othello's condition is in many ways parallel to all three of the cases in this chapter, I decided to see what an expert on the play and the character of Othello has written. Harold Bloom, in his essay on *Othello* in his book *Shakespeare: The Invention of the Human*, says:

> In some respects, Othello is Shakespeare's most wounding representation of male vanity and fear of female sexuality, and so the male equation that makes the fear of cuckoldry and the fear of mortality into a single dread. … We wince when Othello, in his closing apologia, speaks of himself as one not easily jealous, and we wonder at his blindness. Still we never doubt his valor, and this makes it even stranger that he at least matches Leontes [in *The Winter's Tale*] in jealous madness. Shakespeare's greatest insight into male sexual jealousy is that it is a mask for the fear of being castrated by death. Men imagine that there never can be enough time and space for themselves, and they find in cuckoldry, real or imaginary, the image of their own vanishing, the realization that the world will go on without them.

In Norman's statement to the police, he told the truth, extenuating nothing, except perhaps the number of times he stabbed his wife. Since his frail ego could not accommodate the idea that Trish was a separate entity, whose feelings, aspirations and wishes were not necessarily the same as his own, his account of the murder omitted any information that Trish might have added to the full account. One can only imagine the frustrations of an illiterate trying to cope with modern business, modern tax and real estate laws, and the hated VAT. It reminds one of Eunice Parchman, the unfortunate protagonist in the early Ruth Rendell novel, *A Judgement in Stone*. As the first line of the novel tells us: "Eunice Parchman killed the Coverdale family because she could not read or write." Eunice, the housemaid, murders the family to protect her guilty secret. This story has been filmed at least twice: one *Judgement in Stone*, retitled *The Housekeeper* (1986), a Canadian film featuring the English actress Rita Tushingham; the other, *La Cérémonie*, made in France by Claude Chabrol (an admirer of Alfred Hitchcock). Ruth Rendell is not suggesting in the novel that illiteracy leads to murder, of course, but that to some people such secrets need protecting by any means, even violence, even murder. In Alan Norman's case, he wasn't concerned to keep his illiteracy secret, but it dogged his steps in almost everything he attempted. It is well to remember that not all illiterates are as lucky or as clever as the hero of Somerset Maugham's tale of the verger of a fashionable London church, where the lowly functionary loses his position because of his illiteracy, but goes on to great success as the proprietor of a string of cigar stores.

Alan Norman couldn't understand the demarcation where he stopped and his wife began; he took the marriage sacrament of becoming "one flesh" literally.

John Sweeney

In 1982, John Sweeney[15] strangled a beautiful twenty-two-year-old actress named Dominique Dunne in Los Angeles, California. Sweeney was the head chef at the exclusive Hollywood restaurant, Ma Maison. The trial caused a considerable sensation in Los Angeles, because of the famous eatery where the murderer worked, a restaurant so exclusive it had an unlisted telephone number. Equally attention-getting were the literary luminaries surrounding the young victim. Dominick Dunne, the victim's father, is a television and film writer, a former movie executive, a novelist and regular contributor to such magazines as *Vanity Fair*. His brother John Gregory Dunne and his sister-in-law Joan Didion are established writers as well.

There was not much argument in court about what happened on the last day of October in 1982: John Sweeney, the estranged former partner of Dominique, burst into her home and strangled her. A witness saw him do it. She was rushed to Cedars-Sinai Hospital where she was removed from life-support on 4 November. Sweeney didn't deny his guilt. In fact he was already under indictment for assaulting Dominique in the same manner on an earlier date. Both times he used his hands to strangle her.

Sweeney's crime was a passionate one. He didn't plan to commit this crime, although some suggest that his drinking of two martinis prior to making the fatal call on his one-time partner implies that he was steeling himself for some act of violence. But, in the general way in which these cases are looked at, this did not fit the definition of a premeditated crime. He hadn't checked to see whether she was alone, and he hadn't prepared an escape or an alibi. It was raw passion exploding with lethal force.

Some time before the fatal day, in an attempt to show Sweeney where he was going wrong in the relationship, Dominique wrote to him. Whether she sent the letter or not is not known, but it was read at the trial with dramatic effect on the jury:

Selfishness works both ways [she wrote]. You are just as selfish as I am. We have to be two individuals to work as a couple. I am not permitted to do enough things on my own. Why must you be a part of everything I do? Why do you want to come to my riding lessons and my acting classes? Why are you jealous of every scene partner I have?

Why must I recount word for word everything I spoke to Dr. Black about? Why must I talk about every audition when you

Mme Yvonne Chevallier, who came from sturdy peasant stock from the valley of the Loire, near Orlèans, is pictured here at the time of her trial for murdering her successful but unfaithful war-hero husband.

Mme Jeanne Perreau was the beautiful, sophisticated "other woman" in the Chevallier case. Her complaisant husband, a department store owner, was mocked and laughed out of the courtroom, even though he tried to wear his horns with a difference.

Looking like a young Prince Charles, **David Blakely**, poses with **Ruth Ellis**, the woman who loved and murdered him. In 1955, she became the last woman hanged in Britain. She did not appeal her conviction; her justification: an eye for an eye.

Ruth Ellis's execution at Holloway Prison in south London attracted large crowds, most of them protesting the death penalty. She referred to her coming execution as the "doings," and walked bravely to meet Albert Pierrepoint, the official hangman, at the appointed hour.

Jean Harris behaved every inch a lady even in a scrum with reporters and photographers. When her private letters recounting her abuses by her lover were read into the record at her trial, questions were asked about whether or not the "lady" label still adhered.

Hy Tarnower's success as a doctor was considerable even before he published his famous diet book. In his treatment of Jean Harris, Tarnower was revealed to be a detestable cad and an s.o.b.

John Thomas Sweeney was the chef at the exclusive Hollywood restaurant Ma Maison. When his starlet girl-friend, Dominique Dunne, tired of his jealous rages and tried to get rid of him, Sweeney twice tried to strangle her. She died after his second attempt.

Young, beautiful and talented, **Dominique Dunne** is seen here in a publicity photo from *Poltergeist*, the chilling, Spielberg-backed ghost story about an invasion of spirits into the Freeling home. Her ex-lover strangled her because he refused to accept that their affair was over.

O. J. Simpson, in happier days, pictured with his wife, the late **Nicole Brown Simpson**. The case was the trial of the decade. Its coverage brought the world into a U.S. courtroom for a closer look than it anticipated.

The assumption throughout the O. J. Simpson trial was that Nicole Brown Simpson was the intended victim. Little time was spent on the life of **Ron Goldman**, seen here with his girlfriend. Was his death a mere by-blow, the elimination of an unexpected witness to the intended crime, or was he the intended major victim all along?

Edith Jessie Thompson had more imagination than was good for her. She entertained her P & O lover with letters recounting highly dramatic situations drawn from the romantic fiction of the day. Did she intend to provoke the murder of her husband or was she merely having a little macabre frisson with her far-away lover?

Edith and Percy Thompson, as seen on a seaside holiday at Ilfracombe, in Devon, England, before fate played a hand. Percy, the stolid Ilford clerk, was murdered as he walked home one night in 1922 from London's Criterion Theatre. Edith's love letters, produced in court, played a major role in the Crown's case. Her insistence, against the advice of counsel, on going into the witness box was a further blow to her case.

A rare family grouping: two murderers and their victim, if the record is to be believed. Here **Edith** sits between her lover **Freddy Bywaters** reading a slim volume (left) and **Percy**, her husband, lost in a tabloid newspaper (right). It is difficult to read their history without seeing how their Ilford-born middle class values helped shape their destinies.

know it is bad luck for me? Why do we have discussions at 3:00 a.m. all the time, instead of during the day?

Why must you know the name of every person I come into contact with? You go crazy over my rehearsals. You insist on going to work with me when I have told you it makes me nervous. Your paranoia is overboard. ... You do not love me. You are obsessed with me. The person you think you love is not me at all. It is someone you have made up in your head. I'm the person who makes you angry, who you fight with sometimes. I think we only fight when images of me fade away and you are faced with the real me. That's why arguments erupt out of nowhere.

There are echoes here of the frustrations in Trish Norman's final unsent letter. Dominique is more sophisticated than Trish and has a better command of language, but the same fear is there, strong enough to taste.

There are many sources of information about this sad case. One, in particular, is unique: an article called "Justice," written by Dominique's father, Dominick, and included in his collection *Fatal Charms and Other Tales of Today*. Whether an account written by the father of the victim can be relied on is an open question, which the reader is asked to bear in mind. Dominick Dunne's story describes the anguish and heartbreak of having to attend the murder trial, of reopening wounds that had only just begun to heal. For that alone, the article is worth reading. But he has also helped to describe how poorly a courtroom trial can represent the reality of what happened on the day of the murder. He tells how Sweeney's boss at the restaurant set up a skilled and highly professional defense team for the young man, whose own resources were limited. Michael Adelson, an assigned public defender, was supported by the legal firm that handled all of the legal work for Ma Maison: an old and distinguished Los Angeles firm: Donovan, Leisure, Newton, and Irving; with Joseph Shapiro, the legal counsel for the restaurant, keeping an eye on all the moves before and during the trial. Dunne tells how, while Dominique was still on life-support, the defense team was angling to exclude from the trial certain harmful testimony relating to other people Sweeney had attacked or nearly strangled. Through a journalist, they approached the Dunne family, not the district attorney's office, for a plea bargain. Dunne reported this to the prosecutor in the case, assistant DA Steven Barshop. This appeared to be the first salvo of a substantial barrage of legal tricks that had the effect of removing from the prosecution's case all reference to earlier attacks by Sweeney of a similar nature (none fatal) on other people, some of them close friends of his, some casual acquaintances. So the jury only knew about the earlier attack on Dominique and the subsequent lethal one. They tried to bar Dominick Dunne's ex-wife, the mother of the dead woman, from the courtroom, because in her wheelchair (Lenny Griffin Dunne suffers from multiple sclerosis) the victim's mother, they argued, might create a climate sympathetic to the prosecution. They didn't win that one.

In the trial, the presiding judge, Burton S. Katz, said to be the fourth worst judge on a Los Angeles bench—he was later demoted to traffic court before leaving the bench entirely—granted most of the defense's requests. He also struck down the murder one charge, reducing it to murder two or manslaughter. He would not let the jury hear what the victim told her mother about the killer or any of the abundant testimony about how Dominique had been living in fear of Sweeney's sudden return into her life after she had made a clean break from him. She had had the locks on her doors changed expressly to keep him away from her. The jury found Sweeney guilty of voluntary manslaughter in the strangulation death of Dominique Dunne and of a misdemeanor assault in the earlier choking incident. With the time he had already served while awaiting trial, he was out on the street again in less than three years.

John Sweeney's life was not seen by the jury. Perhaps, as the law implies, it is not fair to try a man or woman on all of his crimes at once. Perhaps his history as a violent offender should only have been permitted insofar as it pertained to the single victim, but much of the evidence of his unstable character—his obsessive jealousy, his paranoid preoccupation with all aspects of Dominique Dunne's life in spite of her insistence that she wanted to be left alone—was also barred from the jury.

When the verdict was announced, it was roundly criticized in the media. At the sentencing hearing, Judge Katz appeared to have changed sides: he was appalled at the verdict as well, and couldn't see how such a miscarriage of justice could have come about. He was outraged at the jury and the verdict. At last he was on the side of the angels.

John Sweeney is not the only violent offender to have escaped the heavy hand of the law. In every country these days we read of cases where husbands or estranged partners have, in spite of legal restraints, managed to break through the barrier in order to murder their spouses or former spouses and, sadly, often the children they have had together. Usually in these cases the killer then turns the weapon on himself, preventing a trial that in fact might be useful, bringing to light some of the blind spots in our legal systems, whereby manic behavior, lethal threats, past violent behavior and the pleas of the victims have not been enough to set things in motion to stop these repeated, desperate acts. With Sweeney and people like him, society tolerates time bombs that could go off at any moment. True, a walking time bomb is not a criminal until he detonates, and the police are at a disadvantage when it comes to crimes that have not yet been committed. How many victims of violent crimes have begged the police for protection from abusive husbands and former lovers? In the courtroom, both prosecution and defense teams are hindered by antediluvian views of the human psyche. Mental illness in all its forms is reduced to the old McNaughton Rule: was the accused aware, at the time the crime was committed, that his actions were wrong?

In the interest of trying to understand the sort of perversion that took the life of Dominique Dunne, and to see how his victim perceived the threat she was under, here is another part of the letter that Ms. Dunne wrote to her former lover detailing what frightened her about him:

> The whole thing has made me realize how scared I am of you, and I don't mean just physically. I'm afraid of the next time you are going to have another mood swing ... when we are good, we

are great. But when we are bad, we are horrendous. The bad outweighs the good.

In this note from a young woman to her obsessive lover can be seen something of what potential victims of such crimes face every day. We should take warning from Dominique Dunne's letter. It's never too late to leave town. In this case, changing of the locks on the doors, alerting friends and being young and innocent were not enough.

O. J. Simpson

There are probably few individuals who have been spared the barrage of publicity and hype surrounding the murder of Nicole Brown Simpson and her waiter friend, Ron Goldman, in Los Angeles in June 1994. As a result of the criminal trial verdict, we cannot say that O. J. Simpson committed this crime.[16] But it does seem to fit within the boundaries as a legitimate crime of passion. Although we can't say in print that O. J. killed his wife, without being hauled into court ourselves, it is fair comment to say that the renowned athlete and his wife seem to have been caught up in a passionate and destructive relationship.

Nicole had been dining with friends at an Italian restaurant called Mezzaluna after a dance recital by her young daughter, Sydney. Nicole was the divorced wife of the great former football running back, the sports superstar O. J. Simpson, who was becoming well-known as a sportscaster on TV and to non-football fans through film, product endorsements and television appearances. At 9:30 that night, Nicole called the restaurant because she, or her mother, had left some prescription sunglasses behind. Her friend, the waiter Ron Goldman, offered to bring the glasses to Nicole's nearby condo. He left the restaurant at 9:50 p.m. Neither Goldman nor Nicole Simpson were heard from or seen alive again.

With Muhammad Ali, Michael Jordan, Michael Jackson and the late Martin Luther King Jr., O. J. Simpson was one of the best-known African-Americans in the world, or, if he was not quite that famous before the murders occurred, he was soon to become so. In addition, he was living his life in the fast lane. O. J. exemplified the rogue male: he was tall, handsome, popular, narcissistic and a celebrity; he was also an active extrovert with a well-developed sexual appetite, who could be crude, self-dramatizing and short-tempered. When aroused, he lived at the top of his voice. When he wanted his woman, he could bellow like Tennessee Williams' Stanley Kowalski, moaning for his Stella.

He lived on and off with Nicole Brown from about the time she left high school. She was blonde, beautiful, outgoing, submissive, rich, unsophisticated and, when they met, just nineteen. Because of her early and violent death, it is difficult to imagine the ambitions that death cut in on. She was a party girl who enjoyed the company of people living it up and having a good time. She was content with her high school education, never seriously considering going on in her studies. As a friend said, "She had never prepared herself to live independently in the world. She had no job skills."[17]

When they married, there were already family difficulties. He had the rogue male's wandering eye. When his promiscuity resulted in bad feelings, he took them out on Nicole. As she says, in an undated letter attempting to pinpoint what was wrong with the foundering marriage, "I assumed that your recurring nasty attitude & mean streak was to cover up your cheating & general disrespect for women & lack of manners!"[18]

His repeated infidelity—and there is also some evidence that Nicole was less than a stay-at-home wife with an embroidery hoop in her lap—now added abuse to the unhappy mixture. There were arguments, fights, beatings and then happy reconciliations for a while. In the same letter quoted above, she reminded him, "You beat the jolly hell out of me & we lied at the X-ray lab & said I fell off a bike ... Remember!??"[19] During Nicole's two pregnancies, O. J. was hostile and unsympathetic to his wife's condition. "You wanted a baby (so you said) & I wanted a baby—then with each pound you were terrible. You gave me dirty looks of disgust—said mean things to me at times about my appearance walked out on me & lied to me ..."[20] As Nicole's mother observed at the time: "He actually thinks you can have a baby & not get fat." Nicole's self-esteem, never her strong suit, plunged during O. J.'s bouts of verbal abuse and withdrawal. He didn't fight fair. It was hard for them to pick up the pieces afterwards. To make up to her and assuage his guilt, Simpson bought Nicole expensive gifts and employed members of her family. This apparent contrition is also an attempt at control. According to psychiatrists who have examined this case and others like it, O. J.'s behavior fits into a recognized pattern common among serious abusers. In an uncanny way, the abuser has the ability—for a while at least—to make the victim (almost always the woman in the case) feel guilty about her failures to come up to the abuser's "high standards" of behavior. So low is her self-esteem that she thinks she's guilty of whatever he accuses her of: misconduct, stupidity, unattractiveness, anything, in short, that the abuser brings up in the heat of his anger and frustration. She is apt to see the iniquities of the relationship—his philandering, beatings, absences and abuse in general—as "par for the course."

With the arrival of the two children, Sydney and Justin, Nicole hung on by her optimism, even as the beatings and rows continued deep into the night. She went to see a therapist twice and came away carrying her own share, as she saw it, of the blame for the failing marriage:

> I want to be with you! I want to love you and cherish you, and make you smile. I want to wake up with you in the mornings and hold you at night ... I want us to be the way we used to be. There was no couple like us. I don't know what I went through ... I didn't believe you loved me anymore—and I couldn't handle it ...[21]

Their two separations, estrangements and occasional attempts to start over eventually ended in divorce. Nicole, at the time of her death, was living in a luxury condominium with her children. She had formed no permanent new relationships, although there have been hearsay statements that her friendship with Ron Goldman was more than passing.

There was a suggestion that she was looking towards trying out a *ménage à trois* that included a woman friend as well as Goldman. Poor Goldman. Either his place in the story has been totally missed by all of the investigators, or he was simply in the wrong place at the wrong time. O. J. was living in a walled mansion in Brentwood with Gigi, the maid; Brian "Kato" Kaelin, a friend of Nicole's, was living in a guest house on Simpson's luxury estate, as something in between a friend and a gofer.

Testimony at Simpson's trial attempted to measure the depth of O. J.'s rages and bizarre behavior. The jury heard about the regular physical and verbal abuse, his attempts to control Nicole's life, even after their separations, his demeaning language. An excellent piece of evidence for the prosecution, which Los Angeles County prosecutor Marcia Clark rammed home, was Nicole's 911 call, which she made from her townhouse in October 1993, eight months before her murder. It amply reflects Simpson's violent mood swings and loss of control:

Nicole: Can you send someone to my house?
Dispatcher: What's the problem there?
Nicole: My ex-husband has just broken into my house and is ranting and raving outside [in the] front yard.
Dispatcher: Has he been drinking or anything?
Nicole: No. But he's crazy.

The dispatcher agrees to send a prowl car, but soon Nicole is on the 911 line again:

Nicole: He just drove up again. (She begins to cry) Could you just send somebody over here? ... [He] broke the back door down to get in. ...
Dispatcher: Has he threatened you in any way or is he just harassing you?
Nicole: (Sighs) You're going to hear him in a minute. He's about to come in again.
Dispatcher: OK, just stay on the line ...

Nicole:	I don't want to stay on the line. He's going to beat the (expletive) out of me ...
Dispatcher:	Is he upset with something that you did?
Nicole:	(Sobs) A long time ago. It always comes back. (More yelling)
Dispatcher:	Is your roommate talking to him?
Nicole:	No, who can talk? Listen to him.

With her two children sleeping upstairs, Nicole tried to impress upon the dispatcher the seriousness of her plight, with what appeared to her to be a madman forcing his way into her house. In her replies to the dispatcher, whose repeated questions about whether O. J. has been drinking or is on drugs, Nicole tells the truth: he hasn't been drinking and he isn't, as far as she knows, armed. Her directness and calm, unexcited responses shed a useful light on the woman's character. Many might have exaggerated the seriousness of her situation if only to speed up her delivery from the yelling menace stomping around in her house, shouting abuse. She also admits that a long-ago lapse of hers might be the present reason for O. J.'s fury. *A long time ago. It always comes back.* This clarity, probity even, reappears in a letter Nicole wrote to O. J. some time before their divorce was final:

> If you're totally happy with your life now—I'll understand—especially if you're truly in love and know that's going to work. Then, I can't mess with that. If I don't hear from you soon—then I'll assume that's the case and I'll never bother you ... O. J. You'll be my one and only "true love." I'm sorry for the pain I've caused you and I'm sorry we let it die ...

Because of the 911 transcript, we have a good idea of what happened that October night in 1993. A memo from LAPD Detective Mark Fuhrman, written in January 1989 regarding an investigation he conducted into a reported domestic dispute during the fall or winter of 1985, shows that there was a history of family difficulties that spilled out into the street, well before the murders. Unfortunately, the amount of information available from the scene of the double murder, the entrance sidewalk leading to the door of Nicole's condominium, is limited. We know that Nicole's dog was heard to wail plaintively by a neighbor at 10:15 p.m. on the night of the murders. Forty minutes later, the dog was found unattended, with bloodstained paws. So, we may assume that by 10:15, Nicole and Ron Goldman were already dead. Ron Goldman left the Mezzaluna restaurant, where he worked, at 9:50 p.m., twenty-five minutes before the dog was heard wailing. Five to ten minutes earlier, according to Brian Kaelin's testimony, he and O. J. returned with a bag of McDonald's food, which they ate in different parts of Simpson's house. If that is true, it's difficult to work out how O. J. could have gone to the scene of the crime, committed the double murder and returned to dispose of the murder weapons and clean up without arousing the suspicion of Brian "Kato" Kaelin in another part of the house. No one saw the killings or the escaping murderer or murderers. The bloodstained murder weapons were never seen or recovered. Split-second timing could have put O. J. at the scene, but that would put this very real, very human tragedy into the realm of an Agatha Christie murder mystery, where murders happen all the time with no moments to spare.

That, at least, is how the jury saw it. The evidence against Simpson was circumstantial. He had been part of Nicole's life and he was extremely jealous of his ex-wife's activities that no longer included him. Earlier, he had remarked to Kato Kaelin that Nicole had been wearing a particularly tight outfit that night. He had felt provoked by being excluded from sitting with his ex-wife at their daughter's dance recital at Paul Revere Junior High School. Similarly, he had been excluded from the celebratory dinner that followed Sydney's recital. This was the sort of thing that often angered Simpson.

The trial was a media circus before which all earlier media circuses paled. It occurred in a community where racial tension is always smoldering, and in the aftermath of the trial of the police officers who were seen and videotaped beating an unarmed black motorist, Rodney King, in a cruel and unnecessary manner. When the verdict in the

Rodney King trial vindicated the actions of the Los Angeles Police Department, the resultant riots devastated parts of Los Angeles and spread quickly to other cities with large, poor black populations.

In this atmosphere, it was decided to move the O. J. Simpson trial away from central Los Angeles, but the media had by that time voided any advantage afforded by a change of venue. The sordidness of the crime, its lurid aspects and the lives of all the characters even peripherally connected to the case were exploited in the worst rash of tabloid journalism we have yet seen. Careers were made during the trying of this case. Obscure lawyers, gofers and police officers became household words, not only in the United States but around the world.

On the other hand, the police and forensic work, however meticulously it was done, did not escape criticism at the trial. DNA evidence was discredited. One of the investigating officers was shown to have planted evidence. A bloody glove, that matched a glove found at the murder scene, was found on Simpson's property. Detective Fuhrman's tapes exposed him as a possible racist. In the aftermath of the Rodney King decision, the riots that followed it, and a biased reading of evidence in another, unrelated, case, the whole question of police interference smoldered like a cheap cigar in an ashtray. This was not the finest hour of the LAPD. All this tended to cast doubt on the rest of the evidence against O. J., evidence collected by some of these same officers. The jury—mostly black—felt that there was reasonable doubt, and found O. J. Simpson not guilty of killing his wife and Ron Goldman on 12 June 1994.

In a civil suit brought by Nicole's and Goldman's parents, O. J. was convicted, and required to pay an indemnity. Simpson was ruined financially, and has crept like a pariah through the years since the second trial. He has often tried to exonerate himself of the crime, for his children's sake as well as his own. He hasn't been getting a large audience to hear him and his denials recently. Nor has he signed many contracts for commercial endorsements.

FOUR

Those Old Love Letters

Edith Thompson and Frederick Bywaters

In the drawing rooms, saloon bars and cafés of Britain in 1922, everyone knew about Edith Jessie Thompson.[22] Her name was whispered in the House of Commons and in the House of Lords. Edith Thompson was not a popular writer, a brilliant hostess or silent film star; she was a murderess. Like O. J. Simpson, she saw her case so enlarged and distorted by the press that she literally took her life in her hands to try to explain things, to put things right, to make the world understand. She failed—disastrously.

Edith Thompson was a great reader of novels, novelettes and the romantic magazine stories of the day. If she had had *less* of a flair for the dramatic, *less* imagination, if she had *not* seen herself as the heroine of a fairytale, she might have lived longer than her twenty-eight years. But facts are facts. Edith and her youthful lover, Frederick Bywaters, ended their illicit passion for one another on two scaffolds in two London prisons, at the same hour, in January 1923.

"No execution of a woman in Britain," writes Patrick Wilson in *Murderess*, "has provoked more controversy than that of Mrs. Thompson …" It has inspired both fact and fiction. Novels like F. Tennyson Jesse's *A Pin to See the Peepshow* and the more recent *Fred & Edie* by Jill Dawson are but two of the fictional accounts of the case. *A Pin to See the Peepshow* was also a successful stage play. There have also been several serious non-fiction examinations of the story, notably Filson Young's account in the *Notable British Trials* Series (1923), *Criminal Justice* by René Weis, *Verdict in Dispute* by Edgar Lustgarten and *The*

Innocence of Edith Thompson by Lewis Broad. Bernard O'Donnell, a London police reporter who was on the scene of the murder within an hour of the killing, covered the trial. He watched the faces of the principals as they spoke in their own defense at the Old Bailey. His is the only account that I have read that is unsympathetic to Thompson. He may have been shocked, like the trial judge, by the love letters and the adulterous relationship so freely entered into by the accused couple. His account of the Thompson–Bywaters case in *Should Women Hang?* is the centerpiece of that document. As for his answer to the question in the book's title: he doesn't see why not. The book was published in 1956, at the time of the furor attending the execution of Ruth Ellis, who proved to be the last woman hanged in Britain.

Let us establish a few facts about this deadly triangle. The Thompsons had been married for six years. There were no children. Both Thompsons worked. There seems little doubt that Edith was married to the dullest man in London—"in England," some insist. Percy Thompson was thirty-two, worked as a shipping clerk, and was almost entirely without ambition of any kind; he owned a little house in the suburb of Ilford, a dull place that suited his dull and fussy ways. In Ilford, a little house like that was called a "villa," which failed to deliver on its promise of sunrises over the Adriatic. Ilford tried to forget that Keir Hardie had founded the British Labour Party in West Ham, a short distance southwest, and tried to show to the world, or at least the world that looked in on Ilford, that middle-class values were respected and honored there. Theirs was a suburban life: bridge games, crowded holidays at the seaside and a Sunday joint on the dining-room table. Edith was twenty-eight and employed as manageress and bookkeeper for a wholesale millinery company in the City, where she earned more than her husband. Freddy Bywaters, not quite twenty when he and Edith began their eighteen-month affair, came closest of the three to living an adventurous life. He was a ship's writer on the P&O steamships, doubling as laundry steward. He was mature for his age, not overly bright, handsome and entirely in love with Edith, whom he met on a summer visit to the

Isle of Wight. He and Edith immediately fell in love. When they returned to London they carried on a clandestine affair under Edith's Ilford roof; Freddy became a tenant. Perhaps suspecting something, Percy Thompson after a time told Freddy to shove off. He shoved off and also shipped out, on a P&O liner. His long voyages were made bearable by the letters he received at every port from his beloved. She wrote to him care of shipping authorities at Aden, Marseilles, Port Said, Sydney, Melbourne, Colombo and Bombay. She might as well have been writing to El Dorado, Baghdad or Samarkand. These letters were filled with Edith's devotion to him, her dreams of eventual happiness with him, and perhaps too many references to the things that Percy had a legal right to do with her that the same laws prevented Freddy from doing. The letters show a rather garrulous, managerial woman, who knew how to sugarcoat her reprimands to her young swain. She says in the letters that she put shards from broken light bulbs in her husband's porridge. Sir Bernard Spilsbury, the legendary medical examiner whose evidence in court over a long and distinguished career has brought science into hundreds of cases, said she had done no such thing; he testified at the trial that it would have left traces in the dead man's body, which were not found. Nor did he discover any evidence of poisoning at his post-mortem examination. Edith Thompson lived her fiction every day:

> Your love to me is new, it is something different, it is my life and if things shall go badly with us, I shall always have this past year to look back upon and feel that "Then I lived." I never did before and I never shall again …

> Darlint,[23]
>   It's Friday night—loose end sort of day (without you) preceding the inevitable weekend. I don't know what to do—to just stop thinking very sad thoughts, darlint, they will come, I try to stifle them, but it's no use.
>   Last night I lay awake all night—thinking of you and of everything connected with you and me …

Yesterday I met a woman who had lost three husbands in eleven years, and not through the war, 2 were drowned and one committed suicide and some people I know can't lose one. How unfair everything is ...

... Now I'm going to be cross—*Don't bully me*—I never said or even suggested that I should cultivate the Regent Palace Hotel [a possible rendezvous] and there was no need whatever for you to have hurled forth that edict and then underlined it. Ask to be forgiven—you bully! (Darlint pal) ...

... Yes, darlint you are jealous of *him*—but I want you to be—he has the right by law to do all that you have the right to by nature and love—yes, darlint be jealous, so much that you will do something desperate ...

Peidi [Freddy's name for Edith]

In her final letter to Freddy, written the day before the murder, one gets an insight into Edith Thompson's confused mind. Her energy, her attempts to deceive and her hopes for a happier future together with Freddy are all in turmoil. Here it is, in part:

I tried so hard to find a way out of tonight darlingest but he was suspicious and still is—I suppose we must make a study of this deceit for some time longer. I hate it. I hate every lie I have to tell to see you—because lies seem such small mean things to attain such an object as ours. We ought to be able to use great big things for a great big love like ours. I'd love to be able to say "I'm going to see my lover tonight." If I did he would prevent me—there would be scenes and he would come to 168 [Aldersgate Street, Edith's workplace] and interfere and I couldn't bear that—I could be beaten all over at home and still be defiant—but at 168 it's different. You wouldn't let me live on him would you and I shouldn't want to—darlint its funds that are our stumbling block—until we have those we can do nothing. Darlingest find me a job abroad. I'll go tomorrow and not say I was going to a soul and not have one little regret. I said I wouldn't think—that I'd try to forget—circumstances—Pal, help me to forget again—I have succeeded up to now—but its thinking of tonight and tomorrow when I can't see you and feel you holding me.

Darlint—do something tomorrow night will you? Something to make you forget. I'll be hurt I know, but I want you to hurt me—I do really—the bargain now, seems so one-sided—so unfair—but how can I alter it?[24]

This last letter appears to have been written by someone near the end of her tether. She speaks of wanting to escape the situation in London, to strike out to make a fresh start with Freddy, but "funds" are needed to make this move possible. This doesn't appear to be even a subtle hint for Freddy to do away with her husband. She speaks, in fact, of having to study deceit for longer still before they can make an escape. If there is any incitement to commit a crime in this letter, I would suggest that the crime might be bank robbery, rather than murder, with a hint to Freddy either to go and get drunk or find a prostitute.

Letters, when they become public letters, as these letters did, are a peculiar commodity. The facts in a letter are always debatable. They were not written with the idea that they would be the truth, the whole truth and nothing but the truth. In 1855 Madeleine Smith, a twenty-one-year-old Glaswegian, told her lover in her passionate letters to him that her cruel father had not approved the relationship and would not consent to their marriage. The difference in class between an impoverished shipping clerk from Jersey and the daughter of a socially prominent Scottish architect was insurmountable. On receiving this information, the young lover wrote back that he intended to confront her demon of a father for himself. At this point Madeleine was alleged to have poisoned her lover. It is possible that her letters contained misstatements, exaggerations and lies. For instance, she may never have discussed the matter with her father at all. She simply may have tired of her highly unsuitable lover when a more eligible bachelor presented himself. Who knows what she was doing with the young man's affections? Certainly, a confrontation of the father by the suitor would not improve Madeleine's situation. Letters can never be taken at their surface value. All sorts of motives and games are afoot in written communications. Nowadays, what I've said about written correspondence holds true of recorded communications as well. Madeleine Smith's[25] trial resulted in a verdict of not proven, which, as Julian Symons[26] has interpreted, means: she did it, but he deserved it. Madeleine departed for America where she vanished from sight, probably by changing her name from Smith.

With young Bywaters far away at sea, Edith Thompson could have told stories of attempting to set fire to her husband's bed or trying to push him off London Bridge. Percy Thompson would never see the letters, and Freddy was in no position to see whether the letters were more than, as Pooh-Bah says, "merely corroborative detail, intended to give artistic verisimilitude to an otherwise bald and unconvincing narrative." Edith's letters would have added to her protestations of love and attested to the "proof" that she was trying to see to it that they would have a future together. Edgar Lustgarten said of the letters and their author:

> Facts and reality were no more than a cue for the exuberant fancy of Edith Thompson's mind. When the story fell short she improved it in her letters, until it was a story worth an artist's while; a story replete with sacrifices and violence, with colourful suitors and relentless poisoning wives, with all the trappings of the novels she had read and all the delirium of the love she had imagined. This was the driving force behind the famous letters which the prosecution used to get the writer hanged.

At the trial, both of the accused lovers claimed that Percy Thompson would not discuss any kind of separation or divorce. In Ilford, as in most parts of Britain in 1922, the very word *divorce* was hardly uttered except in whispers.

There is no doubt that Freddy stabbed Percy Thompson as he and his wife made their way home from a night at the theater on 3 October 1922. It was around midnight. About fifty meters from their front door a figure leapt from the shadows and struck Percy several times. Edith recognized the form of her lover, as he made his escape. Edith's screams followed him. She called for the doctor who lived across the street. Neighbors came running, the police were summoned. Edith said nothing about recognizing the assailant. In fact, she said nothing at all about an attack of any kind. Her husband had suddenly slumped against her, she said bleeding from the mouth, as though struck dead by a malevolent deity.

That's a brief account of the situation before the police began to pressure Edith to enlarge her story. Thompson's brother told the authorities about Edith's lover. He was discovered staying at Edith's mother's home, and brought in for questioning. The police allowed Edith to glimpse Freddy Bywaters at the Stratford-East police station. Edith finally broke down and named Bywaters as the attacker. But to what degree was Edith involved? Did she and Freddy plan the murder? Did she dominate her young lover? (Bywaters was eight years younger than Mrs. Thompson.) Had they simply daydreamed about a world without Percy Thompson in it? To what degree was Edith guilty of murder? Were her calls for help at the time of the murder simply *mise en scène*, part of a plan, or was she genuinely shocked and horrified to see one of her daydreams acted out before her startled eyes? Was she the suburban Clytemnestra the newspapers tried to make of her? And what about the use the Crown made of her letters at the trial? To what degree was there murderous intent and encouragement in these love letters written to ports around the world? The jury heard a selection from the letters read out in court. A careful selection from any group of documents, especially personal papers, adds its own color to the impression of the whole group. The use made of them during the trial certainly suggests the use of a shredder in all cases where people put the feelings of their hearts down on paper. Without the letters, Edith

Thompson would not have been convicted. Freddy Bywaters testified that the letters had not influenced him in any way in either forming the idea to commit the crime or in its commission. Another judge would not have allowed the two to be tried jointly. Marshall Hall, a leading barrister of the day, was certain that he could have got her off.

Thirty years after the trial, one of the jurors, or someone *claiming to be* one of the jurors, wrote to the editor of the *Daily Telegraph*:

> Sir—On the direction of the judge about 120 typed foolscap sheets of the whole of Mrs. Thompson's correspondence were handed to the jury to be studied by them, and it was my duty to read them to the members of the jury, which included two women. "Nauseous" is hardly strong enough to describe their contents.
>
> I cannot but feel that if Miss Tennyson Jesse [one of the authors of books about the case] had read the correspondence, and if she been present at the six days' trial, she would, however distressingly, have concurred in the verdict.
>
> The jury performed a painful duty, but Mrs. Thompson's letters were her own condemnation. Yours, etc.,
> ONE OF THE JURY[27]

The writer of this letter may not have been a member of the jury at all, of course, although the *Telegraph* usually checks up on its contributors. In order to boost the effect of nausea, the writer has added a second woman to the jury. Contemporary reports show only one female juror.

The letter, with its use of the word "nauseous," strongly suggests, as Mrs. Thompson's counsel said at the time: "[she] was hanged because of her immorality." As Lewis Broad sees it:

> Morality has as much bearing on the establishment of guilt or innocence as it has on Einstein's theory. Proof of guilt or innocence depends not on morals but on reason and logic. This was one of the failures in the processes of justice that resulted in the woman's conviction …

At the end of his excellent book on the case, with its announced bias in the title, *The Innocence of Edith Thompson*, Lewis Broad agrees that it was Thompson's unconventional life, her immorality, that brought her down with her lover. He says that the judge was no hanging judge, but a man of the most delicate sensibilities, fair-mindedness and integrity, in short, an upright judge in all ways but one. "[I]ntegrity and high moral standards pursued in a life blamelessly lived do produce a consciousness of rectitude and an attitude of mind that is affronted by loose living and loose loving. The gush and sentimentality of Edith Thompson's letters, her adulterous affair and the detestable murder in which it culminated filled her judge with injudicial detestation. Of any scruple of unfairness he was not, we may be sure, conscious. But there is a time when a judge must rise above his own sense of righteousness." In addition to this all important judgment, Broad thought that Edith Thompson had been denied justice for the following reasons:

1) trying both Thompson and Bywaters together handicapped Thompson's defense badly enough to constitute a denial of justice;
2) because of the unfavorable climate created by media, bringing her immorality into the question of her guilt or innocence, prejudiced the minds of those hearing her case;
3) while the letters were properly admitted at the trial, they were allowed to go to the jury "with suspicion taking the place of proof."

In regard to this last point, it may be added that the letters were not used in such a way as to give a context to the murder. Quite the opposite: the murder was used by the Crown to give a context to the letters. With the murder in mind, it was hard for the jury not to see dark meanings in the most ambiguous or innocent phrases. It becomes difficult to read phrases like the following in any other way: "We failed before but there will be no failure next time darlint"; "Be jealous so much that you will do something desperate"; "The best way to disarm any suspicion"; "Think out all the plans and methods for me"; "I'll still risk and try if you will." Lewis Broad continues:

> These letters had been admitted by the Judge as evidence of intention and evidence of motive. The Crown took this as a general licence to use the considerable mass of correspondence as a quarry from which to extract any material that could be made to bear a suspicious, sinister or incriminating construction. The Crown never established that the extracts selected had the meaning and purpose attributed to them. A person on trial for life in the circumstances of this woman should surely have had the right to insist:
>
> If you quote my letters against me, I require you to establish the meaning and purpose I gave to my words when I wrote them. It is not enough for you to say that my words can be made to convey the meaning and purpose you attribute to them as you read them. That does not establish motive against me, that is only your guess. To establish my motive you must first of all prove what my words meant in the sense that I used them when I put them down on paper. Before you can invoke them as proof of motive you should establish that they had the meaning you assert and no other meaning whatever.

Quite obviously, from what has been written above, this was not done.

Another reason, not stressed enough in Lewis Broad's book, is the fact that Edith Thompson made a very poor impression on the jury. It was not a good idea to put her on the stand, and her counsel failed her when he gave in to her wish to be heard. Thompson thought that the simple truth would clear up everything. But she made an incoherent and unconvincing witness.

Bernard O'Donnell, who saw Bywaters and Thompson testify at their trial, shows little sympathy for Edith Thompson. Watching her every day in court, he was reminded of what her employer said in the witness box: "She knows her own capabilities perfectly ..." O'Donnell continues:

> Now she was facing up to the most crucial test she had ever experienced and in the beginning she displayed the confidence of a performer who has zestfully rehearsed her part. She also enjoyed the advantage of having heard the evidence given by Bywaters.

Her counsel led her through all of the evidence, gaining in confidence as she explained away item after item. Then it was the Crown's turn to examine her. O'Donnell continues:

> Throughout this examination Mrs. Thompson was in command of herself. She wept in telling the story of her husband's death and occasionally used a handkerchief to wipe away a stray tear. She dealt as adroitly as she could with the dangers inherent in her letters and was quick to tell the court that she was willing to do what Bywaters thought.
>
> In cross-examination she said she had deliberately told untruths on the night of the tragedy to shield her lover. She had recognized him but had no idea of his intentions before he brushed her aside and attacked her husband. Mrs. Thompson then admitted that she had lied when she told the police she had always been on good terms with her husband and explained that her one thought was to shield her lover and not have his name brought into it.

The Crown prosecutor, who was Thomas Inskip, no less a personage than the solicitor-general himself, pushed Mrs. Thompson to explain why she had, in one of the letters, written, "Why aren't you sending me something—I wanted you to—If I don't mind the risk why should you?" The witness saw the importance of her answer here and the danger. In O'Donnell's words, "She tried to temporize. She had no idea of the nature of the "something" she had asked for but was afraid of it getting into hands other than her own. At last she had to agree that it was something for her to give to her husband.

Crown:	"With a view to poisoning your husband?"
Thompson:	"That was not the idea, that was not what I expected, something to make him ill."
Crown:	"Did the suggestion come from Bywaters?
Thompson:	"It did."

After close questioning, she admitted that at first she rejected Bywaters' suggestion, but in the end acquiesced. There were other attempts to try to hang the witness in a noose of her own words. When the Crown prosecutor, Mr. Inskip, pointed out that she had written to Bywaters that she intended to try using broken glass on her husband again as soon as it was safe, he asked:

Crown:	"When was it likely to be safe?"
Witness:	"There was no question of it being safe. I was not going to try it.
Crown:	"You are representing that this young man was seriously suggesting to you that you should poison and kill your husband?"
Witness:	"I did not suggest that. He said he would give him something."

The "something" was obviously something to make Percy Thompson ill. She admitted that the illness was needed to bring along another heart attack, which would finish her husband off. He could see, as his cross-examination moved towards its conclusion, that Edith was "struggling desperately and hopelessly."

Mr. Inskip continued to question her with regard to the letters and the suggestions which she had made.

"Was that acting or real?" she was asked.

"That was acting for him."

"You were acting to Bywaters that you wished to destroy your husband's life?"

"I was."

"Did you continue the deception right up to the Bywaters' visit to England a few days before the murder?"

Mrs. Thompson paused and counsel repeated the question before she replied, "I never suggested the subject. I suppose he thought I wanted to do it."

Edith Thompson was in tears at the end of the examination, but had recovered by the time her re-examination began. It was plain from her expression that she now realized how badly she had failed in her attempt to simply explain everything.

The fact that the lovers met in a little tea shop earlier on the day of the crime, O'Donnell sees as a meeting of the conspirators prior to "the deep damnation of his taking off." He sees it as likely that Edith told Freddy about the coming excursion to the theater. He sees Thompson giving Bywaters the time and place to commit the crime. She *could* have given this information with felonious intent; she could as easily have given the same information quite innocently, to fill the time, part of the dull pattern of her days. O'Donnell sees Edith Thompson as a cross between Medea and Mrs. Danvers in *Rebecca*, a female Svengali entrapping her young pliable prey in her net of lascivious and illicit pleasures.[28] Certainly, Bywaters is as much to be pitied as Thompson in their fugitive love between a rock and a hard place. But, young, foolhardy, direct and impulsive Freddy wielded the knife. In answering the question "Did she know about it before it happened?" it seems to me there is room for reasonable doubt.

O'Donnell concedes that Mr. Justice Shearman in his summing up "might well have said less about the moral aspect" of the conduct of the two accused lovers. But in general he sees nothing wrong with the way the trial was allowed to proceed:

... never, throughout a long experience [in covering criminal cases and writing about them], have I listened to a case in which the motive was established with greater certitude than that of the Thompson-Bywaters trial. I am as convinced now [1956] as I was at the time, that no other verdict was possible.

Patrick Wilson has recorded the following comments on the case:

No other woman has been hanged since 1843 for a murder committed by a man. The five other women executed with male accomplices had each taken an active part in the killing. The failure to reprieve Edith Thompson was, therefore, a retrogressive step [in the long struggle to do away with capital punishment, at least for women].

The trial and appeal judges differed in what they believed was required to link Edith to the murder. The Lord Chief Justice at the Court of Criminal Appeal said that it was enough to prove that she and Bywaters planned to poison Thompson. Judge Shearman, the trial judge, maintained that it must be proved that Edith knew that her husband would be murdered on the night of his death.

Wilson, in *Murderess*, sums up his impressions of the case:

... Given their two characters, I am certain they also discussed the possibility of Thompson being killed by Bywaters. I do not believe that Mrs. Thompson knew Bywaters would attack Thompson on the night he died, for, while she was quite capable of encouraging her lover to make a gallant gesture, I do not think she would have envisaged the solution Bywaters found. I believe that Mrs. Thompson did administer noxious substances to her husband, but that she did so in doses that she knew— probably subconsciously—would not be fatal ... The Home Secretary showed unusual severity when he failed to reprieve her. However, she certainly brought about the death of Frederick Bywaters, and if she had outlived him, acquitted or reprieved, is it not certain that her sanity would not have survived?

Thirty-three years after the Thompson–Bywaters trial, Ruth Ellis appeared in the Old Bailey to answer a charge of murder. While much was said about Ruth's life of easy virtue, there was little said that utterly condemned her way of life. The Crown readily conceded that the woman had been treated wretchedly. Thirty years had removed the conscious snobbery and holier-than-thou buffer that separated the prisoner's dock from the bench.

Both Edith Thompson and Freddy Bywaters acted foolishly and dangerously. Freddy entangled Edith in his murderous act to clear the way for the two of them. Edith's highly imaginative letters enmeshed her practically minded lover in tangles he could not untie. Edith's middle-class scruples rejected the possibilities of separation or divorce when Percy opposed the idea. At the back of her scheming and plotting was the notion that whatever happened, she wanted to be comfortable. She didn't want to live with her beloved in a garret and be shunned by her good friends. Edith Thompson came from Ilford; and Ilford was part of everything she did. In the end, because of her infamous behavior with Freddy, she may have taught Ilford a thing or two.

FIVE

The Media

The Mannings

The popular press (and through it, history) has dressed some quite commonplace murders in the dramatic hues of crimes of passion. Some needed stretching on the rack of a journalist's imagination to sustain such a description. In the eighteenth century, even the condemned criminals would hardly have recognized themselves from the broadsides published at the time of their executions. Very ordinary thieves found themselves dubbed highwaymen; stupid killings by half-starved, abused and demented wretches became, in the press, misled shepherdesses and betrayed virgins.

Because space was, and is, expensive and scarce, the writers of such chapbooks and broadsides were called upon to simplify the story into quickly digestible bite-sized pieces. Sound familiar? From simplification it is an easy step to exaggeration and embellishment. Facts be damned! Undeservedly, we remember such crimes because of the involvement of the media. While the cases themselves may be common, narrowly or crassly conceived, that is not how they have come down to us. Nasty, greedy crimes, crimes without imagination or romance about them have been changed utterly in the press of the day into the stuff of pulp fiction, novelettes and melodramas. Here events have been recreated in order to sell newspapers. Is there a woman involved? Is there a love triangle? The New York tabloids fed on the lifeblood of Ruth Snyder throughout 1927, during her fight to escape death in the electric chair. (More of this soon.) Eighty years earlier, in

November 1849, Marie Manning and her husband, Frederick, were hanged before a crowd of 50,000 people at South London's Horsemongers' Lane Gaol for the murder of Marie's sometime lover, Patrick O'Connor.[29] Many in the crowd came to watch because of what they had read in the papers about the case.

The crime of the Mannings caught the imagination of Victorian England. Every London paper carried the news. Even *Punch* covered the story, with humor and gibes against capital punishment. There was much speculation about this triangle of lovers. Newspaper reporters and sketch artists like Robert Cruikshank covered the trial as avidly as Charles Dickens did the execution. How odd, how edifying, to see a married couple turned off from the same gallows and left struggling in the air.

Unfortunately for the symmetry of my thesis, the passion of the Mannings was not for one another; nor was Marie's for O'Connor, her murdered lover. It was for his money. O'Connor, who worked on the London docks and in the customs house, had made a great success in money-lending, and often carried large amounts of cash on his person. The crass reality that the crime of the Mannings was one of cold-blooded avarice did not deter the press. Swiss-born Marie de Roux, or as she was sometimes called, Maria Roux without the aristocratic particle, was described as a "beauty." Albert Borowitz, whose book *The Woman Who Murdered Black Satin*, is the best recent account of the case, cynically remarks that when a woman is accused of a sensational murder she becomes a beauty automatically, especially when wearing a veil. Indeed, the trial of the Mannings was turned into something of a fashion show. No story of the trial failed to mention what the accused woman was wearing. Everything was done to milk the romantic as well as the macabre from this rather sordid murder. Still, there was *something* about her. Marie held these two men in what literally amounted to a fatal embrace.

Marie, who had been a lady's maid and a failed dressmaker, had been connected with some of the best families in England by way of the back stairs. (She was present when Queen Victoria was being entertained in one stately home.) This aristocratic connection drew attention to her, as did her foreign, continental birth. These mysterious Swiss origins imparted an extra fillip of sensation. Marie's Catholicism added another ingredient. All of these things transformed her into an exotic creature, as reported by the press. First she was seen as a victim and then, later, as a fiend. This gave a sinister ground bass to the events that brought her and her husband to their appointment with Mr. Calcraft,[30] the hangman. After hearing the sentence of death pronounced by the judge, Marie pleaded "There is no justice and no right for a foreign subject in this country. There is no law for me. I have no protection ... Base and shameful England! ... Damnation seize you all!" Whereupon she picked up a handful of the rue that had been placed about the prisoners' dock as a precaution against catching "jail fever," and threw it at the judge's bench.

Marie first met Patrick O'Connor on shipboard, crossing to Boulogne in the retinue of Lady Blantyre around the year 1842. He fell in love with her, wrote to her and sent her gifts. Her biographer, Robert Huish, who was at least partly a creator of fiction, gives her an exotic invented background and parentage. Why she succumbed to the blandishments of Frederick George Manning, a railway guard on the Great Western Railway, with few prospects, instead of marrying O'Connor we will never know. Manning, a weak man with a weak look about him, had bulging eyes, a fat face and no chin at all. Admittedly twenty years older than Marie, O'Connor was tall, possessed of a prominent nose and chin and carried large amounts of money in his pockets. At the time of his disappearance, his friends advertised his description:

Ten Pound Reward—Missing

Mr. Patrick O'Connor, an officer of the Customs, who left his residence, 21, Greenwood street, Mile-end road, on Thursday morning, the 19th inst., and was seen near Weston street at 5 o'clock on the same afternoon. Description—50 years of age.

5 feet 11 inches high, fair complexion, light hair, stout made, and wears a false set of teeth.

He had secured a lucrative place in the customs house through political connections in Tipperary and added to his income by gouging the people he lent money to. He was a dockside usurer, often drunk and just as often accused of being on the fiddle inside the customs house. With suspicion that Manning had a lively connection to a sensational railway robbery and O'Connor's pursuit of usury and loansharking, there is no one in this story who comes away untinged with criminal activity. Marie made no secret that the aging, sodden O'Connor's bonds held most of his attraction for her.

The banns were read and Marie and Fred Manning were wed. O'Connor, no great believer in the sanctity of marriage apparently, continued to write to Marie and arrange meetings with her at his house. For a time, Marie juggled her two relationships without having the men meet. Later, perhaps to simplify the arrangements, she introduced them to one another. Unfortunately, they either suspected the truth or resented the third wheel. They did not become friends. When Fred paid a visit to the island of Jersey, O'Connor moved into Minver Place with Marie. It was a larger apartment than the last one, and it was hoped that O'Connor would enjoy living closer to his beloved. When Fred returned, Marie tried to dun Patrick for his unpaid rent.

Meanwhile, Fred lost his job. He was suspected by the company and by the police of assisting a gang of train robbers, who had stolen bullion from the Great Western in a daring daylight robbery. Fred was the inside man, the guard who looked the other way when the thieves broke into the bank car after walking along the top of the train cars in a way that was to become a cinematic cliché a century later. After the robbery, Fred was never employed again for long. He lived off the rent he and his wife charged William Massey, a young medical student who rented a room in their house in No. 3 Minver Place.[31]

If there was a reason other than envy of O'Connor's ample funds to justify his murder, it was probably Marie's resentment that he hadn't married her when he could have. She was also angry at him for reneging on a scheme to set up a *ménage à trois* under the roof at No. 3 Minver Place. She had a right to be miffed; the new lodgings were more expensive than the last, and the Mannings needed O'Connor's contribution toward the rent. Marie's pursuit of "the old villain," as she called him, was her assurance that the community knew that she and O'Connor were friends. She would thus never be suspected should the Irish moneylender meet with an accident or simply disappear. There were dockworkers enough owing money to O'Connor and with grudges against his well-thumbed interest to make up a fine list of suspects, should it come to that.

There were several attempts to kill O'Connor. Marie kept inviting him to dine at No. 3 Minver Place. On one occasion, drunkenness kept him away. Another time, he blamed habitual fecklessness. Once he arrived late and in the company of a tipsy companion. The bait held out to encourage these visits was the possibility of meeting the sister of the medical student lodger, young William Massey. Massey's part in the ensuing drama has never been thoroughly explored. Several times he wrote letters, at Marie's behest, inviting the Irishman to come to dine with him and his sister. Since the sister was not in London during the relevant time, one wonders how he was persuaded to write untruths in an innocent way. If not culpable, he was certainly highly gullible, or stupid. But O'Connor's luck in missing so many invitations added only days to his life. One is put in mind of Edith Thompson's reported unsuccessful attempts on her husband's life, as recorded in those damning letters.

The preparations for committing the crime were carelessly made: a crowbar and shovel were bought. Fred made a fuss about the crowbar not being sufficiently wrapped in paper so as to hide its identity. He hadn't realized that to the innocent public of south London, a crowbar was just a crowbar; it took Manning's guilty knowledge of the use to which he and his wife intended to put it, that turned it into "the murder weapon," an object to be hidden from sight. Manning purchased and took delivery in his kitchen of a bushel of quicklime—"the sort which would burn the most quickly."

On the fatal day, Thursday, 9 August 1849, Marie sent a note around to O'Connor. He had missed coming the night before because he hadn't received the letter until it was too late to dine in Minver Place that evening. But the final invitation gave the time of the dinner and he set out with no apparent foreboding. Indeed, he was excited by his opportunity to dine free of charge with the Mannings. In crossing London Bridge, he showed the note, signed "Marie," to friends crossing in the other direction. He was not seen alive after that.

On Friday, the following morning, O'Connor's cousin William Flynn, another customs officer, missed seeing his friend at his usual post. He had not reported for duty. He was not to be found on Saturday either. Friends and relatives called at his lodgings near Mile End Road, and found him absent. Running into the friends who saw him walking across London Bridge, Flynn learned where he had been heading that Thursday evening. Calling again at his house, the friends learned from his landlady that Mrs. Manning had been to O'Connor's rooms on both Friday and Saturday, both times without Patrick. When they called at Minver Place, they found that Fred Manning was away from home on business, and that Mrs. Manning was put out by O'Connor's rude failure to arrive for dinner on Thursday and his lack of courtesy in sending no apology or explanation on Friday or Saturday.

The indefatigable Flynn continued his search through London. (Just as his namesake would search for his crony Ambrose Small,[32] the famous missing theater magnate, seventy years later in Toronto, both this Flynn and the later one alerted the police, but found they were not quick off the mark in starting an investigation.) O'Connor's friend talked to the police at the station near O'Connor's house, to an officer at the station close by Minver Place and finally to Scotland Yard. In company with an officer, Flynn confronted Marie, while the officer placed himself "in order to observe the workings of her countenance."

"Have you seen or heard anything of Patrick O'Connor these last few days?" Flynn demanded, after learning that Manning himself again wasn't home. She denied seeing Patrick after his drunken visit on Wednesday night, 8 August, in company with an inebriated friend. She admitted to having called at O'Connor's house on Thursday after his failure to appear in time for dinner. She remarked that she was surprised by this behavior, "since he is a very regular man." She went on to say that O'Connor was a "very fickle man" who would "frequently come to see us and, after sitting down for a minute or two, he would jump up suddenly and go away." That the same man could be both regular and fickle was not lost on her interlocutors. Always helpful, she suggested that they might look for the missing man in Vauxhall Gardens, on the river above Lambeth.

That was the last time either of the Mannings was seen in Minver Place. After the policeman left, Marie packed two steamer trunks and took them to the continental departures cloakroom at London Bridge Station, where she left them, hoping they would lead pursuers on a wild goose chase across the Channel. She caught a train to Edinburgh. Here she tried to convert some of the bonds she had taken from O'Connor's house. An astute broker contacted the police, who, after questioning Marie, took her into custody.

Earlier, finding his wife had fled, Fred quickly arranged to sell the remaining household belongings to a dealer, since Marie had taken all of the money they had found in O'Connor's japanned cash box. He then escaped himself to the island of Jersey in the English Channel. Here his constant drinking and unpleasant manner drew attention to him. He was recognized from his former visit and the police came up from London to collect him from St. Helier. He was arrested six days after his wife was locked up in Edinburgh.

From the moment the manacles were placed on his wrists, Manning began to talk. "Ah, sergeant, is that you? I am glad you are come. I know what you are come about. If you had not come I was coming to town to explain all. I am innocent." From the start, he saw himself as a friendly witness, as someone the police had rescued from "that bitch." Marie was the devil who made him do what little he had contributed to the death of Patrick O'Connor. At every juncture, Manning claimed, he had preached forgiveness, caution and prudence.

When he learned that Marie was in custody, he exclaimed, "Thank God, I'm glad of it; that will save my life. She is the guilty party; I am as innocent as a lamb."

Gradually the story of what happened when Patrick O'Connor finally turned up for dinner that fatal Thursday in August came out at the trial. Fred tried to be helpful to the Crown. He told how Marie had shot her one-time lover in the back in the basement kitchen where he had been lured to wash his hands. The *coup de grâce* administered by Fred with a crowbar or chisel was simply a humanitarian gesture, to put Pat out of his misery. He told how Marie, after burying the body under the kitchen flagstones, covered with lime and vitriol, slipped out of her bloodstained dress and into another in which she hastened in a cab to O'Connor's lodgings with her victim's keys. Here she liberated the cash and pocketed the bonds. While Manning did all he could to appear to be a Crown witness, he had no such status. His wife, for her part, heaped the lion's share of blame for the deed on her husband, who was a man, after all. She spoke bitterly of his lack of chivalry in not admitting that the whole fantastic adventure was his idea. It was a classic case of the pot calling the kettle black. In the end, the jury found that there was guilt enough to hang both of them.

The story of the romantic Mannings did not end with the couple being condemned to death. The press followed them to their graves. A fictionalized biography of Marie appeared: *The Progress of Crime: The Authentic Memoirs of Maria Manning*. One paper admired Marie's masculine ability to take matters in hand, while rejecting Manning's feminine passivity. There was a paper, a broadside, a chapbook, a literate article for every class and taste. From the moment the body was discovered until the moment the Mannings were turned off into the air at Horsemongers' Lane Gaol, London read about little else. The *Observer* and the *Morning Post* admired Marie's fashions and deportment. The *Observer* added, "There seems to be little doubt that Marie Manning was as treacherous to her husband as she was to O'Connor."

What Marie wore on the scaffold was reported in every account of the execution. (*Punch* carried a mock notice: dress for sale: black satin, only worn once.) Hardly an account of the case, contemporary or modern, fails to remark that the very moment Marie's body fell like a plumb through the gallows' trap, black satin just as suddenly went completely out of fashion. Albert Borowitz uncovered in his exhaustive digging into this century-and-a-half-old crime, that there was no indication that the sale of black satin fell off at all because of its association with what came to be known as "the Bermondsey Horror." But, as H. L. Mencken discovered when he tried to expose his invented account of the origin of the bathtub in America, it is easier to create a legend than to explode it. Borowitz, in his well-researched book, has done the homework that others should have done. While he tends to see Marie as a largely misrepresented creature, noting that the chief evidence against her came from her husband who was trying to save his own neck by accusing his spouse, his book (unlike those written by more excitable historians) is not a rant about justice denied; nor is it an exposé of a notorious failure of the system as it flourished in 1849.

Henry Mayhew, the great London historian, who was the father-in-law of the editor of *Punch*, has left a lingering impression of the murder. In his *London Labour and London Poor*, he quotes a street salesman standing by a placard carrying a pictorial representation of the commission of the murder. He said that people, particularly out-of-town people, greatly admired the picture of Mrs. Manning, beautifully "dressed for dinner" in black satin with "a low front," firing a pistol at O'Connor, while Manning, his jacket removed, watches with stark surprise. The street salesman goes on as Mayhew takes it all down in writing:

> The people said, "O look at him a-washing hisself; he's a doing it so nattral and ain't a-thinking he's a-going to be murdered. But was he really so ugly as that? Lor! Such a beautiful woman to have to do with him." ... "When there's mischief a woman's always the first. Look at Mrs. Manning there on that werry board—the work of one of the first artists in London—it's a faithful likeness, taken from life at one of her examinations, look at her. She fires the pistol, as you can see, and her husband was her tool."

Two final legacies of the famous Manning case have lingered. The effigy of Marie Manning, dressed in her own clothes and in her own kitchen, stood in Madame Tussaud's Exhibition in the Chamber of Horrors at the top of Baker Street for a century and a quarter. It was removed in the 1970s. The last legacy, however, will go on as long as the books of Charles Dickens are read in the world. Dickens modeled Hortense, the villainous French maid of *Bleak House*, on Marie Manning. He found a number of characters in the news of the week. Here he created a female villain who was as ruthless and brutal as any man; quite a change from the conventional Victorian women of fiction. His Inspector Bucket in the same novel was based on the Inspector Field who worked so hard to bring the Mannings to account.

There was so much passion in the contemporary press about the case, including Charles Dickens' own account of the execution and his subsequent letters to the *Times* urging the removal of the gallows from the streets, that merchandising of the murder and the double hanging reached a frantic pitch: a huge array of Mannings-related products were offered for sale, everything from cheap dolls hanging from toy gibbets to finely made Staffordshire figurines of the doomed couple. Dickens failed to mention that he had paid a pretty penny for the rental of a room overlooking the spectacle for himself and a few close friends. The group included John Forster, his own future biographer, who admitted that he had become quite smitten with love for the unfortunate Marie in her last moments. "This is heroine-worship, I think!" he wrote to another writer, along with details of the hanging that even Dickens didn't repeat.

I have taken quite a bit of space to describe a case where greed and money jostled the promptings of sex and dominance for attention. Had it not been for the accident of press coverage inflating the story and pushing it into the area of the classic crime of passion, the case might well be forgotten by now. The press has the power to distort and embellish not only the facts but also the whole atmosphere in which a case is heard and reported.

Ruth Snyder and Judd Gray

The case of Ruth Snyder and Judd Gray in the USA[33] has many similarities to the Thompson–Bywaters case, but never evoked as much outrage. Snyder and Gray did not touch the wellspring of sympathy that so overflowed in the English case. For them there was no petition with fifty thousand signatures protesting the carrying out of the death sentences.

Like Edith Thompson, Ruth Brown Snyder was married to a rather dull, conventional male, who was stuck in a rut and liking it. Bored with a suburban life not so very different from Edith Thompson's life in Ilford, Ruth found a brassiere and corset salesman to lighten the burden of her days with afternoon meetings at the Waldorf Astoria Hotel in Manhattan, a toll bridge away from her husband's Long Island home. Unlike the Thompsons, who were childless, Ruth and her husband, Albert Edward, had a young daughter, Lorraine. Henry Judd Gray was also married with an only child.

Judd Gray was a short, bespectacled, dapper, somewhat prissy fellow. He was a model citizen from East Orange, New Jersey, who had served in the Red Cross during the Great War. "He's as nice appearing a gentleman as you'd want to meet," said the detective who arrested him. His problem was that he had a mother fixation. He needed to be dominated in order to be stimulated. He found in Ruth the perfect dominatrix. He called her "Momsie, my Queen." She called him "Lover Boy." Their liaison brought a certain amount of adventure and stimulation into their otherwise drab lives. Ruth, with her bobbed hair, love of dancing, flirting, drinking and parties running into the small hours of the morning, an aging flapper, tried to evoke the glitter and exuberance of the Jazz Age. But she was no Daisy Buchanan. Scott Fitzgerald would not have found much originality in this thirty-two-year-old suburbanite.

At forty-five, Albert Snyder was thirteen years older than his wife. He was an art editor for *Motor Boating* magazine. Ruth worked as a secretary in the same organization. She was trying to improve on her working-class background, and took a shine to Snyder when Snyder took a shine to her. Ruth found him handsome and enjoyed his company. He was her first lover before they married in 1915. After living in Brooklyn and the Bronx, Albert bought an eight-room house in Queens Village on Long Island. Lorraine was born three years later. Albert saw the house, the address, their car, radio, furnishings and "the little woman" as signs that he was moving up in the world. These were markers of his success. Ruth, however, did not like the isolation of suburban living. Unlike Edith Thompson, she had no job that brought her into town regularly for shopping or work. She felt confined with her baby in boring solitude. At first she fought against the trap of loneliness by becoming the perfect housewife: she cooked, sewed curtains, made clothes for herself and for Lorraine. In 1925, the Snyders were a model family, a monument to success and the "American way." But the appearance was deceiving. Ruth was unsatisfied and unhappy. Snyder had an ugly temper and a gloomy personality. Although he was making a good living, he was disinclined to spend much of it in entertaining his family. His mother-in-law, Josephine Brown, who moved in with them after her husband's death, described Ruth to reporters as gay and fun-loving, while Albert, she said, was almost always glum. Ruth enjoyed people, parties, crowds, dancing, being with her friends, while Albert was a wet blanket: he preferred to stay at home in the evenings; he took little pleasure in restaurants, theater or bridge. She loved children and pets; he was disappointed that the child Ruth gave him was a girl. He wouldn't allow more than a canary in the house. He enjoyed puttering with his motors and making "artistic knickknacks" for the house. Perhaps Snyder was, in the Russian manner, in mourning for his life, or maybe he was still grieving for an old girlfriend, Jessie Guischard, who died tragically before he could marry her. Albert was always throwing up the memory of sensible, stable Jessie, to immature, giddy, fun-loving Ruth. He kept a pin with Jessie's initials inscribed upon it among his treasures.

Whether Ruth and Judd met through Judd's professional dealings in women's underwear or in a less intimate way is unknown. She called at his office at the Bien Jolie Corset Company one day for a fitting. She sent him a note. They had sex. For nearly two years they were lovers, giving and getting what each of them required. Why this wasn't allowed to continue is at the heart of the motive for the crime. Percy Thompson knew about Edith's affair with Bywaters (as Roger Perreau knew about his wife's affair). Thompson disapproved and made himself the obstacle to their happiness. But Albert Snyder did not know about his wife's adultery. The question of divorce—less horrendous in New York than in London, in the second decade of the twentieth century—had never been raised. He was in no way a stumbling block to their regular meetings and lovemaking. But somehow, Ruth decided that Albert had to go. I say Ruth, because she thoroughly dominated Gray, who was afraid of his own shadow most of the time. As far as he was able, he did what he was told. It is not at all unlikely that the killing of Albert Snyder was part of the passionate sexual fantasizing the couple indulged in. It was a task Ruth set for Judd, a kind of debasement that excited both of them.

But Ruth's passion also had a practical side to it. In his bloody leave-taking, Albert was picked to finance the lovers' future. Unknown to Snyder, Ruth had insured his life for $48,000, with a double-indemnity clause in case of accidental death, which raised the total to $96,000. If this sounds a little like the plot of James M. Cain's *Double Indemnity*, you have been paying attention. The details of the story and the setting are different, but the characters—the elderly, dull, unwanted husband, the alluring, unsatisfied wife and the amorous, suggestible salesman—are all there.

In the event, they killed him in his own bed. It was a cold-blooded murder, badly planned, clumsily executed and unconvincingly covered up. Ruth and Judd didn't fool anyone for long. Judd had established an alibi with a friend for the night of the murder. He bought the things they had planned to use to kill Albert, brought them with him to the house in Queens Village, and hid in a closet until the Snyders came home from a late bridge party. Albert went straight to bed. Judd Gray stepped out of his hiding place and smacked Albert over the head with a five-pound window-sash weight, which he used as a cosh or blunt instrument. Albert awoke and started screaming. Judd called out,

"Momsie, Momsie—for God's sake help me!" She did. She gave Albert more blows to the head, used picture wire to strangle him and finished him off with chloroform.

To hide their crime, Judd Gray bound and gagged Ruth with window-sash cord, a necktie and a towel. He left a kerchief, such as he thought immigrants often wore, where it would be discovered, and then made his getaway to Syracuse, where a rented room awaited him in a hotel, with a Do Not Disturb sign on the door. Ruth's banging and kicking awoke her daughter, Lorraine, in the morning. Ruth summoned neighbors, who brought in the police. She told them of the horror of the attack by a tall, swarthy foreigner. She feared that the intruder might have injured her husband. What they found in his bedroom more than confirmed her suspicion.

The police, however, were skeptical of what they saw and heard from the moment they entered the house. Why was only Snyder killed? Why not both or neither? If he was killed during an attempted robbery, why were the "stolen" jewels found under the mattress? Why had Mrs. Snyder not been beaten as brutally as her husband? Why were her bonds, which supposedly held her captive through the night, tied so loose? Why was there no sign of illegal entry? Why did her daughter tell them that Mommy and Daddy argued and fought all the time? That was enough to start with. In spite of Ruth's helpful pointing out of the kerchief on the floor, which corroborated her story, they didn't believe Ruth's account of the crime. Burglars aren't often murderers. Not even desperate foreign ones.

They found Ruth's address book with the names of her close friends inside. One of the investigating officers found a stick-pin, with the initials "JG" inscribed on it. The initials stood for "Jessie Guischard," Albert's dead sweetheart. The police thought at first that the pin could have been dropped by the fleeing murderer, the "swarthy man" that Ruth had described to them. In the address book they found the name Judd Gray, the only entry with a name having those initials. The man questioning Ruth through the night, fishing for suspects, asked her, "What about Judd Gray?"

"Has he confessed?" she asked innocently, a simple question that put her firmly in the electric chair as surely as anything that transpired at the trial—which quickly followed.

During the investigation, both Ruth and then Judd "confessed," but each party to the crime accused the other of the actual murder. It was also discovered that Ruth had tried on several earlier occasions to kill her spouse. In fact, up until the moment of his death, Albert Snyder had been a very lucky man. He had not been poisoned by things Ruth had put in his drinks—he blamed the bad taste of bichloride of mercury on the bootlegger—and had not been asphyxiated either by carbon monoxide when he was trapped in the garage, with the car's motor running, or when the gas heater in the bedroom was turned on with the flame extinguished. Twice!

Given the details above, it is clear that this murder was not the result of an outburst of sudden emotion. Nothing went black. No one was faced with a surprising and frightening situation. There was no talk, no argument, no blows except those delivered to the sleeping figure of Albert Snyder. Except for the passions released in a sexually charged situation of dominance and subservience, except for the passion most of us share—for financial reward—this was no ordinary crime of passion. Taking the unlikely raw material, the media, especially the tabloid press, ran with it and made of it the biggest story in years. In this collection, this case and the preceding one are ugly ducklings dressed by the media to pass for swans. They help to illustrate the press's weakness for making "crimes of passion" out of ordinary sordid murders, reflecting the editors' view that crimes of passion are what people want to read about.

The coverage in the press of the investigation, trial and execution of Ruth Snyder and Judd Gray was from the beginning in the hands of the best and worst of American journalists: Ben Hecht, Damon Runyon, Gene Fowler, all of the big guns of the press of the day were brought in to write daily items as the case developed. Such unlikely people as Mary Roberts Rinehart, D. W. Griffith, David Belasco, Peggy Hopkins, Billy Sunday, Aimee Semple McPherson, Dr. John Roach Straton and Will

Durant covered aspects of the case. There was a large readership for stories like this. They sustained the tabloids. Even the *New York Times*, with its banner slogan "all the news that's fit to print," included coverage. The public had been left high and dry by the inconclusive ending of the Hall–Mills story in 1926, a case involving the death of a prominent clergyman and a female member of his choir, whose murdered bodies were found in a New Jersey lovers' lane in September 1922. Now, in the Snyder–Gray case, they had a sensational new entertainment. In fact, Charlotte Mills, daughter of the murdered woman in the Hall–Mills case,[34] was engaged by one of the papers to follow the Snyder–Gray trial as she had covered the trial of the wife and brothers of her mother's paramour. The Hall–Mills case is said to have had more words written about it than any other murder case up to the time of the murders of O. J. Simpson's wife and her friend in California in the 1990s, but the Snyder–Gray case offered impressive competition. The murder of Albert Snyder and the trial of the lovers who killed him inspired hundreds of thousands of words in the press. As Ann Jones, in *Women Who Kill*, says:

> The newspapers, then, in cooperation with the court, took up the task of excising that social cancer, of reestablishing old standards, of ensuring, as the *Herald Tribune* put it that the "slightly pale yellow dawn of a new decadence, which rose after the lurid sunsets of the war," would deepen "into the clear blue of another, an almost Victorian earnestness." The more respectable dailies tended to serious reflections upon the case while the tabloids went for sensational, and often wholly fictitious, sidelights. Among them all, they turned the Snyder case into one of the top media events of the decade—and its most important morality play, designed like medieval moral drama to point the way to heaven. By the time it was over, all of the papers had written volumes and, incidentally, sold more newspapers than ever before.

At first, Ruth was treated in the press as "the beautiful wife" of the murdered art director. After her confession, the reporters changed their approach, in stages. At first the *Mirror* contrasted Ruth's attractive appearance with the brutal acts she had confessed to. On 24 March 1927, the paper displayed a full-page studio photograph of the accused murderess with instructions to its readers to:

> ... study this face, pretty, soft, smiling, with curling hair and delicate features. One of a loving wife and devoted mother, you would say. Yet it is that of Mrs. Ruth Brown Snyder....

Soon the papers abandoned this tack completely. Now she was depicted as the "Fiend Wife," the "faithless wife," the "blonde fiend," the "marble woman" encased from head to foot in a "mask of marble," "flaming Ruth," a "vampire," and "Ruthless Ruth, the Viking Ice Matron of Queens Village." Again, according to Ann Jones:

> The more sober New York Post found her to be a "hard-faced woman" probably "oversexed" and certainly interested in "power and authority." Physically, the Post said, she was "heavy and coarse." The New York Herald Tribune, apparently casting about for the right approach to the story, called her a "woman of steel" and then criticized her for having rough skin, straight hair, and a wrinkled dress, concluding its report of the first press interview given by the confessed conspirator in murder with the apparently damning judgement: "She was not well groomed."

Ruth was compared through the trial to Lucretia Borgia, Eve in league with Satan, Messalina and Lady Macbeth. Phrenologists were consulted and ample space was given to their findings. The bumps on her head were compared to those of Brigham Young, indicating a "polygamous disposition." Other commentators declared Ruth to be "unfeminine," with a masculine mouth and a hard and granite-like jaw. Soon the tabloids had dubbed her the "Granite Woman." No one saw her as anything but cold-eyed and self-obsessed. The pseudoscientific appraisals of the woman on trial for her life went on and on. Natasha Rambova, the second wife of Rudolph Valentino, the movie star, watched Ruth as she sat in the courtroom: "There is lacking in her character that real thing, selflessness. She apparently doesn't possess it and never will. Her fault is that she has no heart."

Judd Gray's treatment at the hands of the press was less dramatic, but more demeaning. He was seen as "Lover Boy," completely in the power of a female Svengali. Judd Gray's attorney, in summing up the defense, declared:

> That woman, like a poisonous snake, drew Judd Gray into her glistening coils, and there was no escape. It was a peculiarly alluring seduction. Just as a piece of steel jumps and clings to the powerful magnet, so Judd Gray came within the powerful, compelling, attractive force of that woman. She held him fast. This woman, the peculiar venomous species of humanity, was abnormal, possessed of an all-consuming, all-absorbing passion, an animal lust, which seemingly was never satiated....

In her defense, Ruth's counsel presented a case at least as believable as the one drawn by Gray's attorney. Gray had bought the sash-weights. Gray had concocted the alibi. Only Gray's testimony connected Ruth to the murder. But no one bought that argument. The jury appeared to believe it was just one more example of the pot calling the kettle black. Ruth was the siren, singing her song of entrapment to her bespectacled Ulysses. Neither of the accused looked well as their case went to the jury. And into the jury room the jurors went, to ponder not simply the fate of a pair of suburban lovers, but to confront a tangled web of depravity from which some basic human values needed to be redeemed by a guilty verdict, which in due course they delivered.

If sympathy was shown in the press for anyone associated with this sensational trial, it was to the children of the lovers and the mothers of the accused murderers. Judd Gray's mother was photographed sitting on her son's lap.

The last act in this sensational case, where lust for power, dominance and money competed, took place in the Death House of Sing Sing prison at Ossining, New York, on 12 January 1928. As predicted in the papers, Ruth Snyder appeared in the death chamber as a sickly, "disheveled wreck," in a drab prison shirtwaist, her hair now almost totally gray. She had, while under sentence of death, converted to Catholicism, the religion of New York governor Al Smith, an act that was judged more opportunistic than sincere. Up to the last she continued to write to the insurance company, demanding that it honor the double indemnity policy on her husband's life. While in the grip of the electric chair, she continued to mumble the responses to the prayers of her priest. Her last words echoed those of Jesus on the cross: "Father, forgive them; for they know not what they do."

Among the witnesses to her death was Thomas Howard, a Chicago news photographer recently hired by the *Daily News* and unknown to the Sing Sing prison staff. He had been brought in like an out-of-town hit man to take a final picture of Ruth Snyder. He had a trip cable running from a hidden camera strapped to his knee to the release in his pocket. Gene Fowler, another eyewitness, reported that "the body that once throbbed with the joy of her sordid bacchanals turned brick red as the current struck," and during those few moments, Thomas Howard snapped the most infamous photograph in the long and sensational history of tabloid journalism. The next morning it appeared on the front page of the *Daily News*, as an *EXTRA*, displacing photographs of the murderers and accompanied by a single word in giant capitals: DEAD!

SIX

When Newspaper Editors
Were in Season

Henriette Caillaux

Mme Henriette Caillaux (1878–1943) was a woman who sacrificed all for the love of her husband.[35] Was it a true crime of passion in the classic mold? It was certainly the stuff of tragedy. Of opera! But there is a flaw in the pattern: one side of the triangle was not an intimate of either of the other partners in the story. This was a triangle in which one side aggressively, publicly, flaunted the power he had over the lives of the other two. Mme Caillaux freely put her own life on the line when she called upon the editor of *Le Figaro* and shot him dead in his own office. Her exquisite reason? This editor had dared to publish private letters written to her by her new husband, the esteemed minister of finance.

The finance minister was Joseph Caillaux, who was fifty-one years old; the editor was Gaston Calmette, fifty-six. The first account I read of the case was short and touched on the main points, but omitted the details that give it its special quality. This version of the story was true in the main, but, as Mark Twain observed in another connection, the author "stretched" some things, distorting and changing some of the facts, but mainly telling the truth. In this version, I hope I have replaced the divots and restored the picture.

Earlier I noted that the *timing* of a crime may have a great deal to do with the impressions it makes on the public. Much of the impact of Henriette Caillaux's story stems from the date of the crime: 16 March 1914. War clouds were gathering over Europe. The sabers that were rattling were not only those of duelists in the Bois de Vincennes or at Longchamps. The tangle of treaties, ententes and alliances that had slowly been created over the century just past was pulled tight and about to be sundered by a passionate assassin named Gavrilo Princip in Sarajevo, an event that would bring about the Great War in August of that year. With five months to run, the peace was fragile; tension in France, bound to be in the middle of any coming European conflict, was as high as it had been on the eve of the declaration of war against Prussia in July 1870. Intrigue was everywhere. The country, which had been divided since the time of the Dreyfus affair, had become paranoid, suspicious, isolated and unjust.

Le Figaro (six pages, price 15 centimes, circulation 30,000) was (and is) a solid, authoritative, conservative paper. It taught the bourgeoisie middle-class values. Even at this time of international ferment, *Le Figaro* carried less than two percent foreign news, but in this it was no worse than the other eighteen Paris papers. Further, it printed no letters to the editor; *Figaro's* editors brooked no criticism or contradiction. This was the paper that first condemned Alfred Dreyfus, in articles by Léon, the royalist son of Alphonse Daudet, and later lost thousands of subscribers when it supported a call for a revision of Dreyfus' trial. Its move to a more pro-Dreyfus stand also caused it to change editors. But that was all water under the bridge. Gaston Calmette, the editor in 1914, was a first-rate journalist, but like many other newspaper editors in France, he found it difficult to separate the public life of a politician from his private life. *Ad hominem* was a way of life in the French press. Gaston Calmette, in addition, was a bulldog. Once he bit into something, he was unlikely to stop shaking it or turn it loose until the thing had been completely savaged and discredited. For instance, a negative review of the 1912 Ballets Russes' production of *L'Après-Midi d'un Faune*, in which Nijinsky danced without a jockstrap, almost severed Russo-French relations.

Calmette had always wanted to edit a paper of the quality and influence of *Le Figaro*. He got as far as assistant editor on his own merits, then married the daughter of the paper's owner, much the way Harry Comfort Hindmarsh, Ernest Hemingway's *bête noire* in his

Canadian years, assumed the helm of the *Toronto Star*. The marriage succeeded in its cynical purpose but left both of the Calmettes unhappy and unsatisfied. By 1914, Calmette had acquired a mistress, whom he hoped to marry one day.

In March 1914, the favored victim of his editorial attacks was Joseph Caillaux, a former prime minister, twice previously minister of finance and now the *newly* appointed minister of finance. He came from an old, politically active family. His bald head turned a splotchy pink when he was out of temper. And his mustaches were terrible when he was crossed. Caillaux had made himself popular by reducing the tax on beer and wine and increasing it on spirits. This discouraged the drinking of absinthe, which had laid low such people as the poet Verlaine. Caillaux changed French drinking habits. Like Calmette, Caillaux had made an unhappy first marriage, of which now he was happily clear. His new wife, Henriette, shared Joseph's political and social ambitions.

Calmette took his first bite from Caillaux's flank at the turn of the new year, 1914, in a half-column rant. He wrote that Caillaux was "preparing a positive arsenal of new laws" and adjured him to "ask himself whether he is not, with his hate-inspired persecutions, going to dry up the sources of that solidarity, of that fraternity, of that spontaneity whereby good works increase in worth." This public-spirited squib was not an isolated blast. He followed the Friday barrage with another on Saturday, 3 January, and another and another. Almost every day, when the morning paper was opened up on the breakfast table, Calmette savaged finance minister Caillaux, often on the front page. He was anathematized, belittled, berated. He was called "Congo Caillaux," "Germany's Man," "Socialist Dupe," "Shady Financier," and was accused of making money on the Berlin stock exchange. One hundred and thirty-eight articles and cartoons highly critical of the minister were printed in the paper in a period of seventy-four days, not counting incidental references and passing inclusions. Why such a pinpointing of one minister, when there were so many? The reason is still not clear. Caillaux had been called "a madman" by Philippe Berthelot, a hard-line nationalist on foreign policy. He was by no means a popular minister.

They called him "His Self-Sufficiency." He was a dandy, none too honest, and full of himself. It has been suggested, notably by Alister Kershaw and Vincent Cronin, that Calmette resented the fact that Caillaux failed to resign at once, as soon as the attacks began. Perhaps it was easier to ride one hobbyhorse than find another. It may have been a case of *folie de grandeur*. Mme Caillaux heard her husband called horrible names by other spectators in the public gallery at the Chambre des Députés. Caillaux suggested that Calmette might be under the influence of a foreign power, or be acting at the behest of political influences within France that were trying to destroy the Radical-Progressive movement. While Gaston Calmette may have been a monster to Caillaux, he comes off better away from politics. He was, for instance, an early supporter and steadfast advocate of the writing of Marcel Proust: *Swann's Way* is dedicated to Calmette. But, alas, it was his articles about the politician Joseph Caillaux, not his taste for introspective literature, that brought him low.

On Friday, 13 March 1914, a very unlucky day for the Caillaux, Calmette broke his rule about using personal correspondence to make his point on the front page of *Figaro*:

> This is the first time in my thirty years of journalism [the editor wrote unctuously] that I have published a private letter, an *intime* letter, without regard to the wishes of the recipient, the owner or the writer.

He published excerpts from a letter written by Caillaux in 1901 to Berthe Gueydan, then visiting in New Orleans, Louisiana. She was at the time Caillaux's mistress and later became his first wife. In the letter, filling his dear friend ("Ma Riri bien aimée") in on his latest triumphs in the Chamber of Deputies, he wrote:

> I have had a great success. I have crushed the Income Tax Bill while appearing to defend it. I got myself cheered by the Centre and the Right, without too upsetting the Left.

Since Caillaux was currently urging the country to accept income tax, saying it was not something new but just a new name for what had existed in the *ancien régime*, it hurt the minister badly. By naming the source of the letter, with its signature, "Ton Jo," Calmette enraged the minister.

What was he to do? Caillaux's dome was streaked red with embarrassment. He couldn't challenge Calmette to a duel—he had fought several—because it was just not done: an aristocrat didn't challenge journalists any more than he would shoot it out with a coachman or chef. A duel was clearly impossible. "Fit to be tied" scarcely describes the state of M. and Mme Caillaux on reading this letter, knowing that all of Paris was reading it at the same moment. It was an enormous blow to his ego and his credibility as a statesman. Bad as that was, worse was sure to come. Caillaux knew of the existence of two love letters that had passed between himself and the present Mme Caillaux, dating from the time when he was still married to the first Mme Caillaux. He thought that these letters had been destroyed, but he suspected that copies existed. He was right: his first wife's sister had made photographic copies, a fact possibly unknown even to the earlier Mme Caillaux. It had been some years since either Henriette or Caillaux had seen the letters, but under the circumstances, they feared the worst. At the very least he remembered with embarrassment such non-political endearments as: "there is only one consolation" for the stresses of public life, "to think of my little one, to see her in my arms as she was at Ouchy (God! Those delicious moments!) ..." "A thousand million kisses on every part of your adorable little body," recalled the finance minister, never a man to be frightened by high numbers. Ouchy, by the way, is a renowned Swiss resort on the shore of Lac Léman; in the early 1900s it was outside Lausanne, but nowadays it is the Lausanne *plage*.

Meanwhile, Caillaux was not the only one whose reputation was in peril. Henriette, as his wife, shared the social position of her husband, and now her world was threatened. As she said:

One day I was in a fashionable couturier's with a throng of customers. One of two women sitting near me leaned over and said to the other: "You see that lady sitting beside me dressed in black? She's the wife of that crook Caillaux."

Still, most of her fashionable friends stood by her, offering sympathetic encouragement and advice. At a luncheon party given by the Princess de Monaco, two days after the publication of the embarrassing letter, the conversation centered on what the embattled couple could do to protect themselves from further outrages. Henriette was urged to seek legal counsel at the earliest opportunity. An appointment was made to see the judge, Maître Monier, the following day. As "Ton Jo" was busy in the Chamber of Deputies, it was Henriette Caillaux who received the judge in their apartment and consulted him about their options, but to little effect. Monier told her that there was no legal way to call off Calmette's hounds. At the time, public figures could not protect either their private or their public lives from even the worst scandal sheets. The judge told Henriette of his own sad dealings with a hostile press: newspapers had been hawked at the very gates of the Palais de Justice with headlines shrieking: *M. le Président Monier est un Bandit!* He went on to say, according to Henriette Caillaux, that given this state of things, he was surprised that more heads hadn't been broken on the understanding that enough is enough.

When Henriette reported M. Monier's opinion to her husband, the minister was beside himself. He was traduced and betrayed on every side; his fury knew no bounds. Employing language seldom uttered in the Chamber of Deputies, he shouted, "Very well then! If there's no solution, at least I won't let him attack you with impunity—I'll break his neck! *Je lui casserai la gueule.*"

"My God, when?" queried his wife. "Today?" Caillaux's agitation cooled somewhat at this challenge to act at once.

"In my own good time," he told her. "It doesn't concern you." Here we have the reaction of a man out of his mind with rage. At one moment he is about to break Calmette's neck to protect his wife from further harm, the next he tells Henriette that it's none of her business. Obviously, Caillaux was distancing himself from his beloved in order to take the problem, as well as any guilt arising from that problem's solution, upon his own head. "Be innocent of the knowledge, dearest chuck." Macbeth uses the same device to keep his wife in ignorance. Mme Caillaux had reason to be worried about what action her husband might take to Calmette's extended campaign against her "Jo." So far, his only action had been to collect all the information he could find against his adversary. It's odd that it didn't occur to him that, extramaritally speaking, they had a lot in common. Both had been stuck in unwanted marriages. Both had had lovers on the side, waiting to see a bill of divorcement. A beery lunch or a convivial apéritif might have done much to resolve their differences. But it was a question of social spheres again. If a man wasn't gentleman enough to fight a duel with, could one have a drink with him?

In French the phrase "*Je lui casserai la gueule*" may be used with a variety of intentions, from the relatively innocent "I'll give him a black eye!" or "I'll bust him in the jaw!" to the more serious "I'll break his neck!", "I'll smash his face!" or "I'll break his head for him!" The phrase must be judged in the context. The language of diplomacy, renowned the world over for the precision of its codes, has its ambiguities too. (Perhaps this unheralded ambiguity is its secret strength.) These subtleties, however, were beyond Mme Caillaux. Henriette believed her husband's intent was murderous. This was not going to be a slap in the face or a tweaking of noses; to her, it smacked of mortal *arbitrament*. Her husband was going to kill Calmette! She went out of her tiny perfect mind with worry and apprehension. She later said that she considered suicide as a way of stopping the impending horror, although, as Alister Kershaw observes, "how this would have solved anyone's problems is obscure."

At this precise moment, M. Caillaux remembered his duty to his country and returned to the Chamber of Deputies; Mme Caillaux recalled that she required a cook for the dinner party she was preparing for the following evening.

It is hard to believe that it never occurred to Gaston Calmette that the distress, the embarrassment, the punishment he had been dishing out over that long period might rebound upon its author. His almost lunatic persecution of so prominent a figure, in so visible a place as the front page of *Le Figaro*, extending over a period of three months, was rash to a degree seldom achieved. Foolhardy is the word that comes to mind. Kershaw refers to this in his book:

> Rarely does one find so flawless an example of the murderee [asking for it]; and in the journalist's astonishingly complacent belief that he could heap up provocation on this scale and not suffer for it is, perhaps, a clue to that strange section of humanity. An unawareness of danger, a vast conceit, may be the qualities which pre-eminently fit the murderee for his gruesome part.

In law there is a large and growing study that concerns itself with provocation. Crimes of passion are almost perfect examples of what happens when provocation reaches a crisis. Perhaps, while M. Caillaux is meeting with junior ministers and executive assistants, and Mme Caillaux is interviewing cooks, it might be convenient to examine some of what the law says about provocation. Among the recent commentators on the subject of provocation, I found *Provocation and Responsibility*, by Jeremy Horder, in the *Oxford Monographs on Criminal Law and Justice Series*. Horder's short book is about the moral and legal responsibility for provoked retaliation. His interest takes him through a historical review of English law on the subject and on to an examination of the philosophical basis for the reduction of criminal liability for homicide, which, in practice, causes a homicide to dwindle from a murder into manslaughter. Provocation has been with us for the past four hundred years at least. The old stiff-upper-lip advice: "Never apologize, never explain" comes a cropper here, buried in the excuses that tend to mitigate the enormity of a murder. The doctrine of provocation has a long and colorful history, which Horder sets out with the deftness of a master chef slicing smoked salmon. He sees it as another example of the law's failure to deal with the results of anger, "a tragic misunderstanding and distortion of the true ethical connection between anger and mitigating virtue." In the domestic sphere, for instance, he thinks we have so far failed in redressing the problem of unremitting male anger, unleashed as violence towards women. Is anger an irresistible impulse? Certainly the Caillaux were very angry, with each day's morning paper adding insult to injury. Here is Jeremy Horder again:

> It is seemingly not supposed that defendants can ever struggle to control their emotions through the use of reason, but supposed instead that they are carried to inflict instantaneous retaliation in the same way that one might be led or made to drop something on being unexpectedly stung on the hand by a wasp.
>
> This being so, it is not clear why, if anger does indeed take the form of irresistible impulse, a complete acquittal is not the result that should of necessity follow from findings that the defendants acted in anger upon grave and unexpected provocation. For it would be as if they had been charged with criminal damage upon dropping something, and it were found that they had been led to drop the property in question upon being unexpectedly startled or stung. Those who hold the conception of anger as irresistible impulse cannot explain why only mitigation of offence and punishment is thought appropriate where provocation has been successfully pleaded.

It appears that Aristotle and Hobbes are still arguing this question. The jury is still out on where the arguments will go from there.

To return to Paris, 22 rue de Tocqueville, the Caillaux residence, and to French law from English law: the descending action of the play now begins its sharp downward turn towards the catastrophe. After having disposed of the minor matter of finding a cook to provide the planned dinner for Madame's soirée—she interviewed several applicants and settled on one at the employment bureau—it was nearing three o'clock on the afternoon of Monday, 16 March. It was at the agency that "the tragic thought first occurred to me," she later recounted, "and I said to myself, 'Suppose I were to go along to *Le Figaro*?'"

At the same time another thought, an "unrelated thought" suggested itself. "I ought to explain that I always carried a small revolver; it was a habit inculcated in my sister and myself by our father ... I had mislaid my revolver some time before and had been intending to replace it. I had asked my husband, if he should be going to the gunsmith to get me one, as the electoral campaign was due to begin and I should be travelling about alone ..." Alister Kershaw, in his account of the story says that Henriette's movements that fatal day were "tortuous" and "subtle." Perhaps in those days, buying a handgun and shooting an editor could be seen as commonplace, unrelated errands. Perhaps today we might begin to suspect a cause-and-effect relationship between these acts. Here is Kershaw's summary of Henriette's comings and goings after three o'clock that afternoon:

> She had had the idea of calling on Calmette; then she had thought of replacing the revolver—a quite fortuitous reflection; *then* she had had the idea of combining the two notions—of taking the revolver with her when she went to the *Figaro* office and, if Calmette proved refractory, "causing a fuss" by—what? Flourishing the weapon? Firing a shot or two in the air? She was not explicit; but the carefully established time sequence, if accepted, indicated that she had not bought the revolver with the idea of killing the journalist and had thus demonstrably acted with so much less premeditation.[36]

That same afternoon, Mme Caillaux tried out a Smith and Wesson and a Browning handgun in the basement shooting gallery of Gastinne-Renette, gunsmiths. She received doting attention from the fawning salesclerks, who let her charge the Browning to her husband's account. After visiting the gunsmith's, she attended to some banking at Crédit Lyonnais before returning to rue de Tocqueville. Here she changed her dress. She was later to claim that this simple act attested to the muddled state of her thinking at that moment. Was she going to change into an afternoon gown and go to a tea-party she'd been invited to, or was she going to call on M. Calmette at *Le Figaro*? She put on an elegant afternoon dress. Whether or not this change of clothing says anything about her state of mind, is moot. Henriette Caillaux had undoubtedly attended numerous tea parties before, and no doubt knew how to look her best for the Princesse de Monaco and her special friend, the Princess Estradère. On the other hand, she had seldom called upon newspaper editors in their places of employment, with or without a Browning revolver in her muff. Surely on an occasion of this kind, too, a lady of fashion wishes to look her best. Would an outfit suitable for wearing to buy a handgun be appropriate for visiting a newspaper office where she might very well shoot the editor?

It was never determined when exactly Henriette decided to call upon *l'ignoble* Calmette. Before she left the house, she wrote a note to be delivered to Gaston by her daughter's governess on his return to the house. The note reads:

My Beloved husband,

When I told you this morning of my interview with President Monier, from whom I learned that in France there is no law to protect us against the libels of the press, you told me that one of these days you would break the vile Calmette's neck [*tu casserais la gueule à l'ignoble Calmette*]. I know your decision to be irrevocable. From that instant on my mind was made up. I will see that justice is done. France and the Republic have need of you. I will carry out the task! If you should receive this letter it will mean that I have obtained or tried to obtain justice. Forgive me, but my patience is at an end. I love you and I embrace you with all my heart.

Your
Henriette

It was by now getting on towards late afternoon. Mme Caillaux drove to the offices of *Le Figaro*, 26 rue Drouot, and had her driver wait in the car. She asked to see M. Calmette, but declined to give her name to the receptionist, who invited her to wait, since Calmette was not in the building. She told Etienne Nicet, the receptionist, "M. Calmette knows me and will see me," as she sat down outside a door to Calmette's inner sanctum. When Nicet tried again to learn the identity of the caller, he was assured simply that Calmette was acquainted with her. In the end, when Nicet insisted, Mme placed her card in an envelope and gave it to the receptionist after sealing it.

Then she waited. And she waited. Towards the end of an hour, she claims to have overheard a conversation that further enraged her. One man standing in the hall told two others gleefully that "tomorrow we've got a big story on Caillaux." She told this story to the *juge d'instruction* during his investigation into the events that were about to occur. The men in the outer office later denied either making or hearing the remarks alleged to have been overheard. Nevertheless, Mme Caillaux told the judge, "the revelation shattered me. Simultaneously my name was called out. 'Show in Mme Caillaux,' ordered M. Calmette. Realizing that my identity was now known I suddenly understood how indiscreet I had been. I completely lost my head."

Why this chance remark, real or imagined, should have disconcerted her, is a puzzle. She had already read 140 "big stories" on her husband. Why should another "shatter" her and cause her to "lose her head," unless she suspected that the only topper to the printing of one personal letter would be the printing of another. And she knew which letters Calmette had access to.

It was about 6:00 p.m. when Calmette, wearing his pince-nez, his mustaches splendid with well-waxed points, returned to his office with the writer and academician, Paul Bourget, a cynical observer for the *Figaro* of such scenes as the one about to be enacted in Calmette's office. Mme Caillaux might have profited from Bourget's advice about ending awkward situations, however cynical. It would have saved her at least four months in St. Lazare prison and a long and stressful public trial. Calmette had used a door that avoided the hall with the receptionist in it as well as his visitor. On the point of leaving the building again with Bourget, he was intercepted at the top of the stairs by Nicet, who informed him of the mysterious caller and handed him the envelope.

Bourget testified that Calmette shrugged, tossed his head in the manner of a busy man importuned while attempting to make a clean getaway from his daily cares, tore open the envelope and showed some surprise at what he read on the card. Wordlessly, he showed the card to Bourget. Meanwhile, Nicet continued to tell his employer that the lady had been waiting for a long time, over an hour, and that she appeared to have important business to discuss with him.

"But you won't see her?" Bourget asked, apprehensively.

After some hesitation, Calmette said, "Of course. I can't refuse to receive a lady," and asked that the lady be shown into his office. He nodded to Nicet, who went to inform Mme Caillaux. No mention of the lady's name had passed aloud between the two writers in front of the receptionist.

Adrien Sirac, an office boy, led Mme Caillaux to Calmette's door and closed it again after he had allowed the visitor to enter.

"No doubt you are surprised at my visit," Henriette Caillaux began. Her fingers hidden inside her muff felt for the safety-catch on the Browning. She was a fast study, and the instructions of the clerk at Gastinne-Renette's were proving invaluable.

"Why, not at all," the editor said diplomatically.

"Doubtless you know why I'm here?"

"Good heavens, no, Madame. But please sit down." Calmette turned from his guest momentarily to sit down behind his desk. It was now, while the office boy was still closing the door, that Henriette produced the revolver from her muff and began shooting it at Calmette. Sirac turned back into the room: Calmette was crouching behind his desk. Before he could interfere, Mme Caillaux fired again. In all, she fired six shots. Four hit the editor. Sirac grabbed the woman's arm and wrenched the revolver from her grasp. Calmette had not fallen to the floor, but moved himself to an armchair, into which he slumped. Hearing the gunshots, staff members crowded into the office.

"I am Mme Caillaux," she announced to all the gaping faces. "Don't be afraid." She warned Sirac, who was still holding the gun, "Be careful, there may be bullets in it."

While some *Figaro* staffers loosened Calmette's clothing, trying to make him as comfortable as possible, Mme Caillaux was removed to another office to await the police, who had been summoned almost at once. Calmette remained conscious through much of this. "Forgive me for causing you so much trouble, my friends," the mortally wounded man said, echoing both Chesterfield's *politesse* and Claudius, the king, in *Hamlet*, after he had been cut down: "Oh, yet defend me, friends, I am but hurt." Slowly weakened from loss of blood, Calmette slipped into unconsciousness. He was taken by ambulance to the closest hospital, where he died early the following morning.

When a crime occurs in a busy office, accounts of what the accused said immediately afterwards differ. Chaos usually rules. But here in the editorial department of *Figaro*, there were plenty of trained observers and note-takers. All agreed that Mme Caillaux remained calm, even indifferent. (Compare this observation with the deportment of Ruth Ellis, Alpna Patel (see Chapter 11) and Yvonne Chevallier under similar circumstances.) One of the newspaper's executives, M. Giraudeau, swore he heard the lady say, rather like an avenging fury, "It was the only way to put an end to it all." An office boy, probably with the ambition to become a reporter, said that "with a most authoritarian air, with great sang-froid," she had said, "There is no justice—so I gave it." Still another office boy recalled her saying: "I am Mme Caillaux ... It is infamous! There is no justice in France, I had to obtain it for myself." Even more memorable were her words to another of the paper's executives: "Let me go, I am a lady, I am Mme Caillaux. I have a car waiting downstairs to take me to the police station!"

The arrival of the police tended to curtail the histrionics of Henriette, who was still telling anyone willing to listen that, "There is no justice in ..." In this she was interrupted by a heartbroken *Figaro* staff member:

"Be quiet, Madame. After what you have done, the least you can do now is to remain silent." Kershaw says of this, with the twinkle of a true true-crime aficionado, "Mme Caillaux eyed him coldly and 'with some irritation' remarked, 'I was not addressing you.' She turned and led the assembled police down to the waiting car."

The 140 days of being pilloried in *Le Figaro* did not begin to prepare the Caillaux for the explosion of press coverage that followed Henriette's call on Gaston Calmette. It was no longer a French story; it now belonged to the world. Madame's gesture could not have misfired from its purpose more. A black-bordered edition of *Le Figaro* devoted nearly three pages to the shooting. Even the London *Evening Standard* argued in a superior manner that such a thing could not happen in England. The wives of British cabinet ministers simply did not behave that way.

Mme Caillaux's murder of Calmette failed of its object in every way. Instead of clearing the way for Caillaux to continue his political career unharassed by journalists, it ensured that he would tender his resignation the following day. If she thought that by killing Calmette she would stop the publication of documents embarrassing to her husband, she was wrong there as well. The very next day, *Figaro* published a story, supported by a written report, about how pressure was brought to bear on an official in 1911 to delay the announcement of information that would embarrass the government and do serious damage to Caillaux in particular. This was called the "Document Fabre." Ironically, based on available evidence, it is unlikely that, had he lived, Calmette would have used it. When Paris read the news, all were shocked to learn of this interference with due process and of Caillaux's sinister role in it.

In the dimly lit cells at the St. Lazare prison, Mme Caillaux was eating meals sent in from a chic little restaurant nearby. Meanwhile, cards and letters of sympathy were being delivered to the newspaper office from titled dignitaries, princesses, dukes, duchesses and marquises, and also from artists of the likes of Sarah Bernhardt, Edmond Rostand and Camille Saint-Saëns. (Whether Proust sent a note or not, I cannot tell.)

Mme Caillaux made her first appearance before the *juge d'instruction* on 21 March. It was the beginning of a process that was to last four months. It was played against a background of inquiries into the

Document Fabre and the *affaire* Rochette, which lay beyond it. Another doomed newspaper editor, *L'Humanité*'s Jean Jaurès, was appointed to chair a commission looking into these linked episodes of wrong-doing and cover-up, only to resign when pressure was exerted on him from the same corrupt high places: he'd been asked to go easy on Joseph Caillaux. (In fiction, it would be impossible to introduce two newspaper editors, both of them condemned to assassination that same year. It would be too incredible. But facts can be as incredible as they like. In Jaurès's case, it was not an irate reader or even the wife or lover of one, but simply a misguided patriot whose real target was Wilhelm II of Germany, but since the Kaiser was unavailable in Paris, he settled for the charismatic leader of the Socialist movement in France. In his view, the Socialists were getting far too friendly with the Huns.)

It was during the *instruction* period that Henriette introduced evidence not previously heard. She said that she had been shaken badly when she heard her name spoken loudly. She also stated that she had been further confused by the dim lighting of Calmette's office, which threw a murky blanket over everything before her. Of course, she omitted no detail of the long Calvary she and her husband had endured at the hands of *Figaro* and the unspeakable Calmette. Alister Kershaw describes Henriette's recitation of the reasons underlying her assassination of Gaston Calmette as "one of the most skillful self-justifications on record."

> ... tenderly she spoke of her childhood, discreet, guarded; rhapsodically of her marriage to M. Caillaux; then, with lowered voice and faltering accent, she recounted the history of that persecution which she and her husband had undergone at the hands, first of [the first Mme Caillaux] and second of M. Calmette. Precisely punctuating her statement with catches of breath, gestures of anguish, and a recurrent unsteadiness of stance, she led her rapt audience towards the climax: the Princesse de Monaco's luncheon party and her subsequent interview with M. Monier.

It was her version of this event that prompted an exchange which "cannot have failed to win over every virtuous person" in court that day:

> I told my husband of the conversation … He exclaimed: "Very well, then; if there's nothing to be done, at least I won't let him attack you with impunity; if it's like that, je casserai la ——— à M. Calmette," employing a somewhat stronger expression than "je lui casserai la figure."

Such scruples on the part of an accused murderess regarding the use of slang irked the counsel for the *partie civile*: "There's nothing to stop you saying it: *la gueule*: it appears all through the dossier."

The president of the court, genial to a point, but determined to keep to the known facts, urged the accused to use the words that were uttered at the time, not bowdlerize them. "He said, '*je lui casserai la gueule*,' yes?"

"It embarrasses me to use such a phrase in public," she said, wincing.

"She wrote it without any trouble," shouted Maître Chenu, recalling the note the accused wrote before setting out to see M. Calmette.

The woman in the prisoners' box cast a heavy dismissive eye on the counsel for the people. "There are things which one writes to one's husband," she pointed out, "which one does not wish to say in public." She had hit just the right note and a sympathetic murmur of assent rippled through the courtroom.

Having won the point, Henriette Caillaux continued to tell her story, continued to show her *pudeur*, her modesty, sensitivity and reserve, as she approached the fatal act itself. Here her flustered account was of little help in giving a clear picture of what was in her mind as she entered Calmette's office. But her final words to the court came with sufficient clarity and strength to make her position clear to all:

> Try and think how I shall be conscious all my life of having, even though I never wished it, caused a man's death. How can

anyone imagine that I ever intended to commit such an action? But, moreover, apart from the problem of conscience, which is terrible enough, there is a question of logic.

That a woman who has been deprived of everything through a man, who feels herself to be ruined, should have the idea of killing in order to revenge herself—that is conceivable. But I— I had everything I desired, leaving aside the outrageous slanders and the threatened publication of the letters. ... Why should I have wanted to kill? To kill a man—that [the accused continued] is a frightful thing, appalling. I never said that death should be the punishment.

Here the witness swayed slightly, gripped the railing and sat down, while three *agents de police* reported successively on their part in coming upon the tragic circumstances in the newspaper office and their taking Mme Caillaux into custody.

Stripped of its finery, Mme Caillaux's defense comes down to the following: She committed the deed without premeditation and with great provocation; the shooting itself was accidental; the dim lighting in Calmette's office confused her; the whispered conversation mentioning a forthcoming blast at her husband overheard while waiting for the return of Calmette and the noisy calling of her name in the newspaper office unnerved Madame. All of these unaccustomed things had contributed to upsetting her. The gun, she claimed, went off by accident. "The bullets seemed to follow one another automatically" due to her unfamiliarity with the newly purchased Browning. "The sustaining of so profuse—and even contradictory—an array of explanations was inevitably difficult," says crime specialist Alister Kershaw, "And the eye-witnesses did nothing to help." Indeed they did not. The receptionist testified that the lighting in Calmette's office was what one would expect to find in any office; the office boy said that nobody called out Mme Caillaux's name; and another witness, a M. Voisin, reported that no one discussed "tomorrow's big story on Caillaux." There had never been such a discussion, he said.

Mme Caillaux commented: "M. Voisin's friend asked him a question which attracted my attention because he used a term which was unfamiliar to me; he said: 'Is the sheet [*feuille*] ready yet?' M. Voisin replied: 'No, it's only six o'clock. Anyway, we're getting a big story on Caillaux ready for tomorrow,'"

"That's false! Arch-false!" Voisin shouted. One by one, his companions of that late afternoon at *Figaro* agreed.

The most spectacular evidence submitted during the second day of the trial was a signed statement from Raymond Poincaré, "*cinquante-trois ans, Président de la République Française demeurant à l'Elysée*," who said that he had made a thorough inquiry and had ascertained that M. Calmette had planned no further publication of Caillaux's letters. Executives of *Le Figaro* substantiated this.

From here the trial took a side-trip through the murky subtext of Joseph Caillaux's record in government as provided by the notorious Document Fabre, which, while it may have illuminated some of the background of the crime, cannot have failed to confuse the jury with the names of the great and near-great, the well-born and the powerful of the day. The jury heard more of this when M. Caillaux himself rose to speak. He declared that both his private life and his public life were without blemish. (He intended even in the midst of his wife's murder trial to let his name stand for re-election to the Chamber of Deputies.) He spoke on in a manner more suitable for the Académie française than for a courtroom, strewing tags and quotations and references to Gambetta, Parnell, Wilhelm II, Jaurès and Briand in a way that was calculated to put a gilded garland around himself and his adoring wife. To collect the fine phrases and the somewhat self-serving arguments he used, may I suggest you look into the memoirs he published after his wife's death. (See Bibliography.)

The testimony of the first Mme Caillaux (now Mme Gueydan-Caillaux) cleared up the mystery of how the private letters had reappeared, after she had sworn they had been expressly destroyed. Unbeknownst to her, her sister had had the letters photographed, and she herself had had no notion the copies existed. She also maintained that once she became aware of their phoenix-like revival, she "treated with unbending disdain all efforts made by the unrighteous to obtain them." Mme Gueydan-Caillaux went on to tell the court, perhaps unnecessarily, but the distinction was important to her, that when she opened her husband's desk to read the letters in the first place, she used not a false key or a screwdriver, but a key from another desk. With a wonderful innocence she told the court that when she inserted the key, why! the drawer opened "as if," she said wonderingly, "by magic."

After this, when the letters, with their "Ton Jos," were read, they proved rather more tame than had been anticipated. The medical evidence was added to the record by a parade of six doctors, taking the witness stand in turn. Only one of the bullets fired from the Browning had been fatal. That shot had torn up the inside of the editor's pelvis in an irreversible way, hemorrhaging the right iliac artery as it went. This information, dressed up in medical terminology, robbed of the lethal impact the language of the street might have given it, struck only a glancing blow at the jury. It was still reeling from its exposure to high society and political skulduggery. In that mood they retired to reach a verdict.

The jury was asked to answer two questions: Was Mme Caillaux guilty of having, at Paris on 16 March, deliberately murdered Gaston Calmette? Was the alleged murder committed with premeditation? After a suitable interval the jury returned to the courtroom. When the foreman was asked for the verdict he replied that in answer to both questions, "On my honor and conscience before God and Man, the jury's decision is NO."

Mme Caillaux walked from the courtroom a free woman. Whether she enjoyed the champagne party prepared for her without thinking of her own words about being haunted by Calmette's death for the rest of her life, we don't know. We do know that *Le Figaro* was not about to accept the verdict without an editorial counterattack. They obviously missed Calmette. Where was he now that they really needed him to rake over the evidence? Again and again, the surviving writers at *Le Figaro* sifted the ashes, first on the front page, then later on one of the remaining five pages.

Marie Manning was a lady's maid and something of a dressmaker. She had been in service in a noble household and had been present when Queen Victoria visited her mistress' house. She became the model for a character in Dickens' *Bleak House*. For over a century and a half, she has been associated with making black satin unfashionable.

Frederick Manning, was a weak-willed railway guard, who accused his wife, Marie, with forcing him to help her murder her wealthier, one-time lover. He tried to cooperate with the police and later with the Crown, but, while they listened to his story, he was condemned along with his spouse. Frederick may have been the inside man in the first Great Train Robbery.

Patrick O'Connor, as seen in the popular biography of his murderer, Marie Manning, Huish's *Progress of Crime*. O'Connor had a job in the custom's house on the Thames, but added to his income by lending out money at high rates of interest. He postponed his murder several times by falling drunk and missing his appointment with his killers.

Ruth Snyder was a suburban housewife married to the art editor of a magazine devoted to boating. With her daughter and husband she seemed to have achieved the perfect life. Not every stenographer was this successful. But when she met Judd Gray, the home, her child and her husband became redundant. The tabloid newspapers called her "the granite woman" and showed little sympathy for her situation.

Henry Judd Gray, 35, was a rather prissy model citizen from East Orange, New Jersey, a fact that helped make him into a figure of fun for the tabloids. (It didn't help the reputation of East Orange, New Jersey either.) He was a brassiere and corset salesman for the Bien Jolie Corset Company. Exactly how he met Ruth and how the meeting turned into an affair has been fodder for speculation for three-quarters of a century. Their intimacy began shortly after she appeared at the company showrooms for a fitting.

Henriette Caillaux (1878–1943) belonged to the upper reaches of French society. She counted titled ladies among her intimate acquaintances, one a princess! When the editor of *Le Figaro* began to pillory her husband in almost every edition without let-up, surpassing its earlier infamies with the publication of private love-letters, Mme Caillaux bought a gun and waited in the editor's office in order to shoot him. She thought she was defending her husband's honour and good name. Shooting the editor didn't help.

Joseph Caillaux, 51, was a former prime minister of France when he married Henriette, his second wife. When the attacks in *Le Figaro* began, he was the minister of finance. It was March, 1914, the eve of the Great War and politics had become dangerous. When Caillaux threatened to smash the face ("Je lui casserai la gueule!") of the offending editor, Henriette saw his political death foretold, so she did the job herself, but with a brand new Browning handgun.

Gaston Calmette, the murdered editor of *Le Figaro*, was the dedicatee of Proust's *Swann's Way*. "As a token of deep and affectionate gratitude," it read. M. Caillaux's bête noire, Calmette was no philistine. Had it been possible for them to talk over a drink, they would have discovered much in common. Calmette had secured the editorship of the foremost conservative newspaper in France by marrying the owner's daughter. The marriage was dead now and Calmette longed to make his mistress his wife, as Caillaux had done before him.

Diana, Lady Broughton, pictured here with **Lord Erroll**, known among the expatriate Europeans in the White Highlands of Kenya as "Joss." While World War II raged elsewhere, the white planters donned home-guard uniforms and entered into the spirit of the war effort. When Joss Erroll's body was discovered, it was wearing this uniform.

Topham Picturepoint/Ponopresse

Henry, Lord Broughton, appeared to be taking his new wife's public dalliance with Lord Erroll in good part. He was being a sport about this true love-match. He agreed to step aside, wished the lovers joy, and appeared to be as shocked as everybody else when Lord Erroll was unexpectedly found murdered in his car at dawn one day.

The Happy Valley of Central Kenya was a haven for well-born, wealthy Europeans during World War II. If that world of privilege and boredom and vice had a center, it was the Muthaiga Country Club, northwest of Nairobi. Here drink, bridge and intrigue tried to ease the tedium. It was here that Lord Broughton offered his wife and her enamorata, Lord Erroll, a "wedding toast" in front of the crème de la crème of the white colony.

The **Marquis Alain de Bernardy de Sigoyer** was executed in 1947 for the murder of his low-born wife, Janine. He was a complex and repellent killer, whose criminal history will probably never be known in full. It was his boast that an ancestor of his had been engaged to a sister of the Empress Josephine.

To write with accuracy about the Caillaux, it would be necessary to know them better. But since French society of which they were leaders prided itself on reticence and an ability to keep private things private, it is next to impossible to catch more than an occasional moment or two of self-revelation. Did they love one another? Did she really do it for "Ton Jo" or did she do it to protect her own niche in society? Was she trying to preempt her husband's version of her own rash act? In a true crime of passion, according to Anna Freud (as I have said before), the ego disappears in the act of redemption. I cannot altogether see Henriette Caillaux separated from her ego any more than I can see her with her hair falling down.

M. Caillaux's career, so abruptly terminated by his wife's hasty action at the offices of *Le Figaro*, proved to be less than permanent. In the general elections of May 1914, Caillaux was re-elected. But tales of treasonous trade with the enemy still dogged his footsteps, as though Gaston Calmette were still writing stories about him from some celestial editorial room on high. In the end, his allegedly treacherous contacts with the Germans haunted him, until Clemenceau had him arrested for "correspondence with the enemy," for which offense he received a prison term of three years in 1920. There were, in spite of this, partisans, who were certain that politics had brought about this frame-up, and Caillaux continued to be a figure in French public life until his death.

On the day in 1914 that Mme Caillaux was freed from St. Lazare prison, Leopold, Count Berchold, the Austrian foreign minister, let it be known that because of another murder in far-off Sarajevo on 28 June, Serbia and Austria-Hungary were at war. For another week, *Figaro* harped on the "shameful verdict" but after that stories of the coming war undermined even so sensational a case as the murder of their own beloved editor, putting such self-indulgent things as a single death out of their minds. The guns of August would soon speak of the deaths of hundreds of thousands.

SEVEN

Unhappy Valley
and the Red Armchair:
Noblesse Oblige

Lord Broughton

The case of the murder of the twenty-second Earl of Erroll is instructive as well as celebrated. There is just enough ambiguity about what actually happened to keep interest in the case alive; and for years now it has been a source of avid speculation. One of its most irresistible qualities as a story is its illustration of the fact that well-born people lose control of their emotions in a deadly, irreversible and reckless way, just like common folk. It also shows again that men can just as easily as women give way to their passions, and the results may catapult them into the tabloids of the world and into the annals of crime. The story is about people who normally feel themselves beyond the strictures of conventional society. High birth nurtures this view in them, and their wealth helps them to find the best legal assistance when and wherever it is needed.

Lord Erroll was not only the twenty-second earl, but he was also Baron of Kilmarnock, Hereditary High Constable of Scotland. He was born plain Josslyn Victor Hay in 1901. Perhaps *plain* is not the word. He was born to the purple, and had titles and property to look forward to. He was high-spirited and untamed, ran with a wild crowd of young toffs, and as might be expected was expelled from Eton for a misdemeanor that was never made known outside the office of the headmaster. He was in serious debt while still a teenager. He seems to have been a thoroughly detestable fellow, who could nonetheless turn on the charm when he chose to. His family tried to do its best for him. His father pulled enough weight at the Foreign Office to get him a job in 1922, and a year later, the boy eloped to Kenya with a woman eight years older than himself, whose titled husband was not pleased. In those days, people were asked, "Are you married or do you live in Kenya?" Kenya, during the war, was a game preserve for the rich and titled. They wanted no street signs to intrude upon their highland paradise. Their sense of what their freedom encompassed was outraged by the mapping of their tiny, all-white atoll in an overwhelming sea of Kikuyu, Masai and Kamba faces. These white planters were refugees from rules, law and fences of all kinds.

The marriage to Lady Idina Gordon lasted out the decade, at which time the "Passionate Peer" began his pursuit of Molly Ramsay Hill. They married in 1930. One of Molly's attractions was a large lakeside house in central Africa, called Oserian, which she nicknamed the Djinn Palace to the delight of the local white planters. She also had eight thousand pounds a year, which delighted Josslyn Hay, now Lord Erroll. It seemed to be a marriage made in heaven, but unfortunately Lady Erroll took to drink and drugs and died in 1939. Meanwhile, Erroll had been sleeping with practically every pretty woman in the White Highlands of Kenya. It appears that he liked the feeling of dominance and power even more than he enjoyed the pleasures of the flesh. He inherited the Djinn Palace, but the money went elsewhere. He had only three hundred pounds a year to run the place and that was not enough. He was in the market for a wealthy woman to support him in his weaknesses.

In the high country in southwest Kenya, wealthy English expatriates had built a colony called Happy Valley, along rather snobbish lines, that rigidly kept away outsiders and allowed the insiders to get on with their drinking, their drugs and their complicated sexual intrigues. It was the world that Isak Dinesen (Karen Blixen) wrote about in *Out of Africa*. In this world both men and women flew their own airplanes and many changed partners as regularly as they did their imported clothes. Boredom was the enemy; all of the hard work was delegated to hired blacks under white supervisors, and there was nothing to do but play endless rubbers of bridge and drink the evenings away after a day or two on safari or a bit of rough shooting near the Muthaiga Country Club, northwest of Nairobi. Happy Valley was a privileged playground, where eccentricity was encouraged as long as it wasn't boring. Partner swapping was almost *de rigueur*.

The next woman to enter the life of Lord Erroll, Lady Diana Broughton, was almost certainly the reason for his violent and untimely death. She was a twenty-two-year-old blonde beauty, who rode to hounds, piloted her own plane, mixed with the international flying set in Vienna and Budapest, and could drink most men under the table, if she wasn't already under the table with one of them herself. Lady Diana was born Diana Caldwell. For a short time she had been married to a popular musician, Vernon Motion, and had run a popular Mayfair cocktail bar called the Blue Goose. She was more successful at changing her social status than Ruth Ellis, who also managed an after-hours club and dreamed of finding Mr. Right, the savior who would get her out of that sort of life. Diana was chic and amusing, but still, after she had been installed in Kenya as Lady Broughton, mistress of Karen House, women criticized her bold use of make-up—which she wore even while hunting—and they didn't like the way she flirted with their husbands. One acquaintance damned her socially in some quarters for all time with the devastating put-down: "Rather Aldershot," which is as much to say "not quite our class, my dear."

She had married Lord Henry "Jock" Delves Broughton, an apparently vastly wealthy eleventh baronet,[37] on 5 November 1940 in Durban, South Africa. Seven days later they arrived in Mombasa, happy honeymooners on their way to Lord Broughton's farm on Lake Naivasha. While Jock inspected his acres and field hands, Lady Broughton went alone to the Muthaiga Country Club's Caledonian Ball on the eve of St. Andrew's Day (29 November 1940). At that ball, she met Lord Erroll, and they at once fell deeply in love, although her marriage to Lord Broughton was less than a month old. On his return from his inspection tour, Broughton discovered that his wife was enjoying the company of Lord Erroll, who, as an old Africa hand, seemed simply to have befriended a new arrival. He showed the couple around, and was constantly in their company. Diana said, "I had the extraordinary feeling ... that I was suddenly the most important thing in his [Erroll's] life." Lord Erroll said, "Jock could not have been nicer. As a matter of fact, he has been so nice it smells bad."

Erroll attached himself to the couple, as one commentator put it, and cynically set out to bedazzle the taciturn, locally unpopular husband in order to stay close to his wife. The strategy appeared to work. Broughton seemed to be enjoying Erroll's attentions, flattered by this new friendship and entranced by his famous charm. Around Christmas 1940, at a birthday party in honor of Diana given by Gwladys Delamere, the flamboyantly lesbian Mayor of Nairobi, Erroll and Diana danced together so often and so close that it was difficult not to know what was going on. "They were glued together," someone observed. Lady Diana's attractions were obvious. Less obvious, but unforgotten by the lovers, was the tantalizing fact that before they married, Lord Broughton had made a legal pact with Diana: if she left him for a younger man, Broughton would agree to a divorce and give her, into the bargain, five thousand pounds a year for seven years after the divorce. The Passionate Peer knew of this arrangement and must have felt that his money worries were over for the foreseeable future.

June Carberry, a friend of all three corners in this romantic triangle, lent Erroll and Diana her house at Nyeri for the weekend of Friday, 3 January, where the loving couple were unchaperoned and uninterrupted. A week later, Gwladys Delamere felt it was her duty to officially inform Jock Broughton about the affair. She did this at a dinner party at Karen, Jock and Diana's house in Happy Valley. After dinner, when the port was running well and tempers were stretched thin, Gwladys dropped her bombshell.

It may not have come as a great surprise to Lord Broughton: Diana was his wife, after all, and he did have full use of his wits and his senses. Further, he had received the first of three anonymous notes telling him the news:

6 January 1941

> You seemed like a cat on hot bricks at the club last night. What about the eternal triangle? What are you going to do about it?

18 January 1941

> Do you know your wife and Lord Erroll have been staying alone at the Carberrys' house in Nyeri together?

21 January 1941

> There's no fool like an old fool. What are you going to do about it?

Commentators on the case agree that the most likely author of these taunting notes, sent to Lord Broughton at the Muthaiga Country Club, was the esteemed Mayor of Nairobi herself, Gwladys Delamere, who often used the phrase, "What are you going to do about it?" Lord Erroll had earlier paid court to Gwladys, then discarded her. One writer suggested that she might have been afraid that Erroll and Diana might flee the Happy Valley colony and that she might never see Erroll again. The same writer also suggests that Broughton may well have written them himself, to create a back-up motive for what he was about to do. If this were so, then the murder of Lord Erroll becomes not a crime of passion, but rather one of well-calculated revenge.

Whoever wrote the notes, it is plain that Broughton knew of the affair, knew also that it was quickly becoming common knowledge, and felt publicly humiliated by it. On the surface, Broughton was a bluff, Colonel Blimpish sort of man; a man's man in many ways, rather dull in mixed company. His friend, Jack Soames, sometimes joined in with his friend's long days of drinking and self-pity, and he advised Jock at this low point to get over the fact that his wife had a lover, cut his losses, pull up stakes and light out for Ceylon, where he could start afresh. Broughton's despair and gloom were well justified, but he appeared to listen to his friend; he seemed to pull himself together, and threw off his martyred look. He told Diana, who was still living at Karen, their home in Happy Valley, that he intended to honor the pre-nuptial agreement he had made with her, and would stand by her through the process of a divorce. He told Erroll that he intended to leave Kenya as soon as he could put his affairs in order. He was being a brick about the whole thing.

On Thursday, 23 January, Broughton invited Diana, Erroll and June Carberry to a farewell dinner at the Muthaiga Country Club, the scene of so much of this domestic drama. At the table he offered a "wedding toast" to the happy couple, hoping that they would be blessed with a male heir before too long. (Shades of *The Godfather, Part One!*) The other guests stared at their plates, embarrassed by the bizarre per-formance they were witnessing. At 10:30 p.m., the lovers excused themselves from the party to go dancing. Broughton's last words to Erroll were to ask him to be sure to bring his wife home by 3:00 a.m. The Earl of Erroll agreed. Diana was delivered home around 2:30 a.m. During the night, Jock twice knocked on the bedroom door of his house guest, Jane Carberry, "to see if everything was all right."

Everything was, of course, not all right. Half an hour after Lord Erroll brought Diana home, he was found lying dead in his big Buick in a ditch at the side of the road about three miles away from the Broughton house in Karen. The ignition of the car was switched off, but the headlights were still burning and the battery was strong. Early-rising milkmen on their regular round of deliveries stopped their truck and investigated. They found the body of a white man, wearing the uniform of a soldier, crouching on the floor under the steering wheel. The milk truck sped to Karen for help.

To a degree, the investigation of the crime went well. Certainly the authorities began working on it within minutes. The most experi-enced police officers were contacted and they hurried to the crime scene. By dawn, the scene was awash with investigating policemen who mucked up tire tracks and trampled possible clues. The local pathologist, Geoffrey Timms, happened to be driving by the scene, and stopped to have a look at the body. He had it removed from the car and laid out on the unkempt verge of the road. This moving of the body prevented the police from checking a number of factors, such as the trajectory of the shot fired. Superintendents Aristis Bewes and Arthur Poppy of the Nairobi Criminal Investigations Department were on the scene shortly after dawn to take charge of the investigation. Bewes noted that the car's interior reeked of perfume, and that the armstraps had been torn from their moorings. It was already known that the dead man was the twenty-second Earl of Erroll, the locally infamous Passionate Peer.

Superintendent Poppy's first look at the body and the car convinced him that the death was accidental. The wound on Erroll's head looked consistent with the sort of blow that could be sustained in an accident such as appeared to have taken place. But when the wound was washed in the mortuary, it became clear that it was a bullet wound, caused by a gunshot at close range. Powder burns do not lie. Subsequent probing revealed that a single .32 caliber bullet, fired at point-blank range, had traveled through his head almost literally from ear to ear. The pathologist, in ordering the body removed from the car, had harmed the investigation. But he wasn't alone: dozens of police footprints now marred the site, which the warm rains further obliterated. In the car, which was towed from the scene—another piece of improper investigative technique—police recovered a second .32 caliber bullet, a bloody cigarette pack and a woman's hair clip.

In spite of the mangled investigation, Superintendent Poppy was well aware of what had been going on between Lord Erroll and Lady Diana Broughton, and had a good idea about where to look for a leading suspect. Lord Broughton was not arrested until more than forty-five days later, but during his investigation, Poppy uncovered several useful pieces of information about Jock Broughton.

On the morning of the murder, Superintendent Poppy was already sure that he had the right suspect. Lord Broughton was the only one who would benefit from Lord Erroll's death: with him out of the way Diana wouldn't leave him, the five thousand pounds he had promised her would be safe, and his hated rival would never humiliate him in public again. A little checking on Jock Broughton strengthened Poppy's suspicions. Three days before the murder, Broughton had reported the theft from his house of two .32 caliber Colt revolvers. Poppy also learned that Jock had burned up a pair of gym shoes and a blood-stained sock, using aviation fuel he had ordered two days before the murder; and he had been practicing his pistol shooting at Jack Soames's farm earlier in the week. He had the bullets he found at Soames's farm checked against the one found in Lord Erroll's brain and the one discovered in the car. They matched. Pondering the "stolen" Colts, he soon discovered that stealing from himself was an old habit of Lord Broughton's. Back in 1938, Broughton had been the victim of two mysterious robberies: first the heavily insured Broughton pearls, which Diana had been wearing, were stolen from her car outside a restaurant on the Côte d'Azur, and later that year, in October, while Broughton was away in London, his country house, Doddington Hall, was broken into. More jewelry was taken and three valuable and heavily insured paintings—two by George Romney—were cut from their frames and made off with. The insurance companies paid up with hardly a whimper, in spite of the fact that it was well known that Lord Broughton's gambling debts had outstripped his income by a wide margin. His interest in horse racing had drained his resources to a dangerous point. It was also known that he had sold off much of what he had inherited from his father. Some years later, one of Diana's friends from Happy Valley, Hugh Davidson, confessed that he had been the thief, put up to it by Lord Broughton himself. When he delivered the pearls to Broughton, the earl used them to blackmail Davidson into committing the second and more dangerous robbery. Davidson never made a nickel out of these adventures. These two thefts had apparently "baffled" the authorities. It seems more likely that they thought it imprudent to push a case against a well-known nobleman.

Broughton did not emerge from this investigation with his reputation unsullied. After his arrest for the murder of Lord Erroll on 10 March 1941, it was remembered in the press that in the early days of World War I, when the Irish Guards were about to sail for France,

Broughton, an officer in the regiment, came down suddenly with a mysterious illness that required him to be taken from the SS *Novara* as it was about to leave the harbor. A month later, his battalion was cut to pieces on a battlefield. Broughton described his ailment as "sunstroke," and it kept him in hospital until the guns of Europe were hushed. In 1919, when he was discharged, he was hobbled with a limp in his left leg and recurring bouts of amnesia and confusion. There was also a disability pension.

All of this was, of course, highly prejudicial and was not brought to the jury's attention at the trial.

Broughton retained Harry H. Morris, KC, the finest defense lawyer in South Africa, to represent him at his trial. Morris was known to be aggressive, flamboyant and clever. He had secured acquittals for several well-known defendants. His reputation for being rough with witnesses was deserved, but he also knew how to show a gentler side, when it worked to the advantage of his client. He had a fine head for detail and his cross-examinations were devastating; many a witness found himself ensnared by his own ill-considered words. Lady Diana had flown to Johannesburg herself to implore Morris to take the case. He accepted, charmed by her, impressed by the prestigious people involved and the probable publicity and not indifferent to the offer of five thousand pounds for his services.

The trial began on 26 May. The cream of Kenyan society packed the small Central Court in Nairobi. The English tabloid press was well represented. The prosecution was led by Walter Harragin, KC, the attorney-general of Kenya. It was a tidy, watertight case, leaning heavily on Broughton's strong motive to murder Lord Erroll. Harragin buttressed this with a mass of circumstantial evidence: the burned shoe and blood-stained sock, the "stolen" revolvers, and Broughton's uncharacteristic solicitude for the quiet repose of his house guest, Jane Carberry, on the night of the murder. He had knocked on her door twice that night, once at 2:00 a.m. and once at 3:30 a.m. asking, both times "Is everything all right?" Erroll had brought Lady Diana to the door at 2:30 a.m., which meant that Broughton would have had sixty minutes to commit the murder and then return to Karen House in time to check Mrs. Carberry at 3:30 a.m.

Jane Carberry made an ambiguous witness. First she told the court about the bizarre toast Broughton had made to the "happy couple" in the bar at the country club on the eve of the murder. She went on to corroborate Broughton's story about checking on her bedroom twice, but then she told the court that Lord Broughton once asked her whether she thought a man would be hanged if he shot his wife's lover. In summing up for the Crown, Harragin emphasized that this was a case of a jealous man's revenge on his wife's lover. Broughton's attempts to appear older and ailing, reconciled to the affair his new wife was having, ready to forgive and forget, were simply a ruse to ensnare Erroll.

Superintendent Poppy had constructed a convincing recreation of the possible ways in which Broughton could have secretly left and then returned to Karen House without attracting any attention, and he was counting on his presentation to score points with the jury. As I said earlier, it was a tidy case the prosecution presented. But not tidy enough.

When Harry Morris stood up to speak to the jury, he painted a picture of Jock Broughton as an elderly—he was fifty-nine—war veteran, encumbered with wartime disabilities as well as the ravages of age. (It's true that Broughton limped, usually carried a walking stick and had an arthritic arm, but that did not impede his prowess on safari, where he handled a heavy elephant gun with apparent ease and was able to walk for miles, keeping up with the others.) But Morris's chief weapon against the Crown's case was its weak ballistic evidence. Harragin had introduced two ballistics experts' testimony into evidence. Morris, who was an amateur authority on firearms and ammunition, demolished the findings of both, and the conclusions they had drawn from them.

No weapon was recovered, either at the scene of the crime or elsewhere. The only evidence in police hands was the bullets found in the body and in the victim's Buick. These had been compared with bullets found on Jack Soames's farm, and the markings made on the bullets in firing them were found to be similar. These markings, or striations, indicated that the murder weapon was rifled with five right-hand grooves in the barrel. From the powder burns on the head of the victim, the experts said that the propellant used was a black powder. All of this suggested that the weapon was old, out of date and unobtainable in 1941 in Kenya, which meant it had probably been brought to Happy Valley from England. Morris pointed out that while this might be interesting, it proved nothing against his client. He pressed the ballistic experts and got one to admit that the .32 Colts "stolen" from Broughton's house would have been rifled with six left-hand grooves.

Quite certain that the Crown had failed to prove its case, Morris gathered his papers together and left the courtroom. He had already left town when the verdict was announced. At 9:15 a.m. on 1 July 1941, Sir Henry Delves Broughton was found not guilty by a jury of his peers. Later, Jock Broughton remarked to Walter Harragin, the prosecutor, "Bad luck, old boy. You knew I did it, I knew I did it, but you couldn't prove it."

After the trial, Lord Broughton rented Lord Erroll's house, the Djinn Palace, and expected Diana to live with him there. Although his former friends cut him, Jock tried to brazen it out in Happy Valley, shooting, riding and gambling. Before long, Diana went off with a wealthy cattle rancher, Gilbert Colvile. Alone again, Jock suffered first a riding accident and then a bad fall down a railway embankment, in which he injured his back badly. In 1942, on a visit to England, he was arrested for insurance frauds, but released for lack of evidence. By this time, it was common knowledge that he had been looting his estate and also cheating his son out of the bulk of his inheritance. All in all, he had gambled away a million pounds at the tables, the track or in bad investments. On 2 December 1942, he booked a room at the Adelphi Hotel in Liverpool, where his dead body was discovered three days later. He had injected himself with a lethal overdose of Medinal.

It is interesting that the self-assured Lord Broughton should end up killing himself in a provincial hotel room. It brings a note of delayed melodrama to the proceedings. Perhaps it hints at Jock Broughton's slower than average mental processes. Like Othello, another military man, he threw away a pearl, richer than all his tribe. The world view of Lord Broughton and others like him was quickly vanishing from the face of the earth. Money kept it alive in Kenya longer than in other places, but the money ran through their fingers and their aristocratic birth meant little without cash. There would soon be few places left for the Lord Errolls and Lord Broughtons and their kind. Like Othello, too, Lord Broughton was not easily made jealous, but when jealous he was perplexed in the extreme. He worked out his destiny, perhaps never dreaming that he would really get away with it. Perhaps the collection of regulars at the bar of the Muthaiga Country Club acted like a Greek chorus of Iagos. What would they have thought at that bar if they knew that in a few years' time the blacks of Kenya would be sitting in their places contemplating the whirligig of time and its revenges?

On Lord Broughton's death, Lady Diana married her cattle rancher, but only to leave him in 1955 to marry Tom Cholmondley, the fourth Baron Delamere. The rancher, Colvile, loved her so much he let Diana divorce him.

The daughter of Jane Carberry, Juanita, claimed in 1979 that Lord Broughton had confessed to the murder of Lord Erroll to her. She was fifteen years old at the time. She said that he wanted to unburden himself after all the ridicule he had been subjected to.

Lord Broughton's complex character brings into question the nature of the crime he undoubtedly committed. Was it a classic crime of passion? He certainly loved Diana, and she was a trophy worth showing off. He had need of her money to support his habits. He was humiliated by Lord Erroll's attentions to her and the slight to his pride in that small, tight-knit society. He was jealous of his rival's charm, youth, good looks and winning ways—not noticing that for Erroll, Diana was just another pretty face and a large fortune to run through. On the other hand, the crime was not brought off without a certain degree of premeditation. Like Hamlet, Broughton put on a false semblance; he acted the part of a broad-minded man of the world ready to live with and accommodate what he couldn't change. He won both Diana and Erroll over, convincing them that he was not going to make a fuss about the young couple. The murder itself required pre-planning. He needed to find and then later dispose of the revolver. He needed and did set up an alibi at his house with Jane Carberry. And finally, he needed to provide a means to return to the house from the scene of the crime, a point two miles down the road. Some commentators have suggested that he had procured a bicycle, which he used to get to and from the murder scene and then got rid of. At some level, it must have pleased Lord Broughton that he was able to bring it off, that he had acted his part so well.

The Marquis de Bernardy de Sigoyer

While reporters and the regular chaps around the bar at the country club contemplated the not guilty verdict, and watched where the scattered pieces fell, another drama was being enacted in France that claimed, or tried to claim, to involve blood as blue as that of Lord Erroll and Lord Broughton. As a companion piece to the Broughton case, with its thick upper crust, its excesses and eccentricities, let me introduce to you the Marquis Alain de Bernardy de Sigoyer,[38] a man who might have tried to join the group at the bar at the Muthaiga Country Club. He might have been accepted. Unfortunately, the Marquis was not quite as fortunate as Jock Broughton in a court of law. One would think that *two* particles in his name might serve to protect the neck of any post-revolutionary aristocratic Frenchman. In this instance, at least, one would be wrong: M. le Marquis went to the guillotine for the murder of his low-born wife, Janine, in 1947, in spite of his string of seven baptismal names. In almost every way, this case exhibits the banality that attends most domestic crimes. But the high rank of the accused in the case attracted the media in the same way that the death of Lord Erroll did in Kenya. For some reason Western Europeans, the French especially, are fascinated by the doings and undoings of their betters. On almost every newsstand in Paris, Amsterdam, Brussels, Berlin or Madrid, the unnatural foibles of Gilles de Rais, Marie de Brinvilliers, the Marquis de Sade and Vlad the

Impaler are retailed endlessly alongside exposés of Edward, Prince of Wales (Victoria's chartered libertine son), elegies to the hedonistic downfall of Princess Diana, or illustrated articles about Napoleon's alleged poisoning and last days on St. Helena. There are millions of people out there enjoying this material. Their imaginations are ignited; their humdrum or frustrated lives are redeemed by the most sordid secrets of history. And the more exalted the noble sinner, the better they like it.

There is no question at all about the Marquis' credentials as a sinner, but there has always been some question about whether Alain de Bernardy de Sigoyer was truly entitled to style himself a Marquis. Earlier in his career, the rank of baron seemed to suit him. In his final series of court appearances, the judge tried to rid the courtroom of bows of deference and phrases alluding to the defendant's supposed aristocratic status. De Bernardy boasted that an ancestor of his had been engaged for a time to a sister of the Empress Joséphine, and he was certainly related to one of the barristers who defended Louis XVI before the Convention in 1792. Another direct member of his family was an associate of Lafayette during the American Revolution. This man established his family on Réunion, where many years later, in 1905 to be exact, the scoundrel Alain de Bernardy de Sigoyer was born. Some writers of de Bernardy's story reject all of this, except for his birth on the isolated Island of Réunion in the Indian Ocean; they believe he made the rest up out of feelings of inferiority that he was determined to rise above.

Throughout his life he claimed to be an adept at black magic. Whether he picked this up from the natives of Réunion is not known. As a child he used his talk of magic and the black arts to try to dominate his little friends. While still a boy, Alain de Bernardy was orphaned; soon after that he found his way onto a ship bound for Europe. Almost from the day of his arrival, de Bernardy was a bad hat. By the time he was in his twenties, his record of petty crimes was posted in the *commissariats* throughout France. He operated his swindles and scams all over France. The police of Toulon, Aix, Nantes and

Bergerac knew him under one name or another. Authorities in Berlin, Vienna, Budapest, Naples and Sofia kept track of his local thefts, frauds and forgeries. Once, when asked the whereabouts of a missing American, whose papers and passport were found in his possession, he quipped to the police, "Don't bother to look any more; I ate him." De Bernardy might have served as a model for Hannibal Lecter. Twice he spent time in mental institutions. There was almost always a component of sadism in his crimes. He seemed to enjoy not only the money he took from people but also their physical discomfort as well.

Why he ever married Janine Kergot is a good question. Why anyone would marry him is another. He was a handsome enough young man, with a long face, dark hair and solid chin. There was a slight cast to his left eye, which might have been acceptable had his ever-present sneer of superiority not spoiled things. From time to time he wore an imperial beard in imitation of the Emperor Napoleon III. Without a doubt, Janine, his wife, loved him. Less than a year before her death at his hands, she wrote:

> I love you so much, Alain, and with my whole soul. I am sick with love for you and I think of you incessantly. I kiss you a thousand times and with all my heart.

Unfortunately for Janine, there were *always* other women in de Bernardy's life. Whether they thought they were attracted to him by animal magnetism or by one of the black arts he claimed to practice is difficult to determine, but certainly there were always women around when he needed them, as Janine discovered not long into her marriage.

The problem with de Bernardy's marriage persists. It is a puzzle. Why did he *marry* Janine when he had discovered that the virtue of most of the women he desired surrendered without a prolonged siege. Janine Kergot was far below him in the social scale. Her education was slight, her accomplishments meager and her fortune nonexistent. Still, her mother described her at the trial as "healthy, cheerful and sports-loving." Others attest that she was a pretty little thing, with a quick smile and soft brown eyes framed by dark hair. She was simple, quiet, and had no aspirations to become a socialite. With such a character as the Marquis, it is difficult to speak of love in the usual way, but it seems that for this lifelong criminal, to whom betrayal was as customary as an afternoon apéritif, Janine meant something special. In spite of her gorgon of a mother, he adored her. To a point. One is reminded of the wanted murderer who is good to his ailing sister, or the ruthless bandit who, in spite of ample evidence to the contrary, earns a reputation for giving to the poor.

Irène Lebeau, a seventeen-year-old peasant girl, entered the home of the Marquis and Marquise as a maid and general help about the same time (1940) as their first-born son, Simety, was born. The house on the Boulevard de Bercy soon became a *ménage à trois* and remained so for most of the German occupation of Paris. In 1942, the Marquise presented de Bernardy with a daughter. The following year, his mistress similarly obliged. Meanwhile, de Bernardy engaged in a profitable and growing trade with the enemy, selling casks of cognac as a wholesaler to German officers (an act of collaboration). He had taken a tall brick house in the Boulevard de Bercy district of Paris, where wines and spirits in bulk were kept in bonded warehouses behind high walls. He also rented a warehouse, just inside the main gates, on the rue de Nuits.

It was at 7, Boulevard de Bercy that the *ménage* began to unravel. In 1944, the year of the Liberation, Janine had had enough. She left her husband. In fact, she fled, taking the children. Through her lawyer, she asked for and got a legal separation agreement that required de Bernardy to pay her ten thousand francs per month. She and the children moved in with her mother. That left de Bernardy alone with his mistress/housemaid, Irène Lebeau.

Ten thousand francs a month was well within the Marquis' power to pay his estranged wife for the support of herself and the children. (It was estimated that he earned at least thirty million during the Occupation.) No, it wasn't the money, it was the Marquis; he wasn't to be trifled with. "It was his surly boast," wrote Alister Kershaw in *Murder in France*, "that he was not a man to inconvenience." He resented having to pay a *centime* for what he regarded as his rightful *droit de seigneur*. From all that we have learned about de Bernardy, he was, as the French say, *un numéro, un type* (a "character"). As a former colonial he had been raised to think of the Ile-de-France as holy ground, but as usual he rebelled. He wasn't going to be pushed around by a woman no better than an ignorant peasant.

Janine should have known this. Her mother should have warned her that de Bernardy was dangerous and that the money was only money. Unfortunately, for so many victims of crime, the balance between safety and what is rightfully due usually comes down on the side of the cash. Janine telephoned the Marquis, who treated his delinquency in not sending the current payment to her on time as a bagatelle. A tiny oversight. He arranged to meet her at his newly acquired house in the rue Étienne-Dolet, near the cemetery Père Lachaise. When she arrived, he had already left for his warehouse, where with Irène's help he dug a grave under the floor. He told his mistress that he was testing to see whether the warehouse would accommodate additional cellars. Having escaped almost certain death on her first visit, Janine persisted: she called again and agreed to meet Alain at their old house at 7, Boulevard de Bercy at nine the following morning. The date was 28 March 1944.

Janine left her mother's and was seen entering the Boulevard de Bercy house, but was never seen alive again except by her estranged husband and his mistress. The Marquis received his wife in one of the second-floor bedrooms, leaving Irène, in her role as maid, to look after Simety, their son, downstairs. According to her testimony at their joint trial, Irène reported that after a time the Marquis called her to come up. Timidly, she entered the bedroom.

> I found M. de Bernardy behind the red armchair which was in front of the bedroom fireplace, and Mme de Bernardy sitting in the armchair. M. de Bernardy had passed a cord around her neck.

According to another translation of this testimony, Irène stated that the Marquis was in a seemingly playful mood as he slipped a length of clothesline, taken from his pocket, around his wife's neck. In this same vein he quizzed her about whether she was having an affair. "Suppose I strangle you for that?" Smiling, she let him tie the cord loosely about her neck.

For her to allow him to put a rope around her neck suggests that there was a level of depravity in the relationship at this point and that it was an expected and familiar part of their version of the ritual of lovemaking. Otherwise, Janine would have fled for her life.

Here Irène picks up the story again:

> He was right behind her. I could hear the question which M. de Bernardy had put to her:
>
> "Is Brisset your lover?" And Mme Bernardy answered:
>
> "I have nothing to tell you!" As I came further into the room, M. de Bernardy looked as if he were about to pull on the cord. I went up to him and asked what he was doing. He pushed me roughly away and said:
>
> "If you interfere you'll get the same." When I looked round, M. de Bernardy pulled on the cord with his knee against the armchair. Mme Bernardy threw up her hands, her legs were stretched out in front of her … It was all over.

According to Alister Kershaw, again, the Marquis' mistress remembered that when Janine de Bernardy refused to answer her husband's question about whether one Brisset was her lover, her face was momentarily illuminated by a smile. Kershaw speculates that Janine was using the jealousy she awakened in de Bernardy to force him to murder her, thus ending two painful and unhappy lives: her own and, with luck, his. While this notion that Janine brought on her own murder may be a little far-fetched, it is interesting to notice that he turned the act of killing his wife into the form of a crime of passion. He pretended outrage at her supposed infidelity *after* the grave was already dug. His motive for killing his wife was to rid himself of the obligation of paying ten thousand francs a month for her support. Why would he care if she had a lover? Kershaw suggests that he put the act of murdering his wife into the form of a *crime passionnel* as a salve to his self-esteem; "a mock-aristocratic preoccupation with his personal honour." He goes on:

> To kill his wife for money would have been conduct unbefitting a gentleman; to do away with her in a frenzy of high-minded rage at her wantonness almost reflected credit on him. ... There is something singularly shocking in the notion of the creature, his mind already made up, playing out the gruesome comedy until his righteous indignation finally overflowed and he could do what he had all along intended to do, but with a self-congratulatory consciousness of his own feudal integrity. How grateful he must have been when his wife collaborated as she did.

The Marquis and Irène Lebeau carried the body to de Bernardy's van and they successfully buried it in the prepared grave. It wasn't very long after this that Janine's mother began making inquiries. When the Paris police asked de Bernardy a few routine questions, the Marquis showed them papers that showed how thick he was with the German authorities, an action that was remembered after the German departure later that year.

The Marquis was arrested almost on the heels of the retreating Wehrmacht, wearing an armband of the Free French and cheering the Liberation. Suspecting correctly that his wife's maid, his former mistress, might be accused with him, he tried to get word to her that she should seriously heed the lesson of the red armchair.

There is no need to go into the trial: he was defended by the same advocate who defended Pétain, the war hero and puppet head of the Vichy government. The Marquis was at his histrionic best, "I have had nothing to do with this dreadful affair," he shouted at one point. At another, he accused his mistress of shooting his wife. This sent the forensic people back to the exhumed remains. They could find no sign of a bullet or of a bullet wound. The judges disliked the Marquis' aristocratic airs, the jury didn't like his sneer; his collaborationist past put the black cap on it. Significantly, not a word about crimes of passion came up at the trial, although it underlined one strand of the Marquis' defense.

For the Marquis, the drama ended in the courtyard of the Santé Prison, where the guillotine had been assembled, erected, leveled and tested. The blade was to fall twice on the morning of 11 June 1947. De Bernardy de Sigoyer was to share the occasion with another murderer, Marcel Brunet, a man of proletarian tastes and experience. They both drank a shot of grog in the early light and smoked a final cigarette, a Gauloise *bleu*. The working class won out in the matter of precedence as well; Republican France required the less high-born murderer to pre-cede the Marquis to the bascule of the "Widow." De Bernardy watched as Brunet submitted to the professional hands of M. Desfourneaux and his assistants. A few moments later, he nodded in the direction of those whose professional connection with the justice system required their presence in the Boulevard d'Arago at such an early hour, said "*Mes respects, Messieurs*" to the attending officials and walked briskly to the machine. Kevin Kershaw ends his essay on de Sigoyer wondering: "Did some romantic notion of how his real or imagined ancestors had died during the Revolution strengthen him to play the dignified part?" Or was this yet another mask, another bit of play-acting, another false impression of this repellent but fascinating poseur? Like many of the murderers between these covers, the Marquis enjoyed the wearing of masks. He had had to abandon the mask of family and personal honor at the trial, because neither the judges nor the jury were having any of it. They saw through Bernardy de Sigoyer with admirable clarity. His bid to show himself off as an honorable man had no chance of succeeding.

While all of this is part of the large dossier of the case, part of the collection of files that make up what is left of these unfortunate lives, the Marquis, as is usual on these occasions, took no baggage with him.

EIGHT

Disguises and Disappearances

Dr. Hawley Harvey Crippen

In the classic crime of passion, the crime is rarely covered up. The perpetrator often makes no attempt to escape. The mad act, meant to stifle pain, has been performed, and that's usually as far as the thinking goes, if there is any. The murderer and the law are one in their opinion about what should follow. Think of Ruth Ellis, standing over the dead body of David Blakely with a smoking gun in her hand. Don't tell me she thought she could get away with it. She was as likely to be thinking of John Philip Sousa. Think of Henriette Caillaux warning the office boy that the gun he had just taken from her might still be loaded. Murder of this kind is a public act, done in full view of the world, with the world invited to witness both the act and the wrongs that encouraged it.

While the giving of poison is not quite the same as flinging vitriol, picking up a knife, or firing a handgun—it seems to imply premeditation—the possibility that Dr. Hawley Harvey Crippen's wife, Cora, died in a rash and passionate attempt by her husband to escape from an unbearable marriage, a last chance for poor Crippen to capture some happiness in a rather drab life, is the best theory presented so far about his motive.[39] Students of the case remain puzzled by it. The terrain is obscured because the escape of the man responsible and then the capture of the fugitive and his attractive young companion on shipboard make it difficult to find a fair reading of the case today.

Poor Dr. Hawley Harvey Crippen had his classic passion. Married to Cora, a large, overbearing former singer and bottom-of-the-barrel music hall performer, who sometimes used the name Belle Elmore, he lived the life of a Walter Mitty, the James Thurber character, a hen-pecked milquetoast, mild, meek and unassertive to a fare-thee-well, until he met and fell in love with his typist, pretty Ethel Le Neve. For years Crippen had been severely managed at home and belittled in public by his wife. He did the cleaning and housekeeping; she made all decisions and even selected his clothes for him. Smiling Ethel put heart into him. What happened next, according to the official results of a trial by jury in October 1910, is that Crippen willfully, feloniously and with malice aforethought poisoned Cora with hyoscine, or scopolamine, which he was known to have purchased from a wholesale druggist.

At first Crippen gave out the story that his wife had returned to the United States, from whence she had come with her Michigan-born husband in 1900. Something about a sick relative, who needed nursing. Cora's real name was Kunegonde Mackamotzki, but she used several others including Belle Elmore. Hawley Harvey called himself both "Peter," because he preferred that name to his two given names, and "Doctor," because he had a sort of medical degree from the Hospital College of Cleveland. In London, he worked as a homeopathic specialist or quack, and was even listed as such in a published list warning people against him and at least 116 others of his kind. When Cora's theatrical friends pressed to know more about Mrs. Crippen's sudden disappearance, they were told she had perished from pneumonia in the high mountains of California while attending a sick relative. But when Ethel was seen to have moved into Hawley's house and was spotted wearing a brooch and other jewelry belonging to Cora, the police were called in. At first, Chief Inspector Walter Dew of Scotland Yard discovered little; a search of the house revealed nothing. Crippen amended his story: now he said that Cora had run off with someone younger, a story Dew found plausible. Had they sat tight, the ending of the story might have been different. But they took fright and left London. Crippen and Le Neve absconded to Antwerp and sailed for Quebec City on the SS

Montrose. The tempo of the story accelerated. Captain Kendall of the *Montrose* became suspicious of two of his passengers. One, dressed as a boy, was clearly a woman. His trousers, their shape altered by safety pins, revealed a feminine form; his table manners were very ladylike. He wired Scotland Yard alerting them to his suspicions. Crippen's house was again searched, thoroughly this time, and human body parts were discovered buried in the cellar. Dr. (later Sir) Bernard Spilsbury was able to identify Cora by an abdominal scar on a piece of skin, and detected a lethal amount of hyoscine in the viscera. The head, limbs and bones were never found. The Chief Inspector caught a faster ship in order to catch the suspects on the wing, and arrived in Quebec City before the *Montrose.* From there he was able to cable home: "Handcuffs Ldn Eng: Crippen and Lenave arrested wire later. Dew."

Separate trials followed quickly upon the doctor's and Ethel's arrest. Ethel was acquitted; Hawley Harvey Crippen was condemned to death and executed. Since then, speculation about what really happened has continued. Was Ethel blameless, guilty of nothing more than adultery? Was she more innocent than Edith Thompson, whose case would be heard a dozen years later? One of the great advocates of the English bar, Sir Edward Marshall Hall, speculated that Crippen may have given the hyoscine to his wife to weaken her sexual appetite. Hyoscine was known to dampen carnal desires. Since he was now partnered with two women, their joint demands were getting excessive. Crippen's mistake, in his view, was in judging the proper amount. The drug was new in 1910, and its strength and potency imperfectly understood. It is not unreasonable to think that Crippen miscalculated the amount. The rest of the crime was simply a grisly cover-up and flight. In a similar vein it has been suggested that the hyoscine was administered to control Cora's alcoholism. It was when she was drinking that she belittled and humiliated Crippen so terribly that friends winced at her behavior. You may pay your money and take your choice about what really happened.

Part of the appeal and notoriety of this story may be pegged to the technological innovations in the case. Hyoscine, for a start, was new and imperfectly known. While Dr. Crippen leaned back, relaxing in his deck chair, he is said to have often looked up at the radio aerial, muttering, "What a wonderful invention it is!" Meanwhile, the captain of the *Montrose* used the radio to report his suspicions to Scotland Yard. This was the first time that radio had been used in a murder investigation. Then followed a highly exciting chase across the North Atlantic, ending in the interception of the fleeing lovers as their ship approached land at Quebec.

After her acquittal, Le Neve vanished. She was thought to have gone to New York, where she lived out the rest of her long life under an assumed name. Crippen's name was briefly used as an expletive. How odd that this most henpecked of murderers should win that sort of fame. He was buried with a picture of Ethel next to his heart. If Crippen *did* do it, he took a direct way, straightforward if not very far-sighted, of eliminating the person who stood in the way of his future happiness.

Cyril Belshaw

There are many cases—for example, the Belshaw case involving the death of a Canadian professor's wife in Switzerland—where the post-homicide events have obscured the homicide itself.

Cyril Shirley Belshaw[40] was in 1980 a world-renowned anthropologist. He was a professor at the University of British Columbia in Vancouver, where Betty, his wife of thirty-seven years, was also a teacher. Her specialty was the life and work of Katherine Mansfield (1888–1923), the New Zealand short story writer. At the time of Betty's disappearance, they were spending the second half of Cyril's sabbatical year in the ski resort of Montana-Vermala in Switzerland, where between rare sorties to conquer the ski slopes, Betty was working on a biography of Mansfield, who had traveled to Montana-Vermala, Switzerland, in a last desperate attempt to treat her tuberculosis around 1922.

On a shopping trip to Paris, where the Belshaws were staying in a hotel near the famed cemetery of Père Lachaise, they set out together on the morning of 15 January 1979, to accomplish a few errands of no special significance. They took the Métro from Bagnolet. Betty got off at Bourse, where she planned to walk to the Bibliothèque Nationale. She was never seen alive again. She apparently vanished into thin air.

Cyril and Betty Joy Sweetman Belshaw were New Zealanders. Betty was twenty-two when she married Cyril in Christchurch. He had served in the Pacific during the war, and afterwards pursued his studies in London, Australia and finally on Canada's west coast. Together they had done the traveling through Melanesia that resulted in Cyril's book, *Under the Ivi Tree: Society and Economic Growth in Rural Fiji* (1964). Betty went with him everywhere and lived with him under the primitive conditions a field worker learns to live with—or finds something less onerous to do. Betty supported him and his research, while caring for their two young children Diana and Adrian.

Betty Belshaw was a stout woman with reddish hair, a little above average height, who wore glasses with tinted plastic frames. She had the colonial's sense of class differences and tried to make her husband's life everything his scholarly eminence deserved. She was formal with her longtime secretary, with whom she preferred to remain on a footing of reserve even when they were alone. She wished to be addressed as "Mrs. Belshaw," not "Betty."

Belshaw was the very model of a modern scholar: somewhat prim, organized, and in command of his facts. He was short, well-dressed, overweight, polite and—some say—kind. He wore gold-rimmed glasses. When his wife failed to keep the appointment they had made to meet for a pre-luncheon drink at the pub in the Galeries Lafayette, he did not panic. He returned to the hotel and waited. It was early evening when he reported his wife's unexplained absence to the *agent* at the Bagnolet *commissariat*. He returned to the hotel a little put out because the policeman failed to get excited at his news. The officer suggested calmly that if she failed to appear overnight, he should return to the police station prepared to give a thorough description of Betty and of what she had been wearing that morning.

She did not return that night, nor the next. She had simply disappeared. Belshaw was not amused when an *agent* informed him that wives and husbands are always disappearing with no warning. It happens every day. He waited in Paris for four days. When he had reported to various friends and relatives that Betty was gone, perhaps hoping that she had surfaced with them, he informed their grown children, Diana and Adrian, and had spoken about his problem to the Canadian ambassador. Then he drove back to the apartment in Montana-Vermala to watch and wait.

Switzerland is, of course, a country made up of many *cantons*, originally totally independent city-states. Some of this independence remains today. Belshaw had not reported his wife's disappearance to the authorities of Valais, where his Montana-Vermala apartment was located. He defended this omission, when asked, with the logical answer: the disappearance occurred in Paris. Vaud, the *canton* next to Valais, did not hear of it until a report of Betty Belshaw's sudden vanishing from the center of Paris arrived in Aigle, the chief town of Vaud, some three months later. This was significant because female human remains had been recovered from a deep valley near a bridge and lay-by called Le Sépey. That was on 28 March 1979, some considerable time after Betty Belshaw's "Paris disappearance." The partial body—it was badly decomposed and had been eaten by animals—had been stripped of its clothing, watch and rings and placed in plastic bags before being dropped in a gorge.

When the authorities at Aigle learned of a possible Belshaw connection, they asked Professor Belshaw if he would supply dental records to aid the investigation. In due time, the records arrived. The body could not be identified as that of Betty Belshaw.

Nine months after the disappearance, Belshaw had returned to Vancouver, where he tried to put his life back together. Meanwhile, the Swiss police had been busy: they had consolidated the investigation in Vaud, for example, and had established contact with the RCMP in Vancouver. When they contacted Belshaw again for more detailed dental records, he wrote to them the following: "I wish to make the following statement to correct information which was supplied to the Swiss police authorities ..."

In the lines that followed, Belshaw admitted that, through psychological trauma, "on impulse" he had "altered the charts during the copying process." To most people, including most policemen, the altering of dental charts that are to be used to help identify a missing person is a confession of guilt. Belshaw argued that he could not face the possibility that Betty had committed suicide. A remarkably conservative and private person, he could not bear the scandal and criticism that he foresaw happening should the Le Sépey corpse be identified as that of his wife. At all events, it fired up the investigation. The Swiss authorities discovered that there was no way Belshaw could be extradited to aid the investigation. Two Swiss policemen came to Vancouver to question him through an interpreter. When the proper dental records were compared with the dentition of the Le Sépey corpse, a positive identification could be made. The body in the gorge was Betty Belshaw.

At home, the Swiss detectives would have been able to question a witness whether the witness wanted to be questioned or not, whether his lawyer was in attendance or not. After fighting the differences between Canadian and Swiss police procedures, caused by the differences between civil code and common law jurisprudence, the two detectives returned home when neither Belshaw nor the woman he was seeing would talk further to them.

Belshaw, it was discovered, was involved in a long-standing extramarital relationship, which was uncovered almost by accident when a policeman checked a parked sportscar and discovered Prof. Belshaw and a woman in a compromising position. Further checking revealed that the woman, a Mrs. Wilson, had been staying with Prof. Belshaw in Montana-Vermala *before* Betty Belshaw arrived to be with her husband.

From here on, the story is a legal one—and it was simplified when Dr. Belshaw stepped off an Air Canada flight in Paris on 11 November 1979. On his way to a professional meeting, he was immediately taken into custody and ended up in a courtroom in Aigle.

The trial was scrupulously fair, a show trial without the unpleasant associations that phrase gives rise to. The judge explained to the prisoner: "You can be convicted, convicted totally, or acquitted because there is a reasonable doubt and you must be freed." Belshaw insisted that a verdict of acquittal "by reason of doubt," was not what he wanted.

"I had nothing to do with the death of my wife, and only an acquittal would be just." At that moment, he lost his usual calm and controlled manner. He banged his hand on the table, and let his feelings be heard and seen: "It is insupportable that people could suspect me of such a thing!"

It was a difficult case to try. No one could say with any assurance how Betty Belshaw died. No wounds or suspicious marks were found on the body. One pathologist suggested that pinkish markings at the root-ends of her teeth *might* indicate strangulation. If it was murder, there were no witnesses. If there was premeditation, there were no absolute signs of it. If Betty Belshaw's death came about during a violent quarrel, which seemed to match Belshaw's manner better than a well-planned premeditated homicide, her death might easily have been accidental—a fall backwards, her head being fatally injured as it hit a hard object, an argument that ended with his hands tightly encircling Betty's neck.

The president of the tribunal himself suggested that there might have been a quarrel following Betty's discovery that her husband had been staying in Montana-Vermala earlier with another woman, and that Betty's ending up, by whatever means, dead, could have been simple bad luck. If so, the cover-up was masterful.

There remain serious doubts about the case. If Mrs. Belshaw was abducted in Paris, as her husband still maintains, why did her murderer drive to Switzerland and cross a border checkpoint to dispose of the body? How would a chance assassin even know where she came from? It seems more reasonable to believe that the crime was committed in Switzerland, close to where the Belshaws were living. If the murderer was unknown to his victim, why would he remove all traces of identification from the dead body, since none of them could lead to him? And, we are still left with the basic question of why Cyril Belshaw falsified the dental records. This falsification included a dozen changes made to the documents he received from Vancouver. Was this killing a crime of passion? As a writer of crime fiction, I am always asking myself "what if?" questions. It's not the same thing as pointing an accusing finger. It's a sort of game crime writers play. Assuming, for the sake of argument, that Dr. Belshaw is the guilty party, I think it was. I suggest that *if* there was a murder, it occurred in their apartment of Jolilac in Montana-Vermala *not* in Paris. I further suggest that, if he did it, it came about through a sudden lapse in Belshaw's secure, cool, controlled manner.

Cyril Belshaw, as of this writing, still lives in Vancouver. He is retired from the University of British Columbia and is listed there as an emeritus professor with the anthropology department. He is a member of the Royal Society of Canada. He is the holder of life memberships and honorary life memberships in several distinguished scholarly organizations. In addition to his many publications in anthropology, he has also published a dining guide to the better restaurants of Vancouver and for some years wrote a "dining out" column in a local magazine.

Peter Hogg

There is an English case, from 1976, which is of interest in this present connection. A fifty-six-year-old former airline jet pilot, Peter Hogg,[41] confessed to strangling his wife, Margaret, a former airline hostess, during a row in which she threw up to him the name of her lover, Graham Ryan. She had in fact been boasting of the affair to all and sundry in the neighborhood of their £90,000 Surrey home. The marriage had been in serious trouble for some time. Ryan, a banker, admitted at the trial that he and Margaret had been away together in Dorset the week before the fatal argument with her husband.

Margaret Hogg's three-year fling with Graham Ryan was not the first of her marital infidelities. Patrick Back, Q.C., described her at the trial as "a piece of erring humanity." She had had partners before Ryan. But the case still conforms to the triangular form of the crime of passion, the only difference being that one of the sides was interchangeable.

When asked during his Old Bailey trial if he had murdered her, he described how she had flaunted her lover's name during the row: "Murder is not the right word. Certainly she died. I think I strangled her. We had an argument, she did her usual act, she was always throwing things at me … She was scratching my face, kicking me in the crotch and I belted her. She flew at me hitting and kicking, then I grabbed her round the neck and squeezed hard. I realized one of her eyes had glazed and I let her go. She fell back on the floor and I realized that she was dead."

Another killer in a similar situation might send for the police and face the music. Certainly that would be true for one kind of *crime passionnel*. But not Peter Hogg. He was surprised and confused by the fatal outcome of a routine quarrel. Something had to be done about it. As a former airline pilot—he had flown 747s for Air Europe—he knew how to keep cool, how to deal with an emergency one step at a time. He changed clothes, trussed the body up in a blanket or rug and then drove 250 miles north, from Surrey to Cumbria, where under cover of darkness he ditched the body from an inflatable raft into one of the picture-postcard lakes of the Lake District. His choice of location was not chance; as a boy he had attended school in the neighborhood and knew the Scree, or rock-slide area of the Lake District, very well. He weighted the body down with a heavy concrete slab, nearly upsetting the raft as he slid her beneath the black water.

After a wait of a month, he reported his wife "missing" to the Surrey police. And there at the bottom of out-of-the-way Wast Water the body lay at a depth of 110 feet until it was discovered eight years later by scuba divers. In Cumbria, Hogg was the victim of bad luck. How could he have known that amateur divers would be searching the lake for signs of *another* missing woman? Chance decided which of the bodies would be discovered first. The divers were searching for a French tourist, Véronique Marre, who had vanished on a walking tour of the Lake District. Peter Hogg was also unaware that just ten yards beyond the spot where he dumped the carpet-bagged and weighted body of his wife, whom the papers dubbed "the Lady of the Lake," the lake bottom dropped many more feet to a depth where scuba divers rarely ventured in fresh water. He also forgot that the ring on his wife's finger bore both of their initials. Whoever murdered Betty Belshaw could have taught him a thing or two about rings, watches and labels. And wasn't Ruth Snyder caught through the *wrong* construction being placed on initials on a piece of jewelry?

Still, Peter Hogg's luck came back when the Surrey police came calling. First of all, he was granted bail, which is not usual in murder proceedings. And when the trial ended he was found not guilty of murder. He was, however, imprisoned for three years for manslaughter and another year was added for obstructing a coroner and perjury in divorce proceedings. It was a highly civilized court that would render such a verdict. In so many cases in the past, the cover-up of the crime has blurred a true and equitable judgment of the crime itself.

Véronique Marre's body was eventually found, not in the lake, but a thousand feet above the lake at the bottom of a three-hundred-foot rock spur known locally as Broken Rib Crag.

NINE

The Hunger of Love
and a Slice of America

Jean Liger

Nearly nine months before the Reims trial of Yvonne Chevallier, the war hero's wife from Orléans whose story begins this book, a woodsman chopping down trees near the Château de Louveciennes, once the home of Mme du Barry, not far from Versailles, discovered what he thought were a pile of animal bones. His employer thought they looked human enough to inform the police, who soon confirmed that the bones were indeed human. They had been buried in a shallow grave quite close to a ruined marble "Temple of Love" associated with the estate. With the bones were an unlined glove, a green tartan skirt and beige nylon stockings. No store labels or laundry marks survived to aid the police. However, David Rowan, a reporter, had received a routine report of a missing young woman from Wiltshire: Jackie Richardson of Trowbridge. She had been working in France as a children's nurse. Friends of hers in England, after not hearing from her in six months, informed Scotland Yard. Meanwhile Police Commissaire Etienne Vasseur and his assistant Inspector Steiner had concluded that, because the young woman's toes showed signs of nail polish and since the glove was unlined, the death had occurred during the summer months. When Rowan informed the French police about the possibility that it might be the Trowbridge girl, dental records were checked and a positive identification made. The body in question was indeed that of Jackie Richardson, the missing nurse.

The day that the name of the victim was confirmed, the police detained the dead girl's former fiancé, Jean Liger, an artist and decorator.[42] Twenty-six years old, dark and handsome, with a thin mustache, Liger quickly broke down under interrogation and made a full confession, which Rowan was allowed to see. "In it, he said that he first met Miss Richardson in November, 1950," at the château, where she was governess to the two children of the Comte de Bellecombe, the occupant of the château. They fell in love and planned to get married. After she returned to England, where she worked in a famous London hotel as a receptionist, he tried to break off the engagement. They were reunited when she returned to France in July 1951. Liger's confession continues:

On 5th August, 1951 (a Sunday), I had arranged to meet her at the château, where I had some work to do. [The Comte was *his* employer as well as Miss Richardson's.] M. and Mme de Bellecombe were on holiday and we were alone on the estate. Just before lunch, Jackie suggested that we take a stroll in the park and I accompanied her. We had another argument.

Another argument? The young man went on to explain: "Yes, she was of a hysterical nature and became very demanding. We had frequent arguments." This time, according to Rowan, she slapped him and he struck her. She fell to the ground and began screaming. To silence her, he seized her mouth and then her throat. When he let go, she was dead.

We were at the far end of the park and nobody had seen us. I bound the feet of the body with the leather belt that the girl was wearing and dragged the body into the undergrowth. Then I came back to the château, where I found a spade. I went back to the body and started digging a grave. But I hadn't the courage to continue such a job and I decided to return to Paris, leaving the body lying on the ground.

He caught the next train, and emptied the contents of Jackie's handbag out the window of his compartment. He threw her shoes down a sewer and spent the night in a hotel, instead of returning to his parents' house. All night long, he debated with himself about whether or not he should give himself up. In the morning, he returned to the château and finished burying the body.

After making his confession, he was taken back to the scene of the crime, where he showed the detectives and the examining magistrate from Versailles where each of the events leading to the young woman's death had taken place. Judge Pierre Cassagne, the magistrate mentioned above, asked him why he had taken Jackie's shoes. Liger confessed that he didn't know why at the time and he still didn't know. Cassagne had him charged with murder.

The trial of Jean Liger took place at Versailles, beginning 7 February 1955. The reason for this three-year delay—unconscionable in most other countries—was simply the languid speed of justice in France. It was now, at the trial, that the world first learned what the young couple had argued about on that fatal day. What got the young man so upset that his anger proved lethal? Rowan says that this was "almost ludicrously pathetic." Jackie and Jean had made love, after wandering through the majestic rooms in the château, no doubt. Afterwards, Jackie wanted to fool around some more. She was still unsatisfied; she wanted more kisses. Liger, the satisfied male, was hungry and wanted to move on to lunch. The quarrel, with such serious and permanent consequences for both of them, began with a happy love scene. Admittedly, the scene immediately after the loving embraces reversed traditional roles of national stereotypes, with the passionate Englishwoman eager for further carnal explorations, and the frosty Frenchman out of temper after the lovemaking, in need of his lunch. Here were the unsatisfied wife and the henpecked husband in the bud, and, as Terence Rattigan noted in *The Browning Version*, it is more often a theme for farce than for tragedy.

Jean, who had gone nearly bald during his three-year detention, between sobs of remorse and emotional strain, told the judge:

I was hungry and wanted to eat. But she felt romantic. She insisted. So, weakly, I gave in. Then each time I wanted to go and eat, she wanted me to embrace her. Finally I said I was leaving. She slapped my face and ran off. I chased her and grabbed her shoulder. It knocked her off balance.

David Rowan picks up the story Liger told in court:

She fell and her head hit the stone of the Temple of Love. When he found that, in trying to stop her screams, he had strangled her, he concealed the crime "to save my parents from shame."

Liger burst out, as though finally getting the truth off his chest, "It all happened because I became overwhelmed by my pent-up feelings against her. She wanted me to act like an animal instead of a well-brought-up young man. I wanted to show her I was not at her beck and call."

He told the judge that he had given up the idea of marrying Miss Richardson, because her physical demands on him had become intolerable. It would appear that he equated her strong sexual desire with depravity, for he told her that she "was not the type of woman" whom he wanted "as the mother of my children." This uttered, he dissolved in sobs once more and the court waited for him to regain his composure. "I was out of control," he said finally. "For six or seven months I had wanted to break with her. I had had enough. It had gone beyond the limit."

The judge commented that Liger had been brought up very strictly by his parents. (The cover-up of his crime was to spare his parents the disgrace that would follow his arrest. It would be interesting to know whether his parents even knew about his affair with the young Englishwoman. He seems to have been at pains to keep them apart.) The judge noted that the accused was "an atheist with existentialist tendencies," an interesting observation. Would the judgment have been different if he were a former altar boy and strict Cartesian? To be sure, he had rather rigid ideas about morality for a young man of his generation; and, he exhibited a surprising capacity for middle age in one so young. But in the early 1950s, existentialism went hand in hand with atheism: blame it on the war, on Sartre, or on Camus. It had become a second skin to undergraduates and young people in general. One wonders whether the judge had read Camus' *L'Etranger*, in which the existentialist protagonist finds himself entrapped in his own curious passivity.

The court also noted that Jackie Richardson, in spite of the reports of her friends as to her "sweet, timid and reserved" character—quite at odds with Liger's experience of her—had had a number of stormy affairs in Britain. The judge was reading from a Scotland Yard report, the source of this information, more in line with Jean Liger's experience of the young woman as tempestuous, argumentative and demanding. These affairs, the judge stated, often "ended with rows, screams, blows and scandal." The state prosecutor, M. Jean Reliquet, added that "at seventeen she was living with an American at Cambridge. For a while she frequented a house of ill-repute in the hope that she would find a husband there."

In the end, after all the extenuating circumstances, Maître Reliquet said the crime boiled down to this: "It was a sordid and cowardly crime." The accused, he maintained, had strangled the victim to get rid of the marriage problem which his lack of willpower prevented him from solving. Part of this problem was his parents, who either knew nothing of Jackie or hadn't approved of what they had seen. Jean Liger was stuck between two fires, like the protagonist in Theodore Dreiser's *An American Tragedy*: George Eastman had a factory-hand girlfriend pregnant and insisting that George do the right thing by her, while George had scored a social success with a young heiress. His attempt at editing the problem landed him in the electric chair.

In the French case discussed above, the defense pleaded that the tragedy of these two young people resulted from a crime of passion. While the cover-up was cowardly and criminal, the crime itself came about in a whirlwind of anger, frustration and suddenly released emotion. With Jean sexually exhausted and hungry as well, the poor girl had chosen a bad moment for a confrontation. Timing is everything in matters of the heart. It is also interesting to note in passing that the overnight stay in a Paris hotel might have been a rather silly attempt to establish an alibi. While the crime itself shows no sign of having been premeditated, the cover-up was *post*meditated with some care.

The jury agreed with the defense counsel. But, as David Rowan says, "This time there was no question of an outright acquittal. The judgement in the Chevallier case still crackled in the chambers of the courthouses across France. Liger was jailed for seven years. Compared with what he would probably have received in other countries, the sentence may seem mild. Yet, in view of the fact that France recognizes the *crime passionnel* and other countries do not, it was at least more in keeping with the circumstances."

Lorena Bobbitt

The sensational case of Lorena Bobbitt, who was charged with maliciously wounding her husband, John Wayne Bobbitt, has entered the folklore of American humor.[43] John Bobbitt did not die from his wound. This was never a capital charge, yet the case received extensive media coverage from June 1993 to early 1994. You may remember the sallies of wit and humor the attack on her husband's honorable member provoked. Here is one of the rhymes it inspired:

> John Bobbitt was never a loner.
> In fact, he was known as a roamer
> His wife seized his prize
> And cut it to size,
> Now John is his own organ donor.

The case of the severed penis and of its near-miraculous restoration is one of the lighter stories recounted here. True, there is no body. No fatality. No capital crime. The crime of grievous bodily harm, however, when almost any other part of the human body is involved, is serious enough by all accounts, but when the object of the assault turns out to be a penis, unaccountably, our modern patina of civilization cracks asunder and our medieval selves roll out, breaking up with idiotic grins and leers, and begins to cavort before us, drooling and behaving in a manner that is far removed from being politically correct.

His wife seized his prize
And cut it to size ...

Some time after he got off on a charge of marital rape, John Wayne Bobbitt, of Prince William, Virginia, on the night of 23 June 1993, attempted to have sex with his wife Lorena against her will: this was customary with him. He was drunk, or at least he had been indulging in a night of serious bar-hopping. He forced himself upon her, raped her in fact, and promptly fell asleep in the marriage bed when he had had his way with her. Bobbitt had several versions of this: that they had not had sex, that Lorena had initiated the sexual activity, and that he had fallen asleep during mutually agreed-upon sex. In her version, Lorena got out of bed afterwards to get a glass of water from the kitchen, spying the knife on the counter, had thought of all the abuse she had absorbed from her husband over the years, and returned to the bedroom with the weapon. She remembered, "I remember[ed] many things. I remember[ed] the first time he raped me. I remember[ed] the put-downs that he told me. ... I remember[ed] the first time he forced me to have anal sex, the bad things he said. I remember[ed] the abortion. I remember[ed] everything." Then she drew down the sheet and cut off his penis. Somehow, she left the house, got in the car and started to drive. She had no destination in mind. During the drive, she discovered that she was still holding John's bleeding member in her hand. She opened the car window and tossed it into a nearby field. Later, in fact soon afterwards, she informed the police where to find it before it suffered further mischief at the paws of stray pets. A team of surgeons, in an operation that took ten hours, reattached the penis where it belonged.

Of course, Lorena was charged with a class-three felony and faced, if convicted, a fine of up to one hundred thousand dollars and a mandatory prison term of from five to twenty years. The trial lasted nine days, during which the jury of seven women and five men listened to testimony with straight faces, then found the defendant not guilty by reason of temporary insanity. After an examination at a mental institution, where the psychiatrists found that Lorena posed no threat to herself or society in general, she was released to continue receiving outpatient therapy.

John Bobbitt attracted little attention when he was convicted of marital sexual assault. The press had other things on its mind. When it turned all of its attention on Lorena Bobbitt, it was not because she had fought back against the convention that a husband's needs are a wife's tribute to be paid wherever and whenever it pleases her lord. The fuss came about because in severing John's penis, she broke a strong cultural taboo. Had she stabbed him in the heart, the media would have shown interest, but it would have been nothing like the furor she unleashed when she took out her revenge against that part of the offending person that had offered the offense.

"The incident," writes Linda Pershing of the State University of New York at Albany,

> and subsequent media attention became the subject of intense national debate. It also sparked a flurry of jokes, limericks, urban legends, T-shirt slogans, and advertising gimmicks. Bobbitt-related discussions filtered into everyday conversations, office jokes, and electronic mail networks. Children circulated their own Bobbitt folklore. For months, nationally known stand-up comedians and television talk show hosts performed extensive repertoires of Bobbitt jokes, while members of the general public created new lyrics to popular melodies (e.g., "The Ballad of the Bobbitt Hillbillies" sung to the *Beverly Hillbillies* theme song).

Pershing goes on to say that jokes, parodies and slogans often articulate observations of contemporary life that the official culture is still gagging on. To sever a penis is comparable to Alexander the Great's cutting of the Gordian knot. It goes directly to the root of the problem. If man has dominated woman down through the centuries, seeing her as an adjunct to himself in all things, as history shows us he has, Lorena Bobbitt's action figuratively as well as literally cut through a lot of red tape in the history of sexual domination. The case also takes us closer to the root of the problem with the crime-of-passion defense: male control and jealousy. Part of mankind, the female half, may identify with Lorena Bobbitt to a degree. A case of *schadenfreude*, or taking pleasure in the misfortunes of others? Not quite: for women it is not so much malicious pleasure in the downfall of John Wayne Bobbitt as instinctive sympathy with Lorena's neat if bloody solution to all the problems a penis and its possessor can bring into one's life. The Gordian knot again.

At the same time, penises are intrinsically funny. Since they are external, they seem part of the general landscape, not simply the private business of its owner, or in this case, loser. Think of all the names there are for penises in the literature of the street. There must be hundreds. The clitoris and the vulva just aren't in the same league. Or perhaps we are caught in a stage of social evolution: *after* the emancipation of the penis, but *before* the revolution in public reference to female genitalia. I should also add that this society is obsessed with penises. It is not simply a case of Freudian penis envy. It goes further than that. In our society, *men* have penis envy: there is a lucrative market for the plastic surgeon in penises, their extensions, their size and durability. It would be interesting to know whether breast implants and other structural improvements to the female anatomy are in the same money bracket. *Viagra*, the drug that is used to battle impotence, is almost as funny as the penis itself. And, when we have tired of chortling about the member, either in repose or at attention, there is always the knife in the case. It has recently been announced that the knife Lorena used on her husband has been offered for sale by John Wayne Bobbitt. He is asking for *two million dollars*. (How it became *his* knife and not *hers*, I don't know.)

"[N]ot since Lizzie Borden have a woman and her cutlery received so much attention," said one commentator. This attention expressed itself in jokes and one-liners that convulsed America at the office and at the lunch counters as well as on late night television. There was one about Lorena being released on bail over Christmas after promising the judge that she would not hang any balls on the Christmas tree. People talked about cutlery manufacturers who had approached her for endorsements. On Hallowe'en 1993, adult women went from door to door wearing Lorena Bobbitt wigs and carrying long wooden knives. Outside the courthouse in Manassas, Virginia, vendors were selling buttons that read: Lorena Bobbitt for Surgeon General.

The neofeminist author Naomi Wolf says that the amputation of Bobbitt's member was "strictly primitive ... If she wanted to be safe [from John], she could have kneecapped him. The mutilation itself seems to be so clearly a sadistic act ... I have worked in battered women's shelters, and I applaud women who do what they have to do to escape their assailant. There are absolutely situations where a woman has to kill her partner to escape or save her children." She did not believe that such a situation existed on the night Lorena trimmed John's masculinity.

Other commentators have pointed out that while the *New Yorker* was printing cartoons about John Wayne Bobbitt and comedians were having a field day over this one severed and restored penis, thousands of women undergo genital mutilation every day without an editorial word being spoken against it. Still other writers have been speculating on whether this story was destined to have a happy ending. They point out that date rape victims have later re-dated their rapists. Cuckolded husbands have taken their errant spouses back again. There is no way to judge the human ability to deny, or to forgive and forget.

TEN

By Love Obsessed.
Hell Hath No Fury...

Pauline Dubuisson

Pauline Dubuisson, a medical student from Lille, in the north of France, was only twenty-six when she shot her lover, Félix Bailly, another student of the healing arts, in his Paris flat, because he was planning to marry another young woman.[44] After the shooting, she turned on the gas in an attempt to kill herself. This was in March 1951. The court condemned her to life at hard labor. This courtroom apparently hadn't heard about crimes of passion; they acted as though such a thing never existed, as though the *crime passionnel* only belonged in romantic magazines. Yet in spite of the cold reading French law gave her case, it was a classic, and deserves its place in this collection.

To be fair, Pauline's war record was not good; she had been the mistress of a German officer, fifty-five-year-old Colonel Von Domnick, director of the German hospital in Dunkirk, and had been treated as a collaborator at the war's end. Still a teenager, she had been paraded half-nude through the main streets of Dunkirk with other female collaborators, and had had her hair cut off in the main square. Male collaborators were often shot. To make matters worse for Pauline, she had had many lovers before Félix Bailly came along. Her promiscuity, noted first in Dunkirk, continued back at home in Lille, where she began the study of medicine. A report of her conduct at the university goes beyond her grades in histology and anatomy: "... she is well-balanced but haughty, provoking, and a flirt ..." Pauline later maintained that Félix was her true love, that the other men in her life meant nothing to her.

> I wanted to force myself to love other people, in order to persuade myself I was capable of having lasting sentiments for him.

She was imprudent enough to make a list of her lovers, noting the sexual preferences of each of them, along with notes from her spare-time study of the arts of lovemaking, researched in the excellent medical library available to her. When this list was placed in evidence at her trial, it had a damaging effect on her defense. One thinks of the use to which Edith Thompson's letters were put back in the 1920s.

Bailly had been serious about Pauline, without once in two years taking her home to meet his mother, but broke off all contact when he found out about his rivals for her time and attention. Plainly, he was tiring of the relationship, or perhaps he was not up to the gymnastics recommended in the *Kama Sutra*. He then transferred his medical studies to the Left Bank in Paris, where he became romantically involved with Monique Lombard, of whom his parents approved. Their engagement was announced. Meanwhile, Pauline made no attempt to see or have any contact with Félix.

But when she heard about Félix's engagement, she went to Paris, where according to her testimony, unsupported by other independent sources, they resumed their former relationship. That was in March 1951. It was on the tenth of that month that she bought a small .25 automatic pistol. On the mandatory police form, part of the normal procedure in buying firearms in France, she stated that she needed it because she often traveled alone late at night. Pauline left a note in her room, addressed to her landlady, saying that on 15 March she was off to Félix's flat to kill first him and then herself. The landlady read the note and quickly got in touch with both Félix and his parents. For the next couple of days, Félix either stayed away from the flat, or relied on student-friends to run interference for him.

On St. Patrick's Day, 17 March, he opened the door to admit another relay of guardians. Unfortunately for him, it was Pauline. When the expected guardians arrived—they had been delayed in a traffic jam—they found their friend dead on the floor with three bullets in him, and Pauline also on the floor with a gas-pipe in her mouth.

At her trial, Dubuisson held her head high, and moved with dignity and self-possession. She earned the nickname "the Mask of Pride." The jury heard about her wartime promiscuity and her existential list of lovers together with their erotic weaknesses, and was harsh in its judgment. Pauline had been accused not of simple murder, but of assassination, which involved premeditation; a guilty verdict usually brings the death penalty. One commentator, Jay Robert Nash, argues that if they had *really* got tough with her, she would have been condemned to death. The writer saw the case as a breakthrough: a crime of passion in spite of a proven promiscuous lifestyle. It was the lone woman on the jury that influenced the other members to reduce the charge to the less-calculated crime of murder without premeditation. In her own defense, Pauline told the court that Félix persuaded her to come back to his flat one day in early March:

> ... he kissed me, everything was as it used to be ... I felt I was coming out of a nightmare ... then in the morning, he threw me out ... life didn't mean anything any more to me ... it was at that moment I decided to kill us both ...

As Colin Wilson says in his study of the case:

> It is still uncertain whether Dubuisson was motivated by humiliation or jealousy, or even by a grinding and genuine regret for a lost passion.

Pauline was released from prison after serving six years, presumably after the circumstances of the case were looked into by a board of review, and killed herself four years later in 1963. Suicide seems to have been part of her coping mechanism: an earlier attempt to commit suicide had delayed the trial. She was only thirty-six.

In 1914, when Mme Henriette Caillaux, the new wife of the French finance minister, shot Gaston Calmette, the editor of *Le Figaro* for printing one of her husband's passionate prenuptial love letters to her on the front page of the famous newspaper, as soon as she had accomplished her deed, she surrendered the weapon to an office boy—warning him to be careful, there might be a bullet left—and informed reporters that she had her car waiting below to take her to police headquarters. When Ruth Ellis had stopped firing her revolver at the fallen form of David Blakely outside the Magdala pub, she told the first man to reach her, "Now call the police." Although the bath-tub murder of Jean-Paul Marat by Charlotte Corday was a crime of *political* passion, she too, having driven home the recently purchased blade in Marat's heart, calmly made only the most perfunctory attempt to avoid capture. There is in the classic crime of passion something approaching self-immolation.

Mary Eleanor Pearcey

There are cases where the eternal triangle gets bent out of shape. Take, for instance, the case of Mary Eleanor Pearcey,[45] whose passionate affair ended with the murder not only of her rival but of her rival's child into the bargain. Mary Eleanor is something of an exception in the annals of crime. Throat-cutting is a common means of suicide and is a preferred method of the sex-offender. Very few women, however, have cut the throats of their victims. It is rarely seen in domestic cases. But there are always exceptions, and Mary Eleanor Pearcey is one of these. The more one learns about her the more fascinating she becomes. For instance, although she came from the working class, she was highly literate. Either she, or someone near to her, saw that she learned to read and write. She read books and was familiar with popular authors. The notes in her handwriting that have been preserved show an aspiring ladylike hand.

Frank Hogg—yes, another Hogg!—was a laborer and sometime furniture mover who lived in Prince of Wales Road, Kentish Town, southeast of Hampstead Heath in London. He was a weak man, irresolute, but a decent bloke of reasonably temperate habits, who shared his earnings with his mother, his sister Clara, who lived with them, and his wife, Phoebe. Their household in 1890 was enlivened by the presence of their eighteen-month-old infant daughter, who was born six months after the banns were read for Phoebe and Frank. Outside this solid family circle and none too happy about it lived Mary Eleanor Pearcey, who had been Frank's mistress for several years, certainly before Phoebe entered the picture. Mary Eleanor had borrowed the name Pearcey from a former lover. Her real name was Wheeler. She believed that the sickly Phoebe had tricked Frank into marrying her; Frank, she thought, could be depended upon to do the decent thing, and Phoebe had taken advantage. Still, Mary Eleanor remained on friendly terms with the whole Hogg clan, and Frank in return paid regular visits to Mary's house in Priory Road. Since Mary was being maintained by a Mr. Crighton who lived at some distance in the suburbs, and used to visit Mary discreetly once a week, it was necessary for Mary and Frank to have a signal to show that the coast was clear. She left a lighted lamp in her bedroom window to show that the generous Mr. Crighton was not expected. This arrangement worked to the satisfaction of all knowing parties for some time.

Frank's wife was often not well and Mary Eleanor was seven years younger than Phoebe and by general agreement an attractive young woman of twenty-four. She was tall, sturdy and handsome: blue-eyed, with fine russet hair, worn long with a center parting. This went well with her pale skin. Her face had some of the English horsiness noted in many other English women including Virginia Woolf. She felt that Phoebe had outwitted her with her pregnancy ruse, and this left a smoldering resentment for Mary's frustrations to chew upon. She was more than half-mad with jealousy of her rival.

Although relations between Mary and Frank's family were strained by the unspoken fact of Frank's continued attachment to Mary

Eleanor, they tried to continue normal civilized contact. They visited back and forth from time to time. While telephones were still rare in London, the people of Kentish Town still kept in touch by sending notes in charge of small boys, who could be relied upon to guarantee delivery for a small coin. On 23 October 1890, Mary wrote a note to Phoebe:

> Dearest, come round this afternoon and bring our little darling. Don't fail.

Phoebe showed the note to her sister, but did not make the visit.

That same afternoon, Mary, waiting for her reluctant guest outside her front door, talked to her former lover Pearcey, who asked why she kept the blinds drawn. She explained that she was keeping the house dark because she was in mourning: her beloved brother had just died. Pearcey expressed his condolences and went off down the street. This was a curious and telling exchange; Mary's brother had not died. There was no reason for her to explain away the dark house in terms that would not stick, when there were other, less provably false ways to the same end. Another thing, if Mary was already planning to kill Phoebe, as her lame explanation of the darkened house suggests, then it is possible that her plot might already have included the little girl.

The next morning, Mary sent Phoebe another note. This time Phoebe, wheeling the child in a perambulator, did come to visit. It was nearly tea-time when neighbors heard noises coming from Mary Eleanor's house. They heard the sounds of breaking crockery and glass, and the wail of an unhappy baby. The upstairs lodger, returning home, had to squeeze by the perambulator left in the narrow hallway. Since the neighbors believed that Mr. Crighton was Mary's father and that her gentlemen callers were other relatives, they assumed that the noise was simply part of a family row, and dismissed it until the police came knocking on their doors.

Mary Eleanor had attacked Phoebe with all the mad fury of a Norman Bates. She cut the throat of her lover's wife, because she,

Mary, was jealous of the attentions Frank Hogg still lavished upon her. She then mutilated the corpse and loaded it into the perambulator on top of the Hogg's eighteen-month-old daughter, who had been sucking on a toffee, soon to be displayed, along with the perambulator, in Madame Tussaud's Chamber of Horrors. The infant was promptly smothered by her mother's dead weight.

Uncovering the murderer, after first one and then the other body was found, one in Hampstead, the other near Finchley, did not greatly tax the abilities of the Metropolitan Police. Mary was arrested and waiting for her trial less than twenty-four hours after the crime was committed.

She was tried at the Old Bailey before Mr. Justice Denham. Most of the evidence against her was circumstantial, and she stoutly maintained her innocence throughout. As one writer commented, "she never lost her nerve from first to last ..." In those days, of course, a defendant couldn't go into the box to testify on his or her own behalf. That law wasn't altered until 1898. It is interesting to imagine how Mary Eleanor Pearcey would have stood up to serious cross-examination.

The reaction of the press to Phoebe Hogg's brutal murder was more than a little tolerant of the termagant who had killed a mother and child. Their best shots were leveled at those who fought for a place in the courtroom and saw themselves as consumers of the whole story. The *News of the World* commented at

> the sympathetic interest taken by such a large number of the fair sex ... It is to be feared that many women, whose training and social surroundings should teach them better, regard such cases much in the same way as they would a sensational drama at the theatre ...

The trial was well covered you may be sure. And the papers, like the *Pall Mall Gazette*, saw fit to chastise the onlookers:

> no sense of decency restrained them; no amount of personal discomfort kept them outside the doors of the grim forum.

Wives came with their husbands, brothers brought the female members of their families, mothers sat side by side with their young daughters. Hour after hour did these ghoulish women, armed with opera glasses, sherry-flasks, and sandwich boxes, hang with eager curiosity upon every movement and look of their miserable sister, whose fate was so firmly fixed from the outset. To the end they stayed; for the solemn closing scene had special attractions for them. These women were not the wives and daughters of labourers and costermongers, but ladies of gentle birth and no inconsiderable position.

The *Evening News* was of the same opinion:

We would gladly publish the name of every woman who dis-graced her sex by rushing to that wretched sight as if it were the finest kind of raree-show.

Such comments are an interesting gloss to Phoebe Hogg's murder and that of her baby, and the plight of their killer, but quite apart from that, the papers give a fine demonstration of the social constriction within which Victorian women led their lives. A Lorena Bobbitt or two about 1890 might have brought a new perspective to the still largely unspoken debate about women's place. Mary Eleanor achieved one thing in her mad murderous tea party: she became the only mistress of a married man in all the history of English jurispru-dence to kill the legitimate wife. F. Tennyson Jesse, the novelist who made a novel of the story of Edith Thompson, her lover and their crime and punishment, was not a light-headed romantic when she wrote of Mary Eleanor:

She was the victim of the impulse of 'love,' as that term is used in the Police Court; but it would be more possible to sympa-thize with her had Frank Hogg been unique, instead of being one in a more or less paying crowd. Mrs. Pearcey lost her right to any claim on Frank Hogg when she accepted money from another man, and, consequently, lost even that dubious right to strike which some people maintain 'love' bestows.

Waiting for the hangman, Mary tried in vain to get some word or token from her lover, but Hogg refused to visit her. The day before her execution, two days before Christmas in 1890, she wrote to her solicitor saying that she still loved Hogg, but, she added bitterly, "He might have made death easier for me." She told one of the wardresses just before her execution: "The sentence is just, but the evidence was false." Whether this was meant as a criticism of the zeal of the Metropolitan Police or of the Crown's case against her is not known. Nor, under the circumstances, did she have time to elaborate her statement. During her last days, she asked her lawyer to place the following cryptic message in a Madrid newspaper:

M. E. C. P. Last wish of M. E. W. Have not betrayed.

On her way to the scaffold, looking "pinched and wan," she told the wardresses, "You've no need to assist me. I can walk by myself." When they replied that they would accompany her, she said, "Oh well, if you don't mind going with me, I'm pleased." She "submitted quietly" to Mr. Berry's straps and walked with apparent calmness to the drop. "A man who kills his wife's lover," writes Patrick Wilson in *Murderess*,

receives a certain public sympathy, but this is not extended to the woman who kills her lover's wife, and the cruelty of the murders caused Mary to be branded as a monster, yet her letters show a sensitivity and capacity for self-expression which is difficult to accord with the image of a brutal murderess hacking off the head of another woman with a carving knife.

To give some indication of the intensity of Mary Eleanor's love for Frank Hogg, not to justify the violence of her crime, but to glimpse the monomaniacal world of the love-obsessed, let me quote from two of her letters. The first was written before Hogg's marriage to Phoebe:

> Do not think of going away, for my heart will break if you do. Don't go, dear. I won't ask too much, only to see you for five minutes when you can get away, but if you go quite away, how do you think I can live?

The following letter was written after Hogg married Phoebe:

> You ask me if I was cross with you for coming only such a little while. If you knew how lonely I am you wouldn't ask. I would be more than happy if I could see you for the same time each day, dear. You know I have a lot of time to spare and I cannot help thinking. I think and think until I get so dizzy that I don't know what to do with myself. If it wasn't for our love, dear, I don't know what I should really do, and I am always afraid you will take that away, and then I should quite give up in despair, for that is the only thing I care for on earth. I cannot live without it now. I have no right to it, but you gave it to me, and I can't give it up.

Mary Eleanor Pearcey committed one of the most vicious murders in the annals of crime, yet her plea to her lover cannot help but gain some sympathy for the creature who was driven to this act, not for gain, not for power, not to secure the victim's silence, but for the love of a man. While there were many lies told to the police and many more told in court, as there are in most cases, there is a human dimension in Mary Pearcey's letters that has the ability to move, to touch the nub of the human condition. How much more direct and honest are her words, than those of French satirical novelist Paul Bourget:

> When you want to break with a woman … simply take the train without making a long song and dance [*sans tambour ni*

trompette] and allow twenty-four hours for her to get over wanting to shoot you. During these forty-eight hours [*sic*] she shrieks, she storms, she buys laudanum, she poisons herself, she makes a mess of it. As in all things, she doubles the dose, but when you return, you have been replaced.

A politically incorrect male perspective, although written well before the invention of the concept or the phrase. Still, there exists a tension between the cynical views of Bourget and the unbridled passion of someone like Mary Eleanor Pearcey. If the name Paul Bourget sounded familiar, you saw it earlier in these pages: it was he who kept Henriette Caillaux waiting so long for her victim in the offices of *Le Figaro*. I wonder whether that experience burned away any of his cynicism?

Crimes of passion are crimes with a human perspective. We try to understand the crimes by trying to glimpse the passion that brought them about.

ELEVEN

Families,
I Hate You!

History and romance are full of crimes of passion: crimes that are born of passion. Earlier, in the introduction, I referred to Helen of Troy, her warrior husband Menelaus, and the lengths he went to to bring her home to Sparta again. His brother, Agamemnon, wasn't so lucky. The story of Agamemnon's murder by his wife, Clytemnestra, and her lover has filled the theaters of the world for two dozen centuries. That such stories as the tragedies of Pyramus and Thisbe and Romeo and Juliet have lasted down the centuries— Pyramus was a Babylonian; the lovers planned to meet at the tomb of the founder of *Nineva!*—stems from the pity the stories awake in the hearts of new readers. Had it not been for their insensitive relations, all would have been perfect. They came *so* close to the happiness they were seeking. In both cases their hopes were scuttled by their families. Pyramus and Thisbe[46] were neighbors who fell in love, but their families stood in the way of their union. So they ran away, only to meet with bad luck that turned to tragedy because of the depth of their love for one another. Shakespeare has great fun with this old story in his *Midsummer Night's Dream*, where the tradesmen of Athens try to get the story up as a play. In another of his plays, the love that Romeo bears for Juliet is frustrated by their feuding families and everything, as in the former case, comes to grief. The families form the third side of the romantic triangle as effectively as a rival lover. As a result of the obstacles their families set in the path of the lovers, they hit upon stratagems that promise to see them safe and happy beyond the smothering reach of disapproving family connections. But in both cases their plans go awry, and they kill themselves believing their sweethearts are already dead.

Families create problems for lovers. Had Madeleine Smith not been so terrified of her father, she would not have poisoned her lover; but he had threatened to confront the girl's forbidding Victorian *paterfamilias* and tell him about Madeleine's secret life. Had Héloïse's wicked uncle, Canon Fulbert of Notre Dame in Paris, not hired a gang of thugs to break into the scholar Peter Abelard's house and castrate him— a serious criminal act even in the eleventh century—Hèloïse and her philosophical husband might well have lived happily ever after. The play *Hamlet* records the fall of a dynasty. Rival brothers love the same woman and one must die. To protect his guilty secret, the murderer arranges the murder of his stepson, who knows or suspects too much, losing in the bloody dénouement of the story both the woman who inspired both deeds, and his own life.

The title of this chapter (a quotation from André Gide) indicates that the stories told here are family stories, but not in the sense that Proust's great novel is a family story, or that Jane Austen's are. In these cases the families have created a palpable claustrophobia so confining that the affected family members are driven to desperate acts to break away. Robert Browning and Elizabeth Barrett, frustrated by the obstacle of another Victorian monster, Elizabeth's father, simply eloped. A lingering Camberwell sense of propriety in Robert brought them to the altar as quickly as possible. For others, it wasn't that easy.

Alpna Patel

After several days of deliberation in the trial of a twenty-seven-year-old Canadian woman of Indian origin, Alpna Patel,[47] who was accused of stabbing her husband, Viresh, to death, an American jury in Baltimore was unable to agree on whether the accused dentist was guilty or not. It was a hung jury. They were able to agree on some things: they acquitted Alpna of first-degree murder, and also on a related weapons charge. But they couldn't decide whether Dr. Alpna Patel, of Saskatoon, Saskatchewan, was guilty of second-degree murder or voluntary manslaughter. The sole male juror caused a sensation in court when he changed his vote as the jury was being polled by the judge. It left the young defendant *half* cleared of the charges that had been brought against her after the killing in March 1999 of her husband, but not free from the possibility of another trial. While the relations of the couple refused to comment to the press, the accused told the jury that the ten-month marriage had been an arranged one, cobbled together in the traditional way, with the couple's consent, by the two families. The families had used the Internet to locate one another, introducing a modern twist to an ancient practice. Another modern aspect to this traditional union was the fact that the young couple had been turned into minor media stars through their appearance in a documentary film made of the whole process of arranged marriages by the Canadian Broadcasting Corporation. Alpna moved in with her in-laws in Buffalo, New York, while Viresh continued his medical residency in Baltimore, where he was a resident in orthopedic surgery. Alpna did not take to this arrangement. She had lost her family in exchange for an absent husband and a new family, one that hewed closer to the traditions of Hinduism than her own had. She found her husband's family conservative and controlling. In fact, having grown up with the customary freedom of movement enjoyed by most Canadian girls, even those from tradition-conscious families, she was disappointed that the marriage was not turning out to be the blissful arrangement promised by the Internet. Or indeed, as pictured for all to see in the CBC television documentary, she found her new family repressive and unheeding, especially her father-in-law, Nandlal Patel, whose mind, when made up, could not be changed by reason, logic or arguments. He refused to let the newlyweds sleep together until they had returned to Buffalo. He insisted that Alpna live and work in Buffalo, not with her new husband in Baltimore. While her husband's mother got to visit Viresh for weeks at a time, doing the housewifely chores of cooking and cleaning, Alpna rarely was allowed a weekend visit. Alpna also resented the fact that Viresh had not put up more of a fight or insisted on seeing his wife more often. It was as though his father was keeping Viresh's concentration on his medical studies unadulterated by marital interference. Did Nandlal believe that Alpna's presence would compromise his son's progress?

In our culture, where the traditions of romantic love are strong, it is difficult to understand the ramifications of an arranged marriage. Some of these ramifications seem to have also escaped Alpna Patel, whose girlhood dream was to have such a traditional Hindu marriage. Alpna did not date Canadian boys; she was saving herself for the right boy and the right circumstances. "You find the right person, hopefully," she said in an interview about her marriage, "and you make it work." Where does passion fit into such an arrangement? Presumably it must, for passion is a part of human nature, which no tradition can suppress completely. I think we may assume that at the time of Viresh's death, Alpna cared deeply for her husband, though her desire to see him regularly in a normal manner was frustrated by his family. She thought that Viresh's dictatorial father was putting the marriage at risk. He was also stunting Viresh's growth as both a man and a husband. There was an intense pressure of anger and frustration building up in Alpna Patel's tiny frame.

On or about 23 March, Alpna skipped work at her Buffalo hospital clinic, traveled to Baltimore, booked into a hotel, then went to see her husband after she was sure that he had returned from work. She found her mother-in-law on the couch and Viresh in bed, exhausted after a long shift at the hospital. He had to report back in a few short hours. They discussed their dissolving marriage briefly, then fell asleep. In the early hours of 24 March, Alpna claims that she awakened to discover Viresh leaning over her, holding a black-handled steak knife to her throat. She says that the fatal stab wound to his neck occurred during the struggle which followed. The prosecution contended that she had expressly gone to her husband's apartment in the middle of the night to kill him as he lay asleep in bed. William D. McCollum, the prosecutor, contended that Alpna was a "poor little rich girl," upset that she was not getting her own way in the marriage. He also questioned her being able to subdue her nearly six-foot husband during a prolonged struggle. Alpna is barely five feet tall. He went on to dispute her claim that Viresh was able to lunge at her with the knife in his hands after having sustained fatal wounds in his neck. "It couldn't have happened the way she said," he maintained.

Although the accused stated that there was a violent struggle for the knife, the jury had to remember that Viresh Patel bore *all* of the injuries, both the mortal wounds to the carotid artery and the jugular vein and the relatively minor cuts or slashes about the clavicle and forehead. The police evidence did not support the notion of a struggle.

When the accused was allowed to leave the courtroom, at the end of the mistrial, she returned to Saskatoon. When she failed to appear for the subsequent hearing (on the advice of counsel, she said) she was declared a fugitive from American justice and the district attorney's office was given a lesson in across-the-border politics. The prosecutors were frustrated that Alpna couldn't be arrested and delivered to Baltimore. The idea that an international border existed gradually penetrated and calm was allowed to return. After a few days, Dr. Patel surrendered herself and explained to the court why she had not immediately responded to the summons. The judge seemed to be happy with her explanation. There seemed to be a lot of fussing and fuming arising from the discovery that American law did not automatically extend across the 49th parallel into Canada.

When the three-day trial to determine the outstanding point left undecided by the earlier hearing ended, Alpna was convicted of fatally stabbing her husband. The jury called it "voluntary manslaughter." They believed that she killed Viresh Patel in an emotional rage, possibly because he fell asleep as she was reading aloud a long catalogue of grievances she had with the current arrangements. Patel had returned around midnight to his apartment after a long and exhausting shift at the hospital. Her barrage of thirty-three points, recited in her flat, monotonous voice, may have lulled him into insensibility. Life has many painful reminders of the danger of dozing off. To make matters worse, Viresh's mother had telephoned Buffalo, and the young man's father, the author of their troubles, told his son to go to sleep.

Alpna's defense counsel harped away on the necessity of having a reasonable doubt. If such a doubt existed in the jury's mind, they must acquit. When Alpna came to the stand, she told a story that was consistent with what she had told the investigating officers at the scene of the crime. However, she described her attempts to help her dying husband in a way that contradicted her flat, unemotional reaction on the fatal night. The jury did not miss this change in her story. It showed that the accused could lie when pressed.

The chief prosecutor, William McCollum, had some interesting things to say about premeditation in his address to the jury. "There is no magical moment in life when premeditation occurs," he said. "We will never be able to pinpoint when she decided to stab her husband. I will never be able to say to you that she is the Charlie Manson of married couples. All I will be able to say to you is that she decided to kill her husband when he was asleep." Perhaps that might have been a fleeting thought, but hardly a rational one. They were not alone in the apartment: Viresh Patel's mother was sleeping on the sofa in the living room. Could there be a worse place to plan and carry out the murder of her husband? What could she know about what her mother-in-law would say about the conduct of her son's slayer?

On 24 October 2000, on what would have been Viresh Patel's twenty-eighth birthday, Dr. Alpna Patel was sentenced by Judge John Privas to three years in prison. The judge, who admired Alpna's intelligence, said she was a "very civilized woman" who "just snapped." He had taken a month to decide upon the sentence. He justified the three-year term as a general deterrent. Maybe "her suffering will be worth the effort if it stops ... one wife from stabbing her husband," he said. Dr. Patel intends to appeal. She says that she is "remorseful" but insists that she is innocent of any intent to kill her husband. She claims, and has claimed since the fatal night, that she acted in self-defense and that Viresh had attacked her.

Compare this sentence of three years for manslaughter with the "not guilty" sentence rendered in the Lorena Bobbitt case. Bobbitt didn't lose his life or his penis permanently; there was no way to undo the harm done to Viresh Patel.

In the discussion so far, all the accounts have concentrated on Alpna Patel's sudden change of situation: her customary freedom was crushed, her happiness was in the hands of an unreasonable dictator. If actions may be used to explain intent, Alpna's purchase of two airline tickets, one to Buffalo and another to Saskatoon, suggests that she was prepared to be reasonable, but if that was not enough she planned to return to her own family in Canada for a cooling-off period until Viresh was able to choose between his wife and his family. It has hardly been said at all that the unfortunate Viresh was subject to similar atavistic pressures. His father was leaning on him as hard as he was on his daughter-in-law. He was in a cleft stick, between a rock and a hard place. If Alpna has been described as a bomb about to explode; so was Viresh, her husband. His manhood was in the hazard.

Pauline Parker and Juliet Hulme (Anne Perry)

Another case where family opposition to young love led to a tragic debacle was one involving two young girls and the mother of one of them in Canterbury, New Zealand, in 1954. Pauline Parker was sixteen and her friend, Juliet Hulme, fifteen.[48] They had been engaged in a passionate and imaginative friendship with lesbian overtones not terribly far removed from ordinary experimental teenage activity, except for its intensity. Pauline was the daughter of a common-law couple who had been together for twenty-five years. Her mother, Honoria Mary, also known as Mrs. Rieper, was the most anxious of all the parents to break up the relationship. Pauline was a bright, rather bullying girl, who had rather fixed ideas on most subjects. Juliet was her opposite. The daughter of an ex-rector of Canterbury University College in New Zealand, she was polite, meek and quiet where her friend was boisterous and headstrong. The girls first met in 1953 and became fast and exclusive friends. The situation became lethal when the parents of the girls decided to put an end to what they saw as an unhealthy relationship. Honoria, Pauline's mother, took aggressive steps to see that they saw less of one another. Juliet's father announced plans to take his daughter to South Africa.

Such was the emotional and imaginative bond between these two young people that they decided to do whatever they could in order to be allowed to stay together. Their time together was spent in intense creative activity. Like the Brontë sisters in Yorkshire, they wrote novels together, assuming the identities of their imagined characters. Pauline became Lancelot Trelawney, a soldier of fortune; Juliet saw herself as "Deborah, mistress of Emperor Charles II of Borovnia." Lancelot wooed the empress and succeeded her protector to the throne after an exciting struggle. Their fantasies became wilder and wilder, involving real as well as imagined sex. When they slept together, they tried to imagine "how the saints made love." In order to discover how normal heterosexual love worked, Pauline experimented with a boy she knew in order to report her findings to Juliet. They engaged in shoplifting adventures together. They were like Cocteau's *Les Enfants Terribles*, developing and testing their illicit skills and daring one another to take greater and greater risks, taking advantage of the protection their middle-class appearance gave them. They discussed the possibility of supporting themselves on the avails of prostitution, wondering whether blackmail might not be a better money-maker. The girls kept journals. Perhaps they wanted to become well-known writers like Katherine Mansfield, another New Zealander. In hers, Pauline wrote:

February 13th. Why could not mother die? Dozens of people, thousands of people, are dying every day. So why not mother, and father too?

June 20th. We discussed our plans for moidering mother and made them a little clearer. I want it to appear either a natural or an accidental death.

Again later:

> ... We decided to use a brick in a stocking rather than a sand-bag.

On the morning of the crime, she wrote:

> ... I felt so very excited and the night before Christmassy last night. I did not have pleasant dreams, though.

What of Juliet at this time? She too was committed to staying together, and tried to talk her parents into letting her friend come to South Africa with them if they were still set on going. What she thought of the plot to "moider" Pauline's Mom, is harder to assess. The choice of that funny word partly shielded her from the reality. Perhaps she thought that this was more elaborate literary play. Did she think about what all this was coming to?

On the afternoon of 23 June 1954, Pauline and Juliet took Mrs. Parker walking in a Christchurch park. It was a rustic place on several levels with stone steps meandering between them, leading to pools and hidden rockeries. Later in the afternoon, two girls came running into a teashop in the park. They were distraught, apparently, excited, and told a story of how the mother of one of them had suffered a bad fall on the stone steps. She had been seriously hurt, they said. In fact, she was dead. The girls were hysterical, describing the fall first to those who came to help and then to the police, who had been summoned. The body of Mrs. Parker was found stretched out across a path. Her head had suffered recent and severe wounding. "It kept bumping and banging," one of the girls explained. Near the body lay a piece of a brick, wrapped in a bloodstained stocking.

Even before the forensic pathologist's report was put on the desk of Detective Brown, he was highly suspicious of the story the girls had told. He told Pauline that she was under suspicion. Then he demanded:

"Who assaulted your mother?"

"I did," said the girl.

"Why?"

"… I won't answer that question."

"When did you make up your mind to kill your mother?"

"A few days ago."

The two were quickly tried. The defense claimed that paranoia had figured largely in this *folie à deux*, "a paranoia of an exalted type." That they were certifiably insane was the position of the defense lawyers. The prosecution maintained that the crime had been shrewdly plotted and committed in cold blood. The lawyer went on: "This was a callously planned and premeditated murder, committed by two highly intelligent and perfectly sane but precocious and dirty-minded girls." The jury agreed with the prosecution, and they were both found guilty of Honoria Parker's murder. But because of their ages, instead of being sentenced to death or to long prison terms, they were sentenced to be detained "until Her Majesty's Pleasure be made known." Since their release in 1958, one of the girls, Juliet, has become a best-selling novelist under the name Anne Perry. She claims that a rebirth of religious belief is responsible for her rehabilitation. She refuses to speak about the past. It was only shortly before he died that Juliet (Anne Perry) came to terms with her famous—in atomic physics circles—father, who had omitted her existence in his *Who's Who* biographies down the years.

Nor will her one-time partner in crime speak willingly about the past. She has also been touched by renewed religious feeling and taken a new name, Hilary Nathan. She lives quietly and alone, running a riding school near Rochester in Kent. Neither has married. Although they are both living in Britain, they have not met since the trial in Christchurch, New Zealand. The story of these two passionate teenagers was the subject of an award-winning film several years ago, by the New Zealand director Peter Jackson. The film was *Heavenly Creatures* and starred Kate Winslet as Hulme.

Nathan Leopold and Richard Loeb

In many ways, the Parker–Hulme case bears a striking resemblance to the Leopold–Loeb case, which was heard in Chicago in 1924. Here two young men, highly intelligent Nathan F. Leopold and Richard A. Loeb, nineteen and eighteen years old respectively, both college students, both scions of wealthy families, kidnapped and killed a younger acquaintance, fourteen-year-old Bobby Franks.[49] Franks meant nothing to either of them. Unlike the New Zealand girls, Bobby was simply an object; he wasn't an obstruction or an obsession. They were attempting to commit "the perfect crime" to prove their "superiority." Since it was motiveless, they were sure they wouldn't be caught. Loeb stayed close to the police investigation and pointed out "clues" to the investigators. There was no reason for the murder; it was a demonstration of how very much smarter than everyone the two gay killers were. They didn't *care* that it was Bobby Franks that they killed; they selected him only when their first choice, Billy Shawn, didn't appear. Spared an early death, William Shawn grew up to become the legendary editor of the *New Yorker* magazine.

Since there was no real motive for the killing, other than to prove the superiority of Nathan and Dick, there might be a tendency to say they did it on an *uncontrollable impulse*. In the Otto Preminger film, *Anatomy of a Murder*, the lawyer played by James Stewart tries to explain why the accused man delayed in taking revenge upon a bartender who may have tried to rape his wife. Stewart hit upon the idea of an *uncontrollable impulse*, and used it to get the murderer off. There was a precedent for the defense going back to the 1880s. The acquitted killer then ran away without paying for his lawyer, saying that he was doing so on another *uncontrollable impulse*.

There are differences in Leopold and Loeb as well as similarities with the New Zealand girls. The parents of the Americans had not thwarted them in any way; they were not facing a separation, as Hulme and Parker were. But Parker and Hulme do not appear to have received a sexual jolt from their murder, while Leopold and Loeb did.

The trial took place in Chicago before a judge without a jury.

Dr H. H. Crippin in handcuffs is escorted down the gangplank after his arrest on shipboard by **Chief Inspector Walter Dew** of Scotland Yard. Upon being alerted by the captain of the S.S. *Montrose* of his suspicions, Dew set out on a faster ship and intercepted the fleeing couple, **Ethel Le Nave** and Crippen, in Quebec City. Here Le Nave—now in feminine attire—can be seen following Crippen to dry land.

Cora Crippen, who called herself Belle Elmore and whose original name was Kunegonde Mackamotzki, was a very minor music hall entertainer. She was well-liked by more talented theatrical friends, who remembered how she used to belittle her milquetoast husband in public. Belle was identified by scar tissue on a piece of skin buried in the Crippen cellar. Most of the body was never recovered.

We never found out exactly what part **Ethel Le Nave** played in Crippen's crime. She certainly inspired it, but whether her complicity ended there, we can only guess. We know that she wore jewelry belonging to Cora Crippen, but whether she knew why it was now hers, is more than we know. She agreed to flee England disguised as a boy. Was she more credulous than most, or was she fully aware of what the good doctor was up to?

In 1979, anthropology professor **Cyril Belshaw** of the University of British Columbia refused to return voluntarily to Switzerland to face charges stemming from the discovery of his wife's nude and decomposed body near where they had been staying in an Alpine ski resort. He was arrested some time after that, when he travelled to Paris for a conference. The trial, which followed his extradition, was a cliffhanger to the very end.

Betty Joy Belshaw was working on a biography of the writer Katherine Mansfield, a fellow New Zealander, in Montana-Vermala, Switzerland, where she had been staying with her husband during their sabbatical year away from Canada. Mrs. Belshaw's body was discovered stripped of all clothing and rings. She was identified by her dental records, which Belshaw, for reasons never satisfactorily explained, falsified.

Lorena Bobbitt takes the witness stand at her trial for cutting off her husband's penis in 1993. The case caused a great sensation in the media and was the source of much ribald humor at the expense of John Wayne Bobbitt, the unfortunate organ donor.

Looking rather pleased with himself, after getting himself back together again, **John Wayne Bobbitt** found the court sympathetic to his wife's claim of provocation.

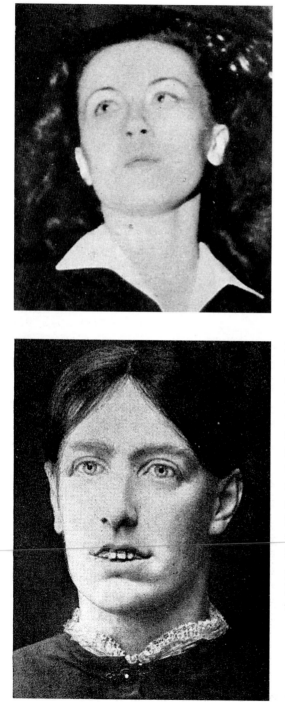

Pauline Dubuisson discovered that not all law courts in France have a sympathetic understanding of crimes of passion. She was a twenty-six-year-old medical student from Lille when she shot her former-lover Félix Bailly when he tried to end their affair.

Mary Eleanor Pearcey was the forty-ninth woman to be executed in Britain after 1843. (There were sixty-eight altogether.) Her passionate affair ended with the murder not only of her rival but of her rival's child. Yet, before that fatal event and afterwards, she appeared to be a literate and civilized young woman, as her letters to her lover reveal.

The Illustrated Police News, Law Courts and Weekly Record was famous for its fanciful illustrations of murder and expiation. Here, from a paper that appeared eleven days after her execution, we see all the steps that led **Mary Eleanor Pearcey** to the gallows. One might wonder at the wisdom of executing people so close to Christmas; there is nothing at all sentimental about the British Home Office.

Alpna Patel, right, the Canadian woman accused of killing her husband of less than a year, walks into the courthouse with her attorney, **Edward Smith Jr**, on August 31, 2000 in Baltimore. Her husband's father imposed conditions on the young couple that finally drove the young wife to drastic measures.

Pictured together in custody, **Juliet Hulme** and **Pauline Parker** admitted killing Parker's mother with a brick wrapped in a stocking because she threatened to separate these passionate teenagers. Freed after serving a term "until Her Majesty's pleasure be known," Juliet turned to writing, where she became famous under her adoped name, Anne Perry. Both now live in England, where Pauline runs a riding academy. They have not seen one another since coming out of prison in New Zealand.

The Day of the Happy Event.

JUNE 1954

22 TUESDAY

I am writing a little of this 173—192 up on the morning before the death. I felt very excited and 'the night before Christmas ish' last night. I did not have pleasant dreams though. I am about to rise.

"*The Day of the Happy Event*" was the day Juliet Hulme and Pauline Parker killed Pauline's mother, Honoria, in a Canterbury park. "I felt very excited and 'the night before Christmas-ish,'" wrote Pauline on the morning of the murder.

In handcuffs, **Susan Smith** leaves the County Courthouse in Union, South Carolina in July 1995. At the end of her tether, and in a desperate bid to win back the affection of her employer-lover who did not want to add Susan's two young boys to his family, Susan allowed her car, with the boys inside, to roll into a lake where the boys were drowned.

Because of their privileged, pampered lives, the two youths were very unpopular with the press. Their clowning during the trial made matters worse for their defense counsel, Clarence Darrow, the esteemed Chicago advocate and humanitarian. "The egg-head killers" barely escaped the death penalty, being given life sentences plus ninety-nine years each for kidnapping. Darrow, after constantly dunning the two families, only received about forty percent of the agreed fee for saving their sons from the gallows.

Loeb, who became an aggressive homosexual in prison, was killed in a prison brawl in 1936, which began when he accosted a fellow inmate in a shower at Stateville Prison. When the tabloids got this news, they printed something like the following:

EGG-HEAD KILLER ENDS SENTENCE WITH PROPOSITION.

Nathan Leopold was released on parole, his fourth try, after serving thirty-four years. His release came in 1958, the same year that Pauline Parker and Juliet Hulme were freed in faraway New Zealand. The American poet Carl Sandburg, speaking in front of the whole parole board, offered to give a home to Leopold if he was released. Leopold married in 1961 and died in Puerto Rico in 1971, where he had been working as a hospital technician.

Lizzie Borden

Another American case, a classic unsolved mystery, which I do not think conforms to the "crime of passion" theme we have been exploring, has one contribution to the notion of family pressure. Lizzie Borden was found not guilty of murdering her father and stepmother in 1892.[50] But *someone* took an axe and beat the heads of Andrew and Abby Borden beyond recognition.

Lizzie was never exposed to romantic passion as far as we know. She was a thirty-two-year-old spinster, whose biological clock was winding down. She had been raised in a household so miserly that its meanness is almost impossible to comprehend. Lizzie was her real name, it wasn't short for Elizabeth or any other given name. The

Bordens appear to have been practical people, not given to waste or frivolities: "If you intend to call the girl 'Lizzie,' why christen her 'Elizabeth'? It smacks of excess and indulgence," Andrew Jackson Borden might have said. She was not an unattractive woman, but instead of beaux calling upon her, she occupied her time and sublimated her sex drive with visits to the Corcoran Art Gallery in Washington and secretarial duties at the Christian Endeavor Society. She might have seen her father and stepmother as standing in her way. Beyond the family, outside the clutch of Andrew and Abby Borden's confining and miserly ways, lay the unknown joys of freedom. Perhaps she thought that with her family out of the way there might be gentlemen callers. It would have taken a stout-hearted suitor indeed to knock on the front door at 92 Second Street in Fall River, Massachusetts, with Andrew and Abby on the other side of it. When parents become the lightning rod for everything that is going wrong with your life, hatred can develop. Lizzie never did approve of Abby, her father's second wife, and *she* believed that the cult Lizzie made of her dead mother was hard-shelled self-indulgence. Andrew Borden, one of the richest men in Fall River, lived on cold mutton and kept a puritanical hold on everything under his roof. The house on Second Street had been heating up with hate for years. Beyond, lay freedom; not just trips, but a chance to breathe freely whenever she chose. I think that Lizzie, a sort of female J. Alfred Prufrock, at the breaking point, on the edge of madness, seized her chance to escape.

Susan Smith

Susan Vaughan Smith of Union, South Carolina, certainly grabbed *her* chance. In the autumn of 1994 Smith was twenty-three, the mother of three-year-old Michael and fourteen-month-old Alex.[51] She allowed her car to roll down a boat ramp into the deep water of John D. Long Lake in order to drown her children, who were strapped into their car seats.

One of the strongest forces in the world is the power of a mother's love for her young children. One wants to know at once: "What force could be stronger than that?" For in Susan Smith's case a stronger power did drive a mother to harm her innocent children.

Smith didn't lose her grip all at once; she was trained for it from an early age. Her father, Harry Vaughan, who had worked as a mill hand in one of the nearby textile mills, committed suicide by shooting himself in the chest with a shotgun when Susan was six, young enough to be deeply hurt by the suddenness and irrevocability of that family-wrenching event. When her mother, Linda Vaughan, married businessman Beverly C. Russell Jr. it made matters worse. Beverly Russell was a molester and an abuser, who bothered Susan regularly when she was fifteen, forcing her to have sex with him regularly until she was eighteen. At that time she confessed "our little secret" to a high school guidance counselor, and her mother, who got her husband, Bev, to confirm the truth of the allegation. When the police were brought in, the principals declined to take matters further. Bev Russell was a member of the state Republican Party executive committee and prominent in the Christian Coalition in Union County.

Susan's family, like many of the families in the area, came from strong Christian roots. This tradition, in the light of her father's suicide, offered her the hope that life after death was within the grasp of the godly, that death was a temporary separation of loved ones. Dying was going to a better place. In heaven, she would be reunited with her dead father. This was a strong element in her faith. She also adhered to the strong moral standards of her church, especially its tenets regarding sexual activity in adults. When she broke the seventh commandment (Exodus 20:14), Susan worried about it. Her marriage to David Smith seemed to steady her for several years. But both of the partners to this marriage eventually sought and found sexual satisfaction outside as well as within the marriage. They had the two children and appeared to take loving care of them as Michael and Alex grew older and looked to them both for love, protection and support. At no time during the investigation preceding Susan's arrest or the trial itself did anyone say or hint that Susan was an unfit mother of her boys. There was never any suggestion in the community of Union, S.C., that she was other than a good, caring parent who doted on her children.

From the age of six, according her old English teacher and a family friend, Susan was given to severe depressions. She thought obsessively about suicide. Dr. Seymour Halleck, professor of psychiatry and law at the University of North Carolina, who spent many hours talking to Susan, testified that he believed that her strong desire to kill herself and her children was overcome by her survival instinct. "I feel that had she been treated with Prozac in the preceding weeks and months, the deaths of her children would never have happened."

When the marriage got in trouble, the Smiths separated, perhaps hoping that a cooling-off period would improve matters. In the summer of 1994 they agreed to divorce. Having witnessed other broken families and read about the unhappy complications that come from contested divorces, they decided to seek an amicable divorce, with neither party being at fault. In August 1994, an attempted reconciliation failed. According to Arlene Andrews, a social worker and a witness at Susan's trial, the failure of this last-ditch attempt to patch the cracks in the marriage began a deterioration in Susan's mental condition. It threw her into a tailspin spiraling down into depression and uncertainty. Out of that came Susan's refusal to go through with the "no fault" deal that had been agreed upon. Now, she was charging David with adultery. Not one to sit passively and let things happen to him without taking action, David, when the opportunity appeared, searched his wife's purse and found a letter from a family friend, Tom Findlay. It was a form of "Dear John" letter, laser-printed like a well-turned-out business letter. It said, in part:

> You will, without a doubt, make some lucky man a great wife. But unfortunately, it won't be me ... Susan, I could really fall for you. You have some endearing qualities about you, and I think that you are a terrific person. But like I have told you before, There are some things about you that aren't suited for me, and yes, I am speaking about your children ... If you want to catch a nice guy like me one day, you have to act like a nice girl ... And you know, nice girls don't sleep with married men ...

The letter, which was dated 17 October 1994, eight days before the murder of the children, also praised Susan for her attempts at improving herself, but suggested that their social worlds were too far apart to make a permanent connection work. Tom, after all was the son and heir of the biggest employer in town and she was the daughter of a former mill worker and suicide. It was a situation right out of Olive Higgins Prouty's *Stella Dallas*. Tom Findlay was Susan's boss. He explained that he was not "Mr. Right" for Susan, because he didn't want to rear another man's children. He also sounded as though he was still angry and embarrassed by Susan's recent behavior at a hot tub party he had thrown. The revelers in the hot tub were naked, but Susan's behavior with one of the men in the hot water was somehow beyond the pale of what constituted a well-run naked hot tub party.

On 20 October, David confronted his estranged wife with the information in the letter and his interpretation of it. He accused Susan of having an affair with Tom. This accusation confused her. Not quite knowing what to say, she confessed to having had an affair with Tom's *father*, J. Carey Findlay, her former employer. Carey Findlay is the owner of Conso Products, a company that makes tassels, piping, cording and braid, far and away the biggest employer in Union. David Smith, still reeling from this news, upped the ante by threatening to inform Findlay's wife about the letter and the relationship between Susan, Tom Findlay and her ex-boss.

Arlene Andrews, who had interviewed Susan on several occasions, said that the young wife and mother was distraught. She didn't know where to turn. "Susan thought she had done something unforgivable," she said. "Her suicidal despair set in and she began to think everything about her was bad." Everything about *her*, apparently, included the children, for five days later they were dead.

During the trial, the prosecution's case depended on showing that the children were murdered in order to clear away the let or hindrance to Susan and Tom Findlay getting back together again. But the children were not Findlay's only objection to continuing his liaison with

Susan. Another objection to her was that she came from the wrong side of the tracks. In a town the size of Union, in spite of its motto:

The City of Hospitality

class is all important. Illicit relationships and hot tub parties were one thing, but a wedding ring and church bells were another.

Susan's problems didn't begin and end with Tom Findlay. She had also been having an affair with his father, with her stepfather and with another man who lived near Union. She had even been sleeping with her estranged husband. In these sexual encounters, psychiatrists, social workers and friends agreed that Susan wasn't promiscuous because she enjoyed the raptures of sexual activity. They seemed certain that what she needed was confirmation that she was liked, needed and appreciated. Susan lost her feeling of self-worth when she was first molested by her stepfather. Her dalliance with other men, especially older men, leads back to the suicide of her father and her sexual awakening at the hands of Beverly Russell Jr., her stepfather.

Susan Smith's trial for the murder of her two sons was to begin on Tuesday, 18 July 1995. It was delayed for a day because of a bomb scare. No one in Union, South Carolina, was surprised by this, because public opinion concerning the fate of Susan Smith had been on everybody's mind for nearly a year. Not just in the Carolinas, not just in the South, but all over the United States and beyond. When special prosecutor Keith Giese, the assistant to solicitor Thomas Pope began making his case for the state, he said:

> For nine days in the fall of 1994, Susan Smith looked this country in the eye and lied … She begged God to return the children to safety, and the whole time she knew her children were lying dead at the bottom of John D. Long Lake …

With due allowance for courtroom hyperbole, what he said was true. After Smith watched her 1990 burgundy Mazda Protegé run down the ramp and plunge into the lake, she ran to a house on the highway where she reported within minutes to the police that her car, with her children in it, had been carjacked by a black man with a handgun. The thief had appeared when she was stopped at a traffic light. He had first of all forced her to drive a few miles and then told her to get out of the car. She pleaded for her children, but the intruder drove off with the two young Smith brothers in the back.

Susan's story electrified Union County. A dragnet was launched. Roadblocks were set up. An all-states bulletin was issued. The FBI sent help. First local radio, then big-city and finally national television took notice. The story of the missing brothers scooped the O. J. Simpson case in the headlines. For the first time ever, Union, S.C., became a well-known dateline. The family was approached by *Larry King Live* and *A Current Affair*. A drawing of the black carjacker was put together from a description Susan gave the police. In Union, and across the state, prayers were said for the safe return of the children. High school teenagers got down on their knees and prayed. Yellow ribbons were worn to show that the whole town was behind Susan and David Smith for the safe return of the boys. But, when after nine days, neither the car nor the children had been sighted and the police were scratching their heads trying to think of what they had left undone, the local Sheriff, Howard Wells, tricked Susan into a confession. When the truth became known, the story which had been growing with every day that passed, burst into the living rooms across the nation, around the world. Meanwhile, black groups everywhere were incensed at being scape-goated, and protested that big lies about blacks were still easily believed south of the Mason-Dixon Line.

When it was over, none of the twelve jurors looked at Susan Smith as they filed back into the courtroom to render their verdict. It had taken them only two and a half hours to decide that the prosecution's view of things was the correct one. The complicated psychiatric assessments presented by the defense might be believed by bleeding hearts, but not these concerned citizens of Union. That wasn't the end of it. The courtroom was filled to capacity again when it was time to decide whether Susan Smith was to live or to die. A crowd of two hundred awaited the news in front of the Union County Courthouse. In this process, the jury decided that she was not a vicious murderer, but a troubled woman who needed help and didn't get it in time to save the children. She was sentenced to life imprisonment, not eligible for parole for thirty years.

In this short account, I have touched on only the main themes of this case. The Internet has all the details, with special aspects spelled out. The race issue alone makes for lengthy reading. The jealousy of David Smith, who hid in a closet in order to catch Susan in conversation on the telephone with her current lover, is a theme that has been touched on in these pages, but since that only intensified the horror Susan was living through, I have not mentioned it until now. Was Susan Smith more or less disturbed than Pauline Dubuisson or Ruth Ellis? Was her act more or less premeditated than Yvonne Chevallier's or Henriette Caillaux's? Than Lord Broughton's or Alpna Patel's? Certainly by killing her children, Smith only advanced her attempt to win back Tom Findlay in one area of his objections to her. More to the point, she deeply wounded David, her estranged husband, for his jealousy, his prying and, unjustly, for her terrible life.

There are classical precursors to the tragedy of the young Smith brothers. Medea, the Corinthian priestess of Hecate, was a poisoner who collected wolfsbane from the foam of the surf on the rocky coast, and is said to have murdered her two sons to pay back Jason, their father, for his unfaithfulness. Not that her earlier career had been without family bloodshed. Once Medea told the credulous daughters of Pelias that she had the skill to rejuvenate the elderly despot. She persuaded them to cut up their father and cook him in a cauldron with certain herbs, Medea having convinced them of the good that would come of it. Later, when Jason ditched her in Corinth for Creon's daughter, Creusa, Medea had her most memorable revenge: she sent Creusa a garment which poisoned her when she put it on, she caused Creon's death, and, for good measure, she murdered her two sons, sired by runaway Jason. The people of Corinth were caught up in the drama and stoned several of the main players. Much later, the good citizens of Corinth bribed the playwright Euripides to soft-pedal Corinthian guilt when he came to write his immortal *Medea*. The whole cycle of myths and legends connected to Theseus, Jason and Medea has more than a taint of family murder and blood sacrifice about it, missing for the most part in the later stories connected to the Trojan War. Medea could have been a character in Shakespeare's early play, *Titus Andronicus*.

Family troubles in high places, of course, didn't stop with Medea. Think of all those Renaissance Italian nobles debauching one another. We were reminded that this sort of thing is still going on when we read of the assassination, on 1 June 2001, of the whole royal family of Nepal. The assassin was the Crown Prince Dipendra, his victims included a brother, Prince Nirajan, a sister, and his mother and father, King Birendra and Queen Aiswarya. The time was around 7:30 p.m. local time, the place the billiard room at the Narayanhiti Palace, the royal residence. The Crown Prince Dipendra had appeared for the regular Friday night family dinner in a surprising state. He had been drinking and smoking cigarettes laced with hashish. He was admonished for his incivility and escorted back to his apartments by his brother, Prince Nirajan and the only eye-witness who survived these tragic events, Dr. Rajiv Shahi, who was only allowed to speak out a week afterwards: "Dipendra," he said, "returned, [to the billiard room] dressed in army fatigues and carrying an M-16 assault rifle." He was also armed with a 9 mm submachine gun, a 12-gauge shotgun and a 9 mm automatic pistol. In a mad frenzy, Dipendra aimed the rifle at his father, the king, and fired. Dr. Shahi attended the stricken monarch, who was bleeding from the neck and stomach. Dipendra walked outside the room firing bursts as he went. It was all over in less than two minutes. When he aimed his weapon at his mother, the queen, Dipendra's younger brother, Prince Nirajan, tried to intercede with his brother, pleading with him to spare their mother, but the drunken assassin was unmoved. He shot his brother in the back and then his mother at point blank range. When he had completed his work of killing, he stepped from the room and shot himself, according to Dr. Shahi. But reports about the prince's suicide were glossed over in the official report of the murders. The only statements that refer to the Crown Prince's fatal shooting is the statement that the only shells recovered came from one or another of the Prince's weapons.

The Crown Prince was not killed outright; he lingered for two days, during which he was the true king of Nepal, although lost in a coma. For that fateful forty-eight hours, while the politicians tried to understand the royal calamity and divine what to do next—could a murderer be allowed to rule?—the people of Nepal were kept from demonstrating by a curfew which kept them at home. Meanwhile banks, stores and offices remained closed throughout the capital and beyond. Even before Dipendra's death at the military hospital where he had been taken, Gyanendra, the murdered king's brother, who was crowned king the moment Dipendra drew his last breath, called for calm in Kathmandu. Ms. Devyani Rana, an intimate friend of the Crown Prince, told the Nepalese authorities gathering information about the royal massacre from New Delhi, where she had fled after the shootings, that Dipendra had called her on the telephone several times before the fatal rampage. She immediately informed the prince's aides that Dipendra sounded sick, that his speech was slurred. The last thing the prince said to her was that he would speak to her the following day.

Nepalese newspapers demanded an explanation of these unhappy events, which must have looked like a Himalayan production of the last act of *Hamlet* or the slaying of the suitors in *The Odyssey*. Several editors and journalists were arrested and charged with sedition and treason.

Is there an explanation for this carnage? Was it simply a drunken spree in the palace, with a firearm going off? Apparently not. The Crown Prince, who was only thirty, had fallen in love with a young woman, Devyani Rana, of whom his mother, Queen Aiswarya and King Birendra did not approve. Families again! The ex-Etonian crown prince had failed to convince his parents of the virtue of his intended. When the discussion was closed, poor Dipendra was forced to seek another solution.

Which reminds me of the tragic story *Mayerling*, an often-staged and filmed tragic love story set among the higher-up Hapsburgs. Rudolf, the only son of the Emperor Franz Josef of the Austro-Hungarian Empire, crown prince, heir apparent, at the age of thirty-one, committed suicide with his lover, the Baroness Marie Vetsera at Mayerling, the prince's hunting lodge, outside Vienna, on 30 January 1889. The two deaths aroused much speculation at the time despite the official announcement that the pair had committed suicide. Had he shot her before taking his own life? This seemed to be the popular theory, although it made the crown prince a murderer at least technically. The Emperor Franz Josef had objected to Rudolf's alliance with the Baroness Marie Vetsera. While the title baroness might seem ample enough for most people, the Imperial Family felt that a look under the skirts of the title left doubts about Marie's antecedents. Franz Josef put his royal foot down. Rudolf didn't think of murdering his father to get rid of the objection. (From what we hear, Rudolf and his father got along well on most subjects.) Rather, he turned in upon himself, removed himself and his beloved to his frosty hunting lodge, where, in the course of the night he killed the girl, who wasn't good enough to become empress, and himself.

The story was filmed in France in 1936 by Anatole Litvak, starring Charles Boyer and Danielle Darrieux. In this version, it was the story of a prince who dared to fall in love with a commoner. Remade in 1968 by a British company, with Omar Sharif and Catherine Deneuve and directed by Terrence Young, it became the story of an Austrian prince who defied convention and his father.

Crown Prince Rudolf's successor as crown prince, the ill-fated Franz Ferdinand, managed his affairs better. When he and his consort were assassinated at Sarajevo in June 1914, Franz Ferdinand still had a widow to mourn him. He had an established morganatic arrangement with another woman: the issue from this union was excluded from the Hapsburg throne. Why didn't young Rudolf think of that? He was considered a bright fellow, had written with collaborators *Die Osterreichisch-Ungarische Monarchie in Wort und Bild* (1886–*et seq.*). And his uncle wasn't the only example on record. Almost all of the sons of

George III of Britain had morganatic marriages, including the father of Queen Victoria. Notoriously, George IV flaunted his Mrs. Maria Anna Fitzherbert at Brighton, where they grew old and fat together. His proper queen, Caroline, was his first cousin. When she began to live a life then considered abandoned, George had her excluded from his coronation and then had her tried for adultery before the House of Lords.

TWELVE

Provocation
and Responsibility

Elizabeth Martha Brown

Early in the morning of 6 July 1856, John Anthony Brown, a
young carter from Birdsmoorgate, Dorsetshire, staggered into
the house he shared with his wife, Elizabeth Martha.[52] He had
been out all night. He was still drunk. When she remonstrated with
him about where he had been, John, Jack or Tony—whatever he was
called in the tiny Dorset community—went on the offensive. He
destroyed a chair by kicking the bottom out of it. As Martha tried to
lead him back to the question she had raised, there were further words
between this husband and wife, which quickly led to blows. He
punched her in the side of the head and then picked up his whalebone
whip, and gave her three good stripes with it, before punctuating this
beating with a solid kick. Then, as she was picking herself up from the
floor, he bent down to get out of his boots. Seeing him occupied for the
moment with the laces, she picked up the coal hatchet, near the fire-
place, and struck him six or seven times. One blow stove in his head
over one eye, another did similar damage to the side of his head. "The
violence of the blows must have been very great," commented one of
the newspapers that reported the homicide.

This murder was the simple crime of a woman, having been beaten
savagely, following many earlier beatings, striking out with the first
convenient weapon to defend herself from further injury. The annals of
crime are full of such cases. These same annals are just as full of the

different ways in which such crimes have been interpreted by law courts and punished. The blows that Martha Brown delivered were passionate, deliberate and immediately followed the beating that prompted them, but whether everything "went black" as she reeled from her husband's kick, before she seized the hatchet, we have not been told. In any case, crimes of this sort are related to the main theme of this book. Abuse, habitual spousal abuse, and the homicides it leads to, represents a large swath of all murders committed by women against men. In looking over the cases going back to a time when a wife's murder of her husband, whatever the provocation, was called "petty treason" and punished by burning at the stake, it is easy to see that such homicides were treated in most cases not only as ordinary murders, but as rebellion against established authority: slave against master, servant against employer, wife against husband, subject against sovereign: blows against the stability and welfare of the community. Just as high treason was an attack on the body politic, the nation itself, petty treason—from the French word *petit*—was an attack not only on another human being, but upon the institution of marriage itself and the institutions whereby married women, by law, submitted to the dictates of their spouses. Such crimes provoked patriarchal rage among the burghers, who saw retaliation by force to male authority and domination as a threat to the fabric of civilization itself.

Nearly every woman executed in Britain after 1843, the year Home Office statistics began recording the gender of criminals, was influenced in her crime by a man. Most of these cases, as Patrick Wilson points out in *Murderess*, concerned women who committed "sanely conceived, premeditated and unprovoked murder," that is, murder outside the scope of this study. Most of the others were hanged for murders that came out of their family situation. Of the sixty-eight women executed in the one hundred and twelve years, until the hanging of women stopped with Ruth Ellis in 1955, many pushed provocation to the limit, helping to define the difference between what a reasonable, sane person might do under extreme stress, and what constitutes unacceptable violence under the circumstances. Most of the cases that could be considered here begin in domestic circumstances not very different from those of John Anthony and Martha Elizabeth Brown.

Apart from an age difference of eighteen years, the Browns were seen by their neighbors as a happy enough couple. They had met when they both worked as servants on a farm near Broadwindsor, Dorset. They had been married five years at the time of the murder. It was suspected that he married her for her money, even though all versions of the story acknowledge that Martha was still a strikingly good looking woman, who did not look her forty-five years. He was a hot-headed young buck, staying out late drinking and spending too much time walking along the roadway with a local woman, Mary Davies. He abused Martha only when he was drunk, it was argued by his supporters. But he drank a lot and the beatings became habitual; while he was asleep or working, she had ample time to heal her bruises and go about her business. He beat her in an orgy of self-disgust, perhaps, but she wore the scars of it. Martha, perhaps as an older woman, had developed a jealous streak; she showed a proprietary interest in the younger women her husband doffed his cap to in the street. She had herself seen her husband with Mary Davies in the village and once through Davies's own window. In Martha's view, Brown may have been an abuser, but he was *her* abuser. Even in cases of extreme abuse, the eternal toxic triangle goes jingle-jangle.

"I had never struck him before, after all his ill treatment," she said, "but when he hit me so hard at this time I was almost out of my senses, and hardly knew what I was doing." She certainly did not. She delayed calling for help for three hours. When it arrived she told a transparent tale of how John Anthony had come home saying that he had been kicked in the head by his horse, and had come from the field bleeding and dying. The helpful young doctor who examined the corpse declared that Brown, in that condition, would have been unable to talk or walk. It was her attempt to hide the crime that sealed her fate. Had she told the truth from the beginning, instead of standing by a tale that no jury would swallow, the story for her might have ended more happily. She finally confessed the truth to her spiritual adviser, the Reverend H. Moule, forty-eight hours before meeting Calcraft, the hangman, at the gallows. On the chance that the truth would save her at the eleventh hour, Moule and others made a dash to London to see the Home Secretary. But all in vain. The Home Secretary was unavailable. They returned to Dorchester with heavy news. "Oh, dear!" she said on the way to the scaffold, "I wish I had spoken the truth at the beginning."

Martha Brown was executed on time at Dorchester prison, where the youthful Thomas Hardy saw her "hanging in the misty rain." He was sixteen. The indelible image stayed with the writer until he exorcized it in the ending of *Tess of the D'Urbervilles* over thirty-five years later.

Elizabeth Workman

There are thousands of stories like that of Elizabeth Martha Brown. The man or woman who strikes out to stop being beaten or to forestall the start of another familiar round of beatings, is in a tradition of murder that is akin to the crime of passion. It sometimes involves a woman losing control completely of what is moral and right in order to stop the hail of blows. Such a person reaches out for the nearest object to fend off the battering. For instance: Elizabeth Workman, of Sarnia, Ontario.[53] Like Martha Brown, Mrs. Workman had suffered regular and habitual physical abuse at the hands of her husband, James, a nasty drunk. On several occasions, the beatings were so severe that she and her children had to take shelter with friendly neighbors. In the small border town of Sarnia, Elizabeth was known as "a kindly, industrious woman, a good mother to her son and a daughter by her husband's previous marriage; and a pious member of the local church." On 26 October 1872, in the middle of another beating, she turned on her tyrant of a drunken husband and hit him with a handy piece of wood. The blow proved to be fatal. The trial ended with Mrs. Workman being condemned to death. In this case, the sudden rage and unthinking desire to get free from the abuser are present, but we know of no jealousy or third party to the relationship. I include the case simply to show how the citizens of Sarnia and Lambton County tried to snatch her from the gallows in vain. Whereas Elizabeth Martha Brown had tried to invent a story that would mask the murder of her husband, and clung to that fiction almost to the foot of the scaffold, Elizabeth Workman had been truthful about the circumstances surrounding her husband's death with the investigators of the crime and at her trial. There was no obfuscation, no attempt to mislead or minimize her part in the fatal encounter. The jury's strong recommendation of mercy, which the trial judge thought would prove useless as an instrument of mitigation, was brought to the attention of the Prime Minister Sir John A. Macdonald, who saw no reason to interfere with the verdict, beyond granting a short reprieve. When the hundreds of petitions seeking clemency failed to prevent the secretary of state from signing Elizabeth's death warrant, the town and county councils appealed directly to the Governor General. This appeal failed as well. The tradition of petty treason was still alive in Lambton County, Ontario, although it was disappearing in Britain. The last woman burned at the stake for murdering her husband there was Christian Bowman, a poisoner, in 1789. In Ireland, very few murderesses were hanged after 1843. The last was Margaret Shiel, who was executed at Tullamore in 1870. This was a land dispute in which a neighbor was shot. In general both in Britain and in the colonies, when reviewing a death sentence in the Home Office or in the cabinet, the deciding official pays more attention to what the sentencing judge said at the trial than to a jury's recommendation of mercy. Certainly Elizabeth Workman saw none.

On the morning of 19 May 1873, Mrs. Workman was hanged. It was a public execution—Britain hadn't seen a public hanging since 1868—with admittance to the walled jail by the presentation of black-edged invitation cards. Very few of the local people cared to attend; they strongly regretted the direction that justice had turned in the case of pitiful Elizabeth Workman. The case left a bad taste in the mouths of all the officials concerned. It was by no accident that the federal government of Canada was deterred from executing another woman for the next twenty-five years.

Violet Watkins

One of the cases Elliott Leyton cites in his book, *Men of Blood*, is a crime of passion as far removed from the raw material of literature as *Romeo and Juliet* is from a barroom brawl. George and Violet Watkins[54] had been married for many years. Both lived in that anonymous community a few streets removed from television's *Coronation Street*. Both were alcoholics in working-class circumstances. Although he regularly beat Violet up, they blamed it on the drink and got on reasonably well the rest of the time. One night, when both had had more than the usual amount to drink, George began to knock Violet about in their council flat after a row began about nothing much. At some point, after having her hair pulled as she tried to escape through the door, Violet found a kitchen knife and stabbed George just once. Like the single thrust Charlotte Corday made over Marat's boot-shaped bathtub, Violet's aim was fatal; George died at once. When questioned by the police, Violet appeared to describe exactly what happened, withholding nothing.

In court, the jury understood the circumstances leading to the death of George, and acquitted Violet of murder. She was sentenced to eighteen months for manslaughter, but this sentence was suspended: there seemed to be little harm in Violet to be expunged.

As in many cases of lover or spouse murder, the murderer—perhaps because of a numbness that sets in following the fatal act—refuses to protect him- or herself. They offer themselves up as sacrifices to help atone for the harm they have done. This seems to be universally the case, except when the murderer tries—as Othello did—to destroy himself.

British society, Elliott Leyton maintains, is far less violent than American society. It is more cowed by the presence of authority and, in general, murders fewer people per thousand. In the U.S., homicide creates less public shock in certain circumstances. For example, in Texas, the law includes classes of murder that are not culpable. Homicides committed to protect home, family or property are not murder. Homicides committed helping the authorities or to stop a fleeing felon or escaping prisoner are not murder. Until the early 1970s, an outraged husband could shoot his adulterous wife and her lover with impunity. It was not murder. In Britain, where the people have more or less delegated the keeping of law and order to the authorities, they are less likely to seek private justice than in the United States, where a type of personal justice that walks around the law, is enshrined in characters like Rambo, the Vietnam veteran, who becomes a one-man army because he has run afoul of a couple of corrupt policemen. In the States, where some murders are condoned by the state as "moral or righteous slaughter," other murders, outside this special category, are similarly viewed as justifiable homicide. In places, according both to Jack Katz (*Seductions of Crime: Moral and Sensual Attractions of Doing Evil*: Basic Books, New York, 1988) and Elliott Leyton, who have studied these matters more than anyone else, the code of honor that justifies such slaughter is medieval.

Ralph Klassen

Susan Klassen was a respected, well-loved occupational therapist who also had established an international reputation as a professional story-teller. She was raised in a solid Catholic home in Edmonton, Alberta, with her five sisters. At thirty-six, she was bright, ambitious and an important part of the growing community of Whitehorse, in Canada's Yukon Territory, where she was coordinator of therapy services for the Thompson Centre, a long-term care facility. In 1982, she married Ralph Klassen,[55] who had grown up in Manitoba. Klassen tried running a Christian Missionary Alliance Church, but failed utterly after a run of seven months. He had taken a bachelor's and then a master's degree in theology. Thereafter, he tried farming, truck-driving, selling cars, carpentry and photography. His inability to find useful employment led to the couple moving around a great deal. The stay of a few months or at most a year or two always led to pulling up stakes and moving on. This is the way it was for most of their twelve-year marriage. Each new situation turned sour after a short try. During this time, Susan appears to have been a good, caring and supportive wife. They moved to Whitehorse in 1990.

The stress of Ralph's almost total lack of success and Susan's record of turning each short stay in another town to account in some way left deep wounds in the marriage. This was aggravated by their inability to have children. Klassen's sperm-count was low, and it is probable that during their many heated arguments this fact was mentioned by Susan as one of the major obstacles to their happiness together. While Susan was friendly, outgoing, a contributing member of the community, through her appearances in local theater projects and story-telling festivals, one of which she founded, Klassen was a stay-at-home, jealous of Susan's local contacts and suspicious of even her women acquaintances. Although the Crown at the trial did not make a point of it, there were several witnesses in Whitehorse who had seen signs of abuse on Susan, although she tried to minimize them, and never named Klassen as the author of her bruises. The couple tried to separate several times. Late in 1995, when Klassen was forty-five, they agreed to a formal separation for a six-month period in order to try to discover what it was they needed. Susan helped Ralph relocate in Alberta and gave him support in establishing himself in this new location. For Susan, it meant an escape from the alleged beatings and Ralph's petty jealousies that had been the bugbear of their life together. For Ralph it added "rejection" to his list of failures.

On 1 November 1995, only a month or two into the agreed separation, Ralph returned to Whitehorse and tried to persuade Susan to take him back. Susan, who knew that Ralph had hardly had a chance to change his spots in so short a time, refused. She didn't, however, send him away from her door. It was late, and he had made no plans to stay anywhere else. After they had retired to bed, she told him she wanted their relationship to stop. We have only Klassen's word for what really happened that night. He told the court that she had upbraided him for his failures, among which his inability to give her children loomed largest. She boasted to him of a new male interest in her life, a local man named Gord. This, he said, drove him mad. He "blacked out," he maintained after getting his hands around his wife's throat. Immediately after killing Susan, Ralph wrote a note, addressed to Gord, in which he apologized for the fit of rage that had resulted in Susan's death, then tried to kill himself by driving his car at high speed into an oncoming propane truck. Miraculously, there was no explosion and neither driver was killed. The driver of the truck received serious injuries which took many months of physiotherapy to relieve. Klassen was never charged with this offense.

Klassen never denied culpability for his crime. The investigating officers found no signs of a struggle on the body or at the scene of the crime. There were no indications that she had tried to fight him off. She may have been asleep when the attack occurred.

He tried to plead guilty to manslaughter, but was formally charged with second degree murder in the death of his wife. Klassen admitted to killing his wife in a fit of jealousy. He told the court how Susan had belittled his virility and boasted of her new lover. On 17 January 1997, a jury found him guilty, not of murder, but of the lesser offense of manslaughter. The next day, he was sentenced to a prison term of five years. (He hadn't sought bail before the trial, so he had been in close custody for thirteen months at the time the case was tried.) It is probable that he is a free man as these words are being written.

Appalled by this verdict and sentence, women's groups across Canada have appealed to have the provocation defense eliminated. Since the victim cannot disclaim or deny the motives, actions or words ascribed to her by the accused, they claim that provocation is a defense that tends to cast the victim in the role of aggressor. This is akin to blaming Dr. Hermann Rorschach for his dirty pictures.

The Criminal Code of Canada does not provide an automatic right of appeal against sentence. Instead, the leave of the court is required for sentence appeals. They did appeal Klassen's sentence, offered new evidence of Klassen's brutality towards his wife, his jealous interference in her movements and his attempts to curtail her involvement in the community. (There is an echo here of the fish-and-chip vendor from Blackpool. Remember Alan Norman and his wife Trish?) But an appeal hearing is only empowered to examine the conduct of the case as far as the *law* is concerned. If no error in *law* has occurred, the right to appeal will not be granted. In Klassen's case, because the five-year sentence given to Klassen had caused such an outcry in the community, the appeal was heard. Afterwards, the appeal court found, according to the evidence presented in the original trial:

> The accused had no criminal record prior to this offence. Since his sentence, there has been some adverse publicity in the local media about the accused having some violent propensities but no such evidence was presented in the trial. Certainly there was no suggestion of violence in the many family victim impact statements provided to the court. This was confirmed by other witnesses who said there was no evidence of violence in this marriage. The Crown not having sought to introduce any such evidence, we are confined to the evidence actually presented at the trial.

Further, the three-judge panel, after examining several similar cases, found that the sentence was not out of line with similar cases heard across the country. A Supreme Court ruling prevented the appeal court from making new law here, by creating a category of offense within a statutory offense for the purpose of sentencing. That left various groups who had brought about the appeal disappointed and unsatisfied. They continued to circulate petitions, circularize two suggested format letters to be addressed to the justice minister, the Ministry Responsible for the Status of Women and to the attorneys-general of all provinces and territories.

According to *The Defense of Provocation and Domestic Femicide*, one of the papers written with this and other similar cases in mind, Andrée Côté says that men who batter women use minimization, confusion, outright denial, intoxication, loss of control and projection to blame their victims and deny their own responsibility. She maintains:

> The statutory provocation defense as it is currently used in femicide/wife slaughter cases inappropriately and unjustly changes the focus of the criminal trial from the behavior of the accused and his intention to murder to the behavior of the victim who

from then on is identified as the one responsible for the accused's violence. The statutory defense of provocation provides a legal excuse for men's anger. It reduces what would otherwise be murder to manslaughter. If the law stops giving men excuses for their violence, they will have no other choice but to take full responsibility for their actions.

In another paper, *Reforming the Defense of Provocation*, by Sheila Galloway and Joanne St. Lewis, the authors pointed out that the defense of provocation is used mostly by men who kill women because they are emotionally unable to accept loss of power and control. When women kill their husbands, it is almost invariably because of a history of battering and abuse. It is an act of self-defense for themselves and their children. "No matter who dies in the relationship, and it is mostly the women who do, it is often reaction to a history of repeated male violence, not female violence." The authors recommended that the defense of provocation be abolished.

The "crime of passion defense," like all defenses, will be taken up by lawyers who see a chance of making it work. An advantage already mentioned is the fact that the victim cannot protest the spin that is put on the facts by the defense attorney. Othello's self-immolation and Klassen's attempt to follow him are open to interpretation. One reading of Othello's suicide is symmetry. He even confesses as much. But one would be foolish indeed to stop looking there and look no further into "these unlucky deeds."

There is much to be said about provocation. The law condescends to those who allow themselves to be provoked, always throwing up to them the unrealistic model of what a reasonable, ordinary person would do under similar stressful conditions. If it is shown that a defendant has done no more than most reasonable people would do, juries may decide that an action is not murder, but manslaughter or even not a crime at all, since what reasonable men do must be some guide to what is legal for all to do. But reasonable people around the world have different standards of what is reasonable behavior in their neighbors. To observers outside the confines of those cultures—and I'm not necessarily thinking of the literal application of Islamic law in Nigeria or Iran or Saudi Arabia—their law seems to work in ways that appear plainly biased against one sex and towards the other.

Kenneth Peacock

Two recent cases from courtrooms in Maryland make their own commentary on the difficulties encountered in finding fair sentences in cases of crimes of passion. In October 1994, Kenneth Peacock, thirty-six years old, was sentenced to eighteen months in prison for shooting his wife, Sandra, in the head after he discovered her in bed with another man. The judge, Robert Cahill, called it an understandable crime of passion as he banged down his gavel. Earlier, the prosecutors had plea-bargained the charge down from murder to voluntary manslaughter, which on conviction carries a three- to eight-year sentence. The sympathetic judge whittled it down further. He said that he couldn't imagine a situation that would provoke "a more uncontrollable rage than this. I seriously wonder," Cahill went on, "how many men, married four or five years, would have the strength to walk away without inflicting some corporal punishment." This questionable statement provoked a considerable protest. The journalist Patrick Cox of *USA Today* wrote about the decision on 20 October of that year. He called the decision "dumb" and the comment "gibberish." He goes on to recall what a judge sitting in an English court said in similar circumstances in 1707: "Adultery is the highest invasion of property … a man cannot receive a higher provocation." Cox goes on to observe:

> This, though, is the 1990s, not the days of scarlet As. Men have no right to treat women as chattel—to have, hold and kill, if they step out of line.
>
> Yet men constantly do.
>
> More than a third of female murder victims are killed by spouses or romantic partners. That's almost 2,000 women a year.

In many of those cases, the murderous husbands and lovers claim they were forced to kill by their spouses' infidelity. All too often overloaded prosecutors, judges or juries buy the story and reduce the charges.

But those men have a simple, non-violent alternative: walk out the door. Get a divorce. No one will kill them if they do.

Patrick Cox goes on to contrast the cuckolded male with battered wives and girlfriends. Men refuse to let their unhappy women go. Some are virtual prisoners, without the means to escape. Such women, when they do get away, are often stalked and some of them are killed. Again, think of the story of Trish and Alan Norman, of the Blackpool fish-and-chip shop.

Patricia Ann Hawkins

In another Maryland courtroom, the same week that Kenneth Peacock was given eighteen months for shooting his wife, Patricia Ann Hawkins, thirty-four, was given twice as much time as Peacock for killing her sleeping husband. Prosecutors knew the woman's long history of abuse at the hands of her mate. It had been going on for years. The day of the killing, he had given her a beating and threatened both her and her children. The prosecutors wanted to let her go in a year. The judge, a woman, gave her the minimum sentence: three years. "The difference in sentences," Cox says, "makes no sense. It just isn't right and betrays an outrageous bias."

After rereading this long catalogue of battering and murder, and coming away with the feeling that the courts will never get it right, that down through history judges and juries have seen things differently in the next town, that the circuit judges have not been able to be supermen and superwomen in their decisions. Their rulings come out of who they are more than where they are. The judge who sentenced Edith Thompson to the gallows had never met a woman like the prisoner at the bar. In spite of her proper Ilford manners, she not only had been taken in adultery, but she defended her antisocial affair. For the judge, she came from a foreign dimension. Maryland courts are not alone in their inconsistency.

When, years ago, I worked as a student at law, one of my tasks was to bring up to date the loose-leaf binders of court decisions in their lower and higher spheres. From the moment I finished discarding the out-of-date pages and replacing them with the current versions, they began to get out-of-date all over again. Keeping up with what is going on in France or Britain or Australia or Italy is a Sisyphus-like task. Judges and juries can only speak for their own communities, measuring guilt and innocence against the standards of their peers. In our human courts, we must try to render godlike justice. How do you do that and remain consistent as well?

Epilogue

I n *Murder and Its* Motives, the English writer F. Tennyson Jesse tries to classify murder by its motives. She breaks it down to six: murder for gain, for revenge, for elimination, for jealousy, for lust of killing and murder from conviction. She goes on to say:

> It will probably be noticed that I do not include what is known
> as the *crime passionnel*. That is because it is not in itself a pri-
> mary division, and it is only sloppy thinking that would make
> it so. A *crime passionnel* always comes under one of the above
> headings—generally under that of revenge or jealousy, occa-
> sionally under that of elimination ... Murders for jealousy run
> the gamut between the *crime passionnel* and a cold-blooded sat-
> isfying of jealousy such as Mrs. Pearcey's.

While hoping to survive the charge of sloppy thinking, I think that the point Jesse is making is that crimes of passion defy classification, ignore definition and will not be pigeonholed. Whether the above pages help or hinder that problem, I will leave to you.

As I approach the end of this not very scientific study, I am forced by convention to look for a message in all of this welter of human tragedy and pain. Like the youthful optimist digging into a mountain of horse manure, certain that with all of that manure there must be a pony, I dip in and come out with two "ponies." The first is Jeremy Horder's conclusion that it is time to shut down and abolish the doc-trine of provocation in murder cases:

... [T]he effect of provocation in murder cases [should be] left as a matter for mitigation in sentence, should the mandatory life sentence for murder ever be abolished. The morality of retribution will then be left to the institutions of state punishment and we shall say to the provoked killer, "Provocation ought no more to be regarded as inviting personal retaliation than a woman's style of dress invites rape. It is one thing to feel great anger at great provocation; but quite another (ethical) thing to experience and express that anger in retaliatory form. For you there can be no mitigation of the offence."

Provoked killings litter this book. Yvonne Chevallier was provoked beyond reason by her war-hero husband. He had a mistress; he was at home in a world of politics, ideas, literature and art, which she could never quite understand. But worst of all, she could see that they had grown so far apart that nothing could ever bring them together again. Their children and their home were no longer enough. Her passionate execution of her once-loving spouse, her righteous and narcissistic anger slaked by the blood she spilled, left her with nothing but guilt and remorse for company. A trifle falling from this table is the fact that such people are rarely ever a public danger again.

The other "pony" is this: There can never be an absolute system of justice. To pretend otherwise is a sham. Justice, man's justice to man, is a groping, unsure approach to the Platonic ideal that is always just out of reach. Lawmakers are moving towards this ideal with the help of everyone in society. Society yells when it feels outraged by a bad sentence or an unfair trial. When the Canadian government failed to heed a jury's recommendation of mercy for Elizabeth Workman, when French courts saw only coincidence in the purchase of handguns by Yvonne Chevallier and Henriette Caillaux shortly before they used them to lethal effect, the people noticed. People keep harping on perceived unfairness. They will keep nagging—and long may they nag!—until the problem has been fixed and the grievance has gone away.

Notes

1. Anna Freud said this in *The Analysis of Defense*. For a complete reference see the Bibliography.
2. Dante Alighieri's *The Divine Comedy* has been translated countless times. The one I used is by C. H. Sisson in the *Oxford World's Classics* series.
3. This is from Yeats' *Leda and the Swan*, third stanza.
4. *Hamlet*, 1.2.76.
5. Tennessee Williams, *A Streetcar Named Desire*, scene 10.
6. Ruth Harris, *Murder and Madness: Medicine, Law and Society in the* Fin de siècle.
7. Jay Robert Nash, the prolific true-crime chronicler, noted this about Catherine Hayes in his useful *Look for the Woman*.
8. My chief source on the Chevallier case is to be found in David Rowan's *Famous European Crimes*.
9. Other sources are Colin Wilson and Patricia Pitman's *Encyclopaedia of Murder*.
10. Of the several books and parts of books that deal with the Ruth Ellis case, I found the following most useful: *Ruth Ellis: The last woman to be hanged*, by Robert Hancock, thought it's a little careless about dates and details; Bernard O'Donnell's *Should Women Hang?* Colin Wilson and Patricia Pitman again; *Murderess* by Patrick Wilson; Jonathon Green's *The Greatest Criminals of All Time*; *The Murderers' Who's Who*, the invaluable crime encyclopedia by J. H. H. Gaute and Robin Odell. *Murder Casebook: Investigations into the ultimate crime* is a British-

produced series, *A Marshall Cavendish Weekly Publication*. Number 11 of the series contains files on Ruth Ellis, Jean Harris and Thompson and Bywaters. Number 35 contains an article on Lord Broughton.

11. He was the son of the Right Honorable David Lloyd-George of Dwyfor (1863–1945), prime minister of the United Kingdom during World War I. Gwilym, 1ˢᵗ Viscount Tenby (1894–1967), sat as a Liberal for Pembrokeshire from 1922 until he became a peer in 1957.

12. Frank MacShane, *The Life of Raymond Chandler,* E. P. Dutton & Co. New York, 1976, pages 236–7.

13. Like Ruth Ellis's biographers, writers have been busy with the story of Jean Harris. Here are a few of their books: Shana Alexandra, *Very Much a Lady*, Dell, New York, 1986; Nan Cobbey, "Jean Harris: A new life after 12 years' prison education," *Episcopal Life*.

14. *Men of Blood: Murder in Everyday Life*, by Elliott Leyton, McClelland & Stewart, Toronto, 1995, became subtitled *Murder in Modern England* on the cover of the Penguin paperback edition of 1997, although the older title prevailed inside. Almost all I know about Alan Norman comes from this source.

15. Dominick Dunne is one of North America's best-known true crime writers as well as the "Boswell of the blue-bloods," whose works have appeared in the best magazines. A collection of his pieces from *Vanity Fair* has appeared under the title *Fatal Charms and Other Tales of Today,* Bantam Books, New York, 1988. This is an unusual source, because the murderer he talks about is the former lover and killer of his daughter, the actress Dominique Dunne.

16. If I were to list all of the sources for this short account of the O. J. Simpson trial, I would add substantially to the length of this book. The Internet alone supplied days of reading. For interested students of this case, I recommend the Internet as a good place to start.

17. An unidentified friend of Nicole's, quoted in a profile of Nicole Simpson by Anne McDermott for CNN, 19 January 1995.

18. The letter was quoted in part in an Internet document known to me only as "http://simpson.walraven.org/nb-to-oj.html". It was an undated letter and, although it is listed as part of the criminal file, it wasn't intro-

duced during the criminal trial. It was introduced during the civil trial on 13 January 1997.

19. Ibid.

20. Ibid.

21. This is from a letter Nicole wrote when she still had some hope of cobbling together their failing marriage.

22. Information about the Thompson–Bywaters case comes from several non-fiction sources and these have been illuminated by two fictional ones. The case is recorded in the *Notable British Trials* series, with a fine introduction by Filson Young. Edgar Lustgarten's *Verdict in Dispute* is another good account, as is Lewis Broad's *The Innocence of Edith Thompson*, Hutchinson, London, 1952; and those of Patrick Wilson in *Murderess* and Bernard O'Donnell in *Should Women Hang?* Colin Wilson and Patricia Pitman include the case in their *Encyclopaedia of Murder*, mentioned above, as do Jonathon Green in *The Greatest Criminals of All Time*; and Leslie Hale in *Hanged in Error*. The Marshall Cavendish Weekly Publication's *Murder Casebook* series treat the case in Number 11 of that publication. Two novels have also been instructive: F. Tennyson Jesse's classic treatment of the case, *A Pin to See the Peepshow*, and the quite recent *Fred & Edie* by Jill Dawson.

23. "Darlint," in the private language of the lovers, meant "darlingest."

24. All of Edith Thompson's letters are included in the *Notable British Trials* series as well as in Lewis Broad's *The Innocence of Edith Thompson*, Hutchinson, London, 1952.

25. This case is treated in Wilson and Pitman and in *The Murderers' Who's Who*.

26. Julian Symons, late dean of British authorities on everything that has to do with murder, was a fine practitioner of crime fiction himself and often represented British authors abroad at conferences at the request of the British Council. Mainstream fiction writers didn't seem to mind.

27. Quoted in Lewis Broad's *The Innocence of Edith Thompson*, page 12.

28. Alfred Hitchcock's first film made in the United States was this almost all-British production—English setting, book and cast—makes me wonder what the master of suspense might have done with the Thompson case. Imagine Edith Thompson as a Hitchcock blonde.

29. The sources to the case of Marie and Frederick Manning are abundant. The easiest to find are: the impressive *The Woman Who Murdered Black Satin: The Bermondsey Horror,* by Albert Borowitz, Ohio State University Press, Columbus, 1981; *Twisting in the Wind, The murderess and the English press,* University of Toronto Press, Toronto, 1989; Bernard O'Donnell's useful *Should Women Hang?;* Patrick Wilson's *Murderess;* as well as Wilson and Pitman; Goate and Odell; Jay Robert Nash's *Look for the Woman; Lord High Executioner,* by Howard Engel, Key Porter Books (Firefly in the U.S.), 1996.

30. William Calcraft served as the hangman for London and Middlesex for longer than any other. He was appointed in 1829, paid a guinea a week plus a guinea per execution, and held his post, in spite of regular bungling, until 1874. He was given a pension of a guinea a week, which he drew until his death in 1879, at his home in Hoxton.

31. Three different authorities give three different versions of the fatal Bermondsey address: Minver, Miniver, and Minerva. The scholarship of crime is often dependent on research found in indifferently written contemporary newspaper reports. As mentioned in the text, even the name of the main figure in this story is confused. Is it Marie or Maria?

32. Canada's famous man who wasn't there. See *The Strange Case of Ambrose Small* by Fred McClement, McClelland and Stewart, Toronto, 1974.

33. The Snyder–Gray case is described in Wilson and Pitman, Goate and Odell, Jay Robert Nash's *Look for the Woman* and *Murder, America; A Pictorial History of Crime,* by Julian Symons, Bonanza Books, New York, 1966. .

34. Also called the Crabapple Tree murder, because the bodies the Reverend Edward Wheeler Hall and his parishioner and paramour Mrs. Eleanor Mills were discovered under such a tree in New Brunswick, New Jersey, in September 1922. The case has never officially been solved, although S. S. Van Dine, the creator of the gentleman sleuth Philo Vance, attempted to do so in his first mystery novel. Van Dine was the pseudonym of Willard Huntington Wright (1888–1939). After several years' delay, Reverend Hall's widow, two of her brothers and a cousin on the New York Stock Exchange were tried for the double murder. All four were found not guilty.

35. Henriette Caillaux's case is well-documented. Accounts of the case appear in *Murder in France* by Alister Kershaw; Wilson and Pitman; Jay Robert Nash's *Look for the Woman; Paris on the Eve: 1900–1914* by Vincent Cronin; Goate and Odell; and *A Pictorial History of Crime* by Julian Symons.

36. See Kershaw.

37. Lord Broughton and his Happy Valley friends are the subject of an article in *Murder Casebook, A Marshall Cavendish Publication*, printed in Britain. Number 11 in the series treats the murder of Lord Erroll. Other sources are Goate and Odell.

38. The Marquis Bernardy de Sigoyer (1905–1947) is well-reported in Alister Kershaw's *Murder in France*, Constable & Co. London, 1955; and David Rowan's *Famous European Crimes*, Frederick Muller Ltd., London, 1955.

39. Crippen may be tracked to the following dark corners among many others: Wilson and Pitman, Julian Symons, Goate and Odell, and Jonathon Green.

40. My debt to Ellen Godfrey for the known facts of this case is total. Her excellent, calm, meticulous reporting of the case is a model for writers to follow. The book is *By Reason of Doubt: The Belshaw Case*, Clarke, Irwin & Co., Toronto, 1981. Recent information about people in the case comes from Janet Friskney and *Who's Who in Canada*, University of Toronto Press, Toronto, 1989.

41. The case of Peter Hogg is not as well known as most of the others in this collection. My information comes from a three-page account of the case from a tourist magazine seen on the Internet. It is unsigned, but traceable through www.lakestay.co.uk.

42. David Rowan concluded his exposition of the Yvonne Chevallier case with a brief treatment of Jean Liger, another case that was tried soon afterwards with quite another result. He suggests that the verdict in the earlier case influenced the court in trying the second case. Both are set forth in Rowan's *Famous European Crimes*.

43. Again, the Internet has provided my basic research. Linda Pershing of the State University of New York at Albany has published an informative, factual and funny item on Lorena Bobbitt's crime in the *NWSA*

Journal, Vol. 8, No. 3. Rights and permissions to reprint the article may be had by contacting Rights and Permissions, Journal Division, Indiana University Press, 601 North Morton St., Bloomington, IN 47404. Fax: 812 855 8507, E-mail: journals@indiana.edu. Other sources are listed in the Bibliography.

44. David Rowan has written an effective account of the short and unhappy life of Pauline Dubuisson in *Famous European Cases*. See also *L'Affaire Pauline Dubuisson* by Serge Jacquemard, Fleuve noir, Paris, 1992. Shorter accounts appear in Jay Robert Nash's *Look for the Woman*; Wilson and Pitman; Julian Symons and Goate and Odell.

45. Mary Eleanor Pearcey's story is, like so many of the others, available from many sources. Here are a few of them: Goate and Odell, Jay Robert Nash's *Look for the Woman*, Jonathon Green, Judith Knelman, Patrick Wilson and Bernard O'Donnell.

46. Shakespeare's source for the Pyramus and Thisbe story in *A Midsummer Night's Dream* was Ovid. So is he mine, in the Ted Hughes translation, *Tales from Ovid*.

47. Alpna Patel's story is told in more places than I have been able to use. The following sources were useful: "A Deadly Arrangement" by Brian Hutchinson appeared in the 21 October 2000, issue of *Saturday Night Magazine*, published by the National Post Company, Don Mills, Ontario; on the Internet files from Agence Presse; Robert Russo, Canadian Press; "An Untraditional Death" by Maureen O'Hagan, Washington Post Staff Writer; C. K. Arora in Washington; Piya Chattopadhyay in a television documentary for the *National Magazine*, Canadian Broadcasting Corporation.

48. Pauline Parker and Juliet Hulme appear as short articles in Wilson and Pitman; Nash's *Look for the Woman*; Julian Symons; Goate and Odell; Jonathon Green.

49. Accounts of Leopold and Loeb's crime will be found in Julian Symons; Goate and Odell, *Murder, America*; and *Almanac of World Crime* by Jay Robert Nash; Jonathon Green; and Wilson and Pitman. There is an article on the case in *The Encyclopedia of American Crime* by Carl Sifakis. *Compulsion* (1956), a novel by Meyer Levin, is a fictionalized version

of the story. "Its originality," as Julian Symons has written, "lies in the psychoanalytical interpretation of the murderers' actions, which is both relentless and persuasive." This was the first of the books that mingled fiction and non-fiction to enhance the understanding of an apparently senseless and unprofitable crime. It was filmed with the legendary Orson Welles playing the part of Clarence Darrow.

50. Arnold R Brown has written what he hopes is the "Final Chapter" in this famous case. The book, *Lizzie Borden: The legend, the truth, the final chapter*, Dell, 1991, presents the basic facts, then adds speculation and background that doesn't in the end illuminate anything very important. Other sources are the reliable ones cited above: Goate and Odell; Jonathon Green; Nash's *Almanac of World Crime*; and Wilson and Pitman; to which I would add *The Encyclopedia of American Crime* by Carl Sifakis, Facts on File, New York, 1982.

51. For the Susan Smith case I have used material from the Internet exclusively. I have read files written by Heather Brooke; Ralph Greer, Jr.; Reginald Fields; Chase Squires; Suellen E. Dean; Clay Murphy; Janet Spencer; Molly McDonough; Shelly Haskins; Gary Henderson of the Spartanburg, South Carolina, *Herald-Journal*; David Stout, New York Times News Service; and Jesse J. Holland, Associated Press. Books about the case include: Maria Eftimiades' *Sins of the Mother*; George Rekers' *Susan Smith: Victim of Murderer*; and *Beyond All Reason: My life with Susan Smith*, by David Smith with Carol Calef. The part of the "Dear John" letter that I have seen was in an Associated Press report, signed Rachel Pergament. I have also seen two articles from *TIME* Magazine: "Sex, Betrayal and Murder," by Elizabeth Gleick, 17 July 1995, Volume 146, No 3; and "Elegy For Lost Boys," by Steve Wulf, 31 July 1995, Volume 146, No 5.

52. Patrick Wilson has something to say about Elizabeth Martha Brown in *Murderess*, as has Howard Engel in *Lord High Executioner*. Robert Gittings came across the case while pursuing his research on *Young Thomas Hardy*.

53. I wish I could have found out more about this case. My only source is Frank W. Anderson's *Hanging in Canada*.

54. Elliott Leyton examines the unfortunate end of George Watkins at the hands of his wife (Violet Watkins) in his *Men of Blood*.

55. Ralph Jake Klassen has been written up in the newspapers of the Yukon, but my chief source is a six-page account of the case put together by the court. I got it through an Internet service called QUICKLAW, which I recommend. Material regarding provocation comes from Jeremy Horder's book, *Provocation and Responsibility*.

Bibliography

Alexander, Shana. *Very Much a Lady*. New York: Dell, 1986.

Anderson, Frank W. *Hanging in Canada*. Calgary: Frontier Press, 1973.

Beattie, J. M. *Crime and the Courts in England: 1660–1800*. Princeton: Princeton University Press, 1986.

Bloom, Harold. *Shakespeare: The Invention of the Human*. New York: Riverhead Books, 1998.

Borowitz, Albert. *A Gallery of Sinister Perspectives: Ten Crimes and a Scandal*. Kent, Ohio: Kent State University Press, 1982.

———. *The Woman Who Murdered Black Satin: The Bermondsey Horror*. Columbus: Ohio State University Press, 1981.

Broad, Lewis. *The Innocence of Edith Thompson: A Study in Old Bailey Justice*. London: Hutchinson, 1952.

Brown, Arnold R. *Lizzie Borden: The Legend, the Truth, the Final Chapter*. New York: Dell, 1992.

Dante Alighieri. *The Divine Comedy*. Trans. by C. H. Sisson. Oxford: Oxford University Press, 1993.

Dawson, Jill. *Fred & Edie*. London: Scepter, 2000.

Dempewolff, Richard. *Famous Old New England Murders: And Some that Are Infamous*. Brattleboro, Vermont: Stephen Daye Press, 1942.

Dunne, Dominick. *Fatal Charms and Other Tales of Today*. New York: Bantam, 1988.

Eftimiades, Maria. *Sins of the Mother*. New York: St. Martin's Paperbacks, 1995.

Emsley, Clive. *Crime and Society in England: 1750–1900*. London and New York: Longman, 1987.

Engel, Howard. *Lord High Executioner: An Unashamed Look at Hangmen, Headsmen and Their Kind.* Toronto: Key Porter Books, 1996.

Faber, John. *Great Moments in News Photography.* New York: Thomas Nelson & Son, 1950.

Freud, Anna, with Joseph Sandler. *The Analysis of Defense: The Eye and the Mechanisms of Defense Revisited.* New York: International University Press, 1985.

Gaute, J. H. H., and Robin Odell. *The Murderers' Who's Who.* Montreal: Optimum Publishing Company, 1979.

———. *Murder 'Whatdunit': An Illustrated Account of the Methods of Murder.* London: Harrap, 1982.

Gittings, Robert. *Young Thomas Hardy.* London: Penguin Books, 1975.

Godfrey, Ellen. *By Reason of Doubt: The Belshaw Case.* Toronto: Clarke Irwin, 1981.

Green, Jonathon. *The Greatest Criminals of All Time.* New York: Stein and Day, 1982.

Grierson, Francis. *Famous French Crimes.* London: Frederick Muller Limited, 1959.

Guillais, Joëlle. Trans. by Jane Dunnett. *Crimes of Passion.* Cambridge: Polity Press, 1990.

Hale, Leslie. *Hanged in Error.* Harmondsworth: Penguin Books, 1961.

Handcock, Robert. *Ruth Ellis: The Last Woman to Be Hanged.* London: Weidenfeld and Nicolson, 1963.

Hargroder, Charles M. *Ada and the Doc: An Account of the Ada LeBoeuf—Thomas Dreher Murder Case.* Lafayette: Center for Louisiana Studies, University of Louisiana, 2000.

Harris, Ruth. *Murder and Madness: Medicine, Law and Society in the* fin de siècle. Oxford: Clarendon Press, 1989.

Heppenstall, Rayner. *French Crime in the Romantic Age.* London: Hamish Hamilton, 1970.

Hodge, Harry, editor. *Famous Trials I.* Harmondsworth: Penguin Books, 1954.

Horder, Jeremy. *Provocation and Responsibility.* Oxford: Clarendon Press, 1992.

Jacquemard, Serge. *L'Affaire Pauline Dubuisson*. Paris: Fleuve noir, 1992.

Jesse, F. Tennyson. *A Pin to See the Peep-Show*. Harmondsworth: Penguin, 1934.

———. *Murder and Its Motives*. 1924.

Jonas, George, editor. *The Scales of Justice: Seven Famous Criminal Cases Recreated*. Toronto: CBC Enterprises, 1983.

———. *The Scales of Justice (Volume II): Ten Famous Criminal Cases Recreated*. Toronto: Lester & Orpen Dennys/CBC Enterprises, 1986.

Jones, Ann. *Women Who Kill: A vivid history of America's female murderers from Colonial times to the present (with a special new chapter on the Jean Harris case)*. New York: Fawcett Columbine, 1980.

Joyce, James Avery. *Justice at Work: The Human Side of the Law*. London: Pan Books, 1957.

Kershaw, Alister. *Murder in France*. London: Constable & Co., 1955.

Knelman, Judith. *Twisting in the Wind: The Murderess and the English Press*. Toronto: University of Toronto Press, 1998.

Leyton, Elliott. *Men of Blood: Murder in Everyday Life*. Toronto: McClelland and Stewart, 1996.

Loomis, Stanley. *A Crime of Passion*. Philadelphia and New York: Lippincott, 1967.

Lustgarten, Edgar. *A Century of Murderers*. London: Eyre Methuen, 1975.

McDade, Thomas M., editor. *The Annals of Murder: A Bibliography of Books and Periodicals on American Murders from Colonial Times to 1900*. Norman: University of Oklahoma Press, 1961.

MacShane, Frank. *The Life of Raymond Chandler*. New York: Dutton, 1976.

Nash, Jay Robert. *Almanac of World Crime*. Garden City, N.Y.: Anchor Press, 1981.

———. *Look for the Woman*. New York: M. Evans & Co., 1981.

———. *Murder, America: Homicide in the United States from the Revolution to the Present*. New York: Simon & Schuster, 1980.

O'Donnell, Bernard. *Should Women Hang?* London: W. H. Allen, 1956.

———. *The Old Bailey and Its Trials*. London: Clerke & Cockeran, 1951.

Reker, George. *Susan Smith: Victim or Murderer*. Lakewood, Co: Glenbridge Publishing, 1996.

Rhodes, Richard. *Why They Kill: Discoveries of a Maverick Criminologist.* New York: Vintage Books, 1999.

Rowan, David. *Famous American Crimes.* London: Frederick Muller, 1957.

———. *Famous European Crimes.* London: Frederick Muller, 1955.

Sharpe, J. A. *Crime in Early Modern England: 1550–1750.* London & New York: Longmans, 1984.

Sifakis, Carl. *A Catalogue of Crime.* New York: Signet, New American Library, 1979.

———. *Encyclopedia of American Crime.* New York: Facts on File Inc., 1982.

Smith, David, with Carol Calef. *Beyond All Reason: My life with Susan Smith.* New York: Kensington Books, 1995.

Symons, Julian. *A Pictorial History of Crime.* New York: Bonanza Books, 1966.

Vandrome, Nick. *Crime and Criminals.* Edinburgh, New York, Toronto: Chambers, 1992.

Wilson, Colin. *Written in Blood: A History of Forensic Detection.* London: Grafton Books, 1990.

———. *The Mammoth Book of True Crime,* (2 vols). London: Robinson, 1988.

Wilson, Colin, edited with Damon Wilson. *Murder in the 1940s.* New York: Carroll & Graf, 1993.

Wilson, Colin, and Pat Pitman. *Encyclopaedia of Murder.* London: Pan Books, 1961.

Wilson, Colin, and Donald Seaman. *Encyclopaedia of Modern Murder: 1962–1983.* London: Pan Books, 1986.

Wilson, Patrick. *Murderess.* London: Michael Joseph, 1971.

Periodicals, Newspapers and the Internet:

Andersen, Erin. "Thatcher Hearing: Killer sought outings for pleasure." *Globe and Mail*, 2000.

Appleby, Timothy. "When love turns deadly." *Globe and Mail*, 7 December 1999.

Arora, C. K. *Washington Post*.

Chattopadhyay, Piya. Television documentary for *National Magazine*.

Cobbey, Nan. "Jean Harris: A new life after 12 years' prison education." *Episcopal Life*.

Cox, Patrick. "Again, a 'passion killer' gets away with murder." Electric Library Canada, 28 June 2000.

Decker, Shelly. "A dark secret for Anne Perry." Murderess Ink. 26 October 1998.

Re Crown Prince Dpendra [Unsigned] "Pakistanis targeting 'honour killings.'" *Globe and Mail*, from Agence France-Press and Associated Press, 11 January 2001.

Gleick, Elizabeth. "Sex, Betrayal and Murder." *Time Magazine*, 17 July 1995.

An out-of-the-way item on Peter Hogg: http://www.lakestay.co.uk/was.htm An unsigned piece, "Wasdale's Lady in the Lake Mystery."

Hutchinson, Brian. "A Deadly Arrangement," *Saturday Night Magazine*, 21 October 2000. Don Mills, Ontario: The National Post Co.

R. V. Klassen. Account of 1997 trial in Whitehorse, YT. Quicklaw.

———. Supreme Court of Canada, 1997.

Koring, Paul. "Patel gets 3 years in husband's death." *Globe and Mail*, 25 October 2000.

Lu, Jao. "Parker-Hulme Murder Exclusive." *Woman's Weekly (NZ)*. The Borovnian Archives. http://www.domusaurea.org/borovnia/hilary.html.

McDermott, Anne. Quoting from Nicole Simpson's friend, on CNN, 19 January 1995.

Mitchell, Alanna. "Girl's murder a turning point." *Globe and Mail*, 11 January 2001.

Murder Casebook: Investigations into the Ultimate Crime. Nos. 11 and 35. London: A Marshall Cavendish Weekly Publication, n.d.

O'Hagan, Maureen. "An Untraditional Death." *Washington Post*.

Other unsigned items about Parker and Hulme (Perry) appear under name:
    http://www.geocities.com/Hollywood/Studio/2194/faq2/Section_3/3.2
    .7.html.

Pershing, Linda. [re Lorena Bobbitt] *NWSA Journal* 8: no. 3. State
    University of New York at Albany. Indiana University Press.

Russo, Robert. Several files on Alpna Patel for Canadian Press.

For O. J. Simpson coverage on the Internet, try:
    http://simpson.walraven.org as the basic request, then follow the leads.
    Try also http://www.cnn/US/OJ.

Re Susan Smith, I have read files by Heather Brooke; Ralph Greer Jr.;
    Reginald Field; Chase Squires; Suellen E. Dean, Clay Murphy, Janet
    Spencer, Molly McDonough, Shelly Haskins and Gary Henderson of the
    Spartanburg, South Carolina, *Herald-Journal*; David Stout, New York
    Times News Service; Jesse J. Holland, Associated Press.

Wulf, Steve. "Elegy for Lost Boys." *Time Magazine*, 31 July 1995.

Index

A

Abelard, Peter, 183
abused women, 44–45,
 55–57, 69–73, 166–170,
 205–211, 212, 214–215,
 217
accomplices to murder. *See*
 Thompson, Edith Jessie
Acquaviva (lawyer), 35, 38
Adelson, Michael, 65
Aegisthus, 18
Agamemnon, 18, 182
Aiswarya, Queen of Nepal,
 201, 202
Albert and the Lion (Edgar),
 55
alcoholism, 44–45
Allemand, Mme., 37
An American Tragedy
 (Dreiser), 165
Anatomy of a Murder, 192
Andrews, Arlene, 196, 197
appeal of sentence, 213–214
L'Après-Midi d'un Faune,
 110
arranged marriage, 184–185
Aurnou, Joel, 51
avarice, crime of, 91–99,
 102, 104

B

Back, Patrick, 158
Bailly, Félix, 171–174
Ballets Russes, 110
ballistics evidence, 139–140
Barrett, Elizabeth, 183
Barshop, Steven, 66
beauty, 91
Bedford Hills Correctional
 Facility, 54
Belasco, David, 104
Belshaw, Betty Joy
 Sweetman, 153–158, 160
Belshaw, Cyril Shirley,
 153–158
Bentley, Derek, 47
"Bermondsey Horror," 98

de Bernardy, Janine, 142,
 144–149
de Bernardy, Simety, 145,
 146
de Bernardy de Sigoyer,
 Alain, 142–149
Berry (hangman), 179
Berthelot, Philippe, 110
Bewes, Aristis, 136
Bien Jolie Corset Company,
 101
Birendra, King of Nepal,
 201, 202
black magic, 143
black satin, 97–98
Blackpool, 55
Blakely, David, 42, 44–45,
 150, 174
Blantyre, Lady, 92
Bleak House (Dickens), 99
Blixen, Karen, 131
Bloom, Harold, 62
Bobbitt, John Wayne,
 166–170
Bobbitt, Lorena, 166–170,
 187
Bolen, George, 52
Borden, Abby, 193–194
Borden, Andrew Jackson,
 193–194
Borden, Lizzie, 193–194
Borowitz, Albert, 91, 98
Bourget, Paul, 120–121,
 180–181
Bowman, Christian, 209
Boyer, Charles, 203
Bride of Lammermoor
 (Scott), 20
Broad, Lewis, 76, 82–83, 84
Broughton, Lady Diana,
 132–142
Broughton, Lord Henry
 "Jock" Delves, 130–142
Brown, Elizabeth Martha,
 205–208
Brown, John Anthony,
 205–208

Brown, Joseph, 101
Browning, Robert, 183
The Browning Version
 (Rattigan), 163
Brunet, Marcel, 149
Bucket, Insp. (*Bleak House*),
 99
Bywaters, Frederick, 75–89,
 102

C

Cahill, Robert, 216–217
Caillaux, Henriette, 24,
 109–129, 150, 174, 220
Caillaux, Joseph, 109–129
Cain, James M., 102
Calcraft (hangman), 92
Caldwell, Diana. *See*
 Broughton, Lady Diana
Calmette, Gaston, 109–129,
 174
Canada, executions in, 209
Canadian Broadcasting
 Corporataion, 184
Carberry, Juanita, 141
Carberry, June, 133, 135,
 138–139, 142
Carmen, 17
Caroline, Queen of England,
 204
Cassagne, Pierre, 163
La Cérémonie, 63
Chabrol, Claude, 63
Chamber of Horrors, 99
Chandler, Raymond, 43, 46
Château de Louveciennes,
 161, 162
Chenu (lawyer), 125
Chevallier, Mathieu, 30
Chevallier, Pierre, 27–31
Chevallier, Yvonne, 24,
 27–40, 122, 161, 220
children, murder of,
 194–201
Cholmondley, Tom, 141
Christian Coalition, 195

Christmas clemency appeals, 54
Clark, Marcia, 71
class, 198
clemency, appeal for, 54
Clytemnestra, 18, 182
Colvile, Gilbert, 140
Conley, Morris, 44
Conso Products, 197
Corday, Charlotte, 174, 210
Côté, Andrée, 214–215
Cox, Patrick, 216–217
Crime of Passion: Murder and Murderer (Lester and Lester), 22–23
crime of passion defense, 21, 24, 32, 215
Criminal Justice (Weis), 75
Crippen, Cora, 150–153
Crippen, Hawley Harvey, 150–153
Cronin, Vincent, 112
Cruikshank, Robert, 91
Cumbria, 159–160
Cuomo, Mario, 54
Cussen, Desmond, 44

D

da Rimini, Francesca, 14, 16–17
Daily News, 108
Daily Telegraph, 82
Dance with a Stranger, 43
Dante, 14, 16, 17
Darrieux, Danielle, 203
Darrow, Clarence, 193
Daudet, Léon, 110
Davidson, Hugh, 137
Davies, Mary, 207
Dawson, Jill, 75
de Bellecombe, Comte, 162
death penalty, 41–42, 46–47, 76, 88, 108
Defense of Provocation and Domestic Femicide (Côté), 214–215
defense to crime of passion. See crime of passion defense
Delamere, Gwladys, 133, 134
Deneuve, Catherine, 203
Denham (judge), 177
dental records, falsification of, 156, 157–158

Desfourneaux (executioner), 149
Dew, Walter, 151
Dickens, Charles, 91, 99
Didion, Joan, 64
Die Österreichisch-Ungarische Monarchie in Wort und Bild (1886-et seq), 203
diminished responsibility, 47
Dinesen, Isak, 131
Dipendra, Crown Prince of Nepal, 201–202
divorce, 80
Djinn Palace, 131, 140
DNA evidence, 74
Document Fabre, 123, 124, 127
domestic violence, 57, 67, 205–208
see also abused women
domination, 100, 102, 104
Donovan, Leisure, Newton and Irving, 65
Double Indemnity (Cain), 102
Dreiser, Theodore, 165
Dreyfus, Alfred, 110
Dubuisson, Pauline, 171–174
Dunne, Dominick, 64, 65
Dunne, Dominique, 63–68
Dunne, John Gregory, 64
Dunne, Lenny Griffin, 66
Durant, Will, 104–105

E

Eastman, George (*An American Tragedy*), 165
Edgar, Marriott, 55
"egg-head killers," 193
the ego, 36, 129
electric chair, 108
Ellis, George, 44
Ellis, Ruth, 41–48, 51, 76, 89, 122, 150, 174
Elmore, Belle. See Crippen, Cora
England, view on crimes of passion, 41–48
Erroll, Earl of, 130–142
Euripides, 200
Evans, Timothy, 47
Evening News, 178
Evening Standard, 123
existentialism, 163–164

F

Famous European Crimes (Rowan), 33
Fatal Charms and Other Tales of Today (Dunne), 65
father's account, 65
Field, Insp., 99
Le Figaro. See Calmette, Gaston
Findlater, Anthony ("Ant"), 45
Findlater, Carole, 45
Findlay, J. Carey, 197
Findlay, Tom, 196–197, 200
Fitzherbert, Maria Anna, 204
Flynn, William, 95–96
Forster, John, 99
Fowler, Gene, 104, 108
Franks, Bobby, 192–193
Franz Ferdinand, Crown Prince, 203
Franz Josef, Emperor, 203
Fred & Edie (Dawson), 75
French law, 21, 26, 27–40, 117
Freud, Anna, 16, 36, 129
Fuhrman, Mark, 72, 74
Fulbert, Canon, 183

G

Galloway, Sheila, 215
Gastinne-Renette, 118
gender, and justice, 23–26
George, Sir Gwilym Lloyd, 41–42, 47, 48
George III, King of England, 203–204
George IV, King of England, 204
Giaour (Byron), 20
Gide, André, 183
Giese, Keith, 198
Giraudeau, M., 122
Goldman, Ron, 68, 70–71, 74
Gollancz, Victor, 43
Gordon, Lady Idina, 131
Granier, Camille, 23–24
Gray, (Henry) Judd, 100–108
Gray, Judd, 18, 19
Great Western Railway, 92–93
Griffith, D. W., 104
Gueydan, Berthe, 112, 127–128

guillotine, 149
guilt, 40
Guischard, Jessie, 101, 103
Gyanendra, King of Nepal, 202

H

Hall, Sir Edward Marshall, 82, 152
Hall-Mills story, 105
Halleck, Seymour, 196
Hamlet (Shakespeare), 183
hanging, death by, 46–47, 179, 208, 209
hanging, execution by, 43, 47–48, 88, 97, 99
Happy Valley, 130–142
Hardy, Thomas, 208
Harragin, Walter, 138–139, 140
Harris, Jean, 48–54
Harris, Ruth, 25
Hawkins, Patricia Ann, 217
Hay, Josslyn Victor, 130–142
Heavenly Creatures, 191
Hecht, Ben, 104
Helen of Troy, 17
Héloïse, 183
Herald Tribune, 105, 106
Hill, Molly Ramsay, 131
Hindmarsh, Harry Comfort, 110
Hogg, Frank, 175–181
Hogg, Margaret, 158–160
Hogg, Peter, 158–160
Hogg, Phoebe, 175–181
Holloway, Stanley, 55
Holloway Prison, 46, 51
Home Secretary, 41–42
Hopkins, Peggy, 104
Horder, Jeremy, 116, 117, 219–220
Hortense (*Bleak House*), 99
The Housekeeper, 63
Howard, Thomas, 108
Huish, Robert, 92
Hulme, Juliet, 188–191
hyoscine, 151, 152–153

I

Ilford, England, 76, 89
immorality, 82
incitement, 78
infanticide, 42, 47
Infanticide Act, 47

Inferno (Dante), 17
The Innocence of Edith Thompson (Broad), 76, 83
Inskip, Thomas, 85–86
insurance money, 102, 108

J

Jackson, Peter, 191
Jadin, Raymond, 32, 33
"jail fever," 92
Jaurès, Jean, 124
Jesse, F. Tennyson, 75, 82, 178, 219
Jones, Ann, 105, 106
A Judgment in Stone (Rendell), 63
Juliet (*Romeo and Juliet*), 182–183
justice, 220
"Justice" (Dunne), 65
justifiable homicide, 211

K

Kaelin, Brian "Kato," 71, 73
Karen House. *See* Broughton, Lord Henry "Jock" Delves
Katz, Burton S., 66, 67
Katz, Jack, 211
Kenya, 131–142
Kergot, Janine, 142, 144–149
Kershaw, Alister, 112, 115, 116, 118, 122, 124, 126, 145, 147–148, 149
Kilmarnock, Baron of, 130–142
King, Rodney, 73–74
Klassen, Ralph, 210–216
Klassen, Susan, 210–216

L

Lambton County, 208–209
Lebeau, Irène, 145, 146–147, 148
Leopald, Nathan, 192–193
Leyton, Elliott, 57, 61, 210, 211
Liger, Jean, 161–166
Lindon (lawyer), 37–38
the Little Club, 44
Litvak, Anatole, 203
Loeb, Richard, 192–193
Lombard, Monique, 172
London Labour and London Poor (Mayhew), 98
Long Island, 100–101

Los Angeles, 63
love letters, 77–82, 180
Lustgarten, Eric, 75, 80

M

Ma Maison, 63, 65
MacDonald, Sir John A., 209
Mackamotzki, Kunegonde. *See* Crippen, Cora
MacShane, Frank, 46
Madame Tussaud's Exhibition, 99
Madeira School, 49
the Magdala, 41
Malatesta, Giovanni, 14, 16–17
Malatesta, Paolo, 14, 16–17
male control, 169, 215
see also abused women; provocation
male perpetrators, 24, 130
Manning, Frederick George, 18, 19, 90–99
Manning, Marie, 18, 19, 90–99
Mansfield, Katherine, 153, 189
Marat, Jean-Paul, 174, 210
Marre, Véronique, 159, 160
"Mask of Pride," 172
Massey, William, 93, 94
Maugham, Somerset, 63
Mayerling, 203–204
Mayhew, Henry, 98
McCollum, William D., 185–186, 187
McNaughton Rule, 67
McPherson, Aimee Semple, 104
Medea of Hecate, 200–201
media circus, 73–74, 75, 90–91, 97–99, 104–108, 142–143
Medical Health Act (U.K.), 60
Men of Blood: Murder in Modern England (Leyton), 57, 210
Mencken, H. L., 98
Mezzaluna, 68, 73
Midsummer Night's Dream (Shakespeare), 182
Mills, Charlotte, 105
Minver Place, 93–95, 96
Mirat (lawyer), 36

the *Mirror*, 106
miscarriage, 42, 47
Monier (judge), 114
Montrose, S.S., 151–152
morganatic marriages,
   203–204
Morning Post, 97
Morris, Harry H., 138, 139
mother fixation, 100
Motion, Vernon, 132
Moule, H., 208
Murder and Its Motives
   (Jesse), 219
Murder in France (Kershaw),
   145
Murderess (Wilson), 42, 47,
   88, 179, 206
Murders and Madness
   (Harris), 25
Muthaiga Country Club, 135

N

Nairobi. *See* Broughton, Lord
   Henry "Jock" Delves
Narayanhiti Palace, 201
Nash, Jay Robert, 25–26, 173
Nathan, Hilary, 191
Nepal, royal family of,
   201–202
Le Neve, Ethel, 151–153
New Guinea penal colony,
   40
New York Post, 106
New York Times, 105
News of the World, 177
Nicet, Etienne, 120–121
Nijinsky, Vaslav, 110
Nirajan, Prince of Nepal, 201
Norman, Alan, 55–63, 217
Norman, Patricia (Trish),
   55–60, 65, 217
Notable British Trials Series
   (Young), 75

O

Observer, 97
O'Connor, Patrick, 91–99
O'Donnell, Bernard, 76,
   84–85, 87
Olga (sister of Trish
   Norman), 56
Orléans, France, 27–28
Othello (Shakespeare),
   60–62, 140–141
Ouchy (resort), 113

Out of Africa (Dinesan), 131
Owen, Frank, 47
*Oxford Monographs on
   Criminal Law and Justice
   Series*, 116

P

Pall Mall Gazette, 177–178
Parchman, Eunice (*Judgment
   in Stone*), 63
Parker, Honoria Mary,
   188–191
Parker, Pauline, 188–191
partner swapping, 132
"Passionate Peer." *See* Erroll,
   Earl of
Patel, Alpna, 122, 183–188
Patel, Nandlal, 184
Patel, Viresh, 183–188
Peacock, Kenneth, 216–217
Peacock, Sandra, 216–217
Pearcey, Mary Eleanor,
   174–181, 219
Peidi. *See* Thompson, Edith
   Jessie
penis, severed, 166–170
Perreau, Jeannette, 29, 31,
   33, 34–35
Perreau, Roger, 32, 33,
   34–35, 102
Perry, Anne, 188–191
Pershing, Linda, 168
"petty treason," 206, 209
phrenologists, 106
A Pin to See the Peepshow
   (Jesse), 75
Pleven, René, 29
Poincaré, Raymond, 127
poisoning, 150–153
police interference, 74
Poppy, Arthur, 136, 139
popular literature, 22
post-homicide events,
   153–158
premeditation, 19, 32, 150,
   187
Preminger, Otto, 192
Princip, Gavrilo, 110
prison conditions, improve-
   ment of, 54
Privas, John, 187
private justice, 210–211
*The Progress of Crime: The
   Authentic Memoirs of Maria
   Manning*, 97

Proust, Marcel, 112
provocation, 20, 48,
   116–117, 205–218
   defence of, 213–215,
   219–220
   see also crime of passion
      defense
Provocation and Responsibility
   (Horder), 116
psychiatric opinion, 36
Punch, 91, 97–98
Purchase, NY, 48
Pyramus, 182

Q

Queens Village, 101
quicklime, 95, 97

R

radio, 153
Rambova, Natasha, 107
Rana, Devyani, 202
Rattigan, Terence, 163
*Reforming the Defense of
   Provocation* (Galloway and
   St. Lewis), 215
Reliquet, Jean, 165
Rendell, Ruth, 63
reprieves, 42
Republican Party, 195
Réunion, Island of, 143
revenge murders, 19
Richardson, Jackie, 161–166
Rieper, Honoria. *See* Parker,
   Honoria Mary
Rinehart, Mary Roberts, 104
Romeo, 182–183
Rousseau, Yvonne. *See*
   Chevallier, Yvonne
de Roux, Marie. *See*
   Manning, Marie
Rowan, David, 33, 35, 161,
   162, 163, 164, 166
Rubio, Luigi, 14
Rudolf, Crown Prince, 203
rue, 92
Runyon, Damon, 104
Russell, Beverly C. Jr., 195,
   198
Ryan, Graham, 158

S

Sandburg, Carl, 193
Sarnia, Ontario, 208–209
Scarsdale Medical Diet, 48

second degree murder,
51–52
*Seductions of Crime: Moral
and Sensual Attractions of
Doing Evil* (Katz), 211
self-defense, 215
see also abused women;
provocation
self-immolation, 174
sentencing discrepancies, 23,
216–218
Shahi, Rajiv, 201
*Shakespeare: The Invention of
the Human* (Bloom), 62
Shapiro, Joseph, 65
Sharif, Omar, 203
Shawn, Billy, 192
Shearman (judge), 83, 87–88
Shiel, Margaret, 209
Should Women Hang
(O'Donnell), 76
Simpson, Justin, 70
Simpson, Nicole Brown,
68–74
Simpson, O. J., 18, 68–74,
105
Simpson, Sydney, 70, 73
Sing Sing prison, 108
Sirac, Adrien, 121
Small, Ambrose, 95
Smith, Al, 108
Smith, Alex, 194–200
Smith, David, 195–197, 200
Smith, Madeleine, 78–79,
183
Smith, Michael, 194–200
Smith, Susan Vaughan,
194–200
Snyder, Albert Edward,
100–108
Snyder, Lorraine, 100, 101,
103
Snyder, Ruth Brown, 18, 19,
90, 100–108, 160
Soames, Jack, 134, 137
sons, murder of, 194–201
Spilsbury, Sir Bernard, 77,
152
St. Lazare prison, 123
St. Lewis, Joanne, 215
Steiner, Insp., 161
Stewart, James, 192
Stranger in Two Worlds
(Harris), 54
Straton, John Roach, 104

Streetcar Named Desire
(Williams), 22
suicide, state as means of,
41, 47
Sunday, Billy, 104
Swann's Way (Proust), 112
Sweeney, John, 63–68
Switzerland, 155
Symons, Julian, 80

T

tabloid coverage. See media
circus
Tarnower, Herman, 48–50
Taylor, Charity, 46–47
Tenby, Lord. See George, Sir
Gwilym Lloyd
Tess of the D'Urbervilles
(Hardy), 208
*They Always Call Us
Ladies—Stories from Prison*
(Harris), 54
Thisbe, 182
Thompson, Alan, 45–46
Thompson, Edith Jessie,
75–89, 94, 100, 102, 172,
178, 217–218
Thompson, Percy, 76, 80–81,
86, 102
throat-cutting, 174
The Times, 99
timing of the crime,
108–109, 166
Timms, Geoffrey, 135–136
"Ton Jo." See Caillaux,
Joseph
Toronto Star, 111
train robbery, 93
La Traviata (Verdi), 21–22
Tryforos, Lynne, 49, 53
Tushingham, Rita, 63

U

uncontrollable impulse, 192
*Under the Ivi Tree: Society and
Economic Growth in Rural
Fiji* (Belshaw), 154
Union, South Carolina. See
Smith, Susan Vaughan
United States, 210–211
USA Today, 216

V

Vasseur, Etienne, 161
Vaughan, Harry, 195

Vaughan, Linda, 195
Verdict in Dispute
(Lustgarten), 75
Vetsera, Baroness Marie, 203
Viagra, 169
Victorian England, 91
Victorian women, lives of,
178
Voisin (reporter), 126–127
Von Domnick, Colonel, 170

W

Waldorf Astoria Hotel
(Manhattan), 100
Watkins, George, 210–211
Watkins, Violet, 210–211
Weis, René, 75
Wells, Howard, 199
Westchester County, NY, 50
Wheeler, Mary Eleanor. See
Pearcey, Mary Eleanor
Wilson, Colin, 172
Wilson, Mrs., 156
Wilson, Patrick, 42, 47, 48,
75, 88, 179, 206
Winslet, Kate, 191
Wolf, Naomi, 170
*The Woman Who Murdered
Black Satin* (Borowitz), 91
women
abused. See abused women
bias against, 216–218
execution of, 76
last executed, in England.
See Ellis, Ruth
last executed, in France, 39
as perpetrators, 23–25
as property, 216–217
see also abused women;
domestic violence
and throat-cutting, 174
Women Who Kill (Jones), 105
women's shelter, 56
Workman, Elizabeth,
208–209, 220
Workman, James, 208–209
World War I, 109–110

Y

Young, Brigham, 106
Young, Filson, 75
Young, Terrence, 203
Yule, Gladys Kensington, 41,
45, 47